Brian Hart
with Herbert Puchta and Jeff Stranks

English in Mind

Teacher's Book 4

CAMBRIDGE
UNIVERSITY PRESS

Contents

Map of Student's Book 4
Introduction 6

Teacher's notes and keys

Module 1	The wonders of the mind	10
	1 Super brains	11
	2 Mind over matter	18
	3 Brainwaves	25
	4 Time travellers	31
	Module 1 Check your progress	37
Module 2	The way we are	38
	5 Personalities	39
	6 In and out of fashion	45
	7 Kindness matters	50
	8 Peacemakers	55
	Module 2 Check your progress	60
Module 3	Making a difference	61
	9 Get involved	62
	10 SOS Earth	68
	11 Stars step in	73
	12 The global village	79
	Module 3 Check your progress	83
Module 4	Around the world	84
	13 Language	85
	14 The wonders of the world	92
	15 Movie magic	99
	16 Music in the air	105
	Module 4 Check your progress	111

Projects 112

Workbook key 114

Acknowledgements 128

Unit	Grammar	Vocabulary	Pronunciation
Module 1 — The wonders of the mind			
1 Super brains	Tense revision: present tense forms Tense revision: past tense forms	Expressions with *mind* Expressions with *brain*	/ð/ <u>th</u>e and /θ/ <u>th</u>ing
2 Mind over matter	Passives review Passive continuous tenses	Health and medicine Feelings Everyday English	Consonant clusters
3 Brainwaves	Relative clauses review: defining/non-defining	Sports equipment / places	Intonation in questions
4 Time travellers	Reported speech review Reporting verbs review	Expressions with *time*	Schwa /ə/ teach<u>er</u>
Module 1 Check your progress			
Module 2 — The way we are			
5 Personalities	*what* clauses Verbs + gerund/infinitive review *Try* + infinitive v. *try* + gerund	Personality adjectives	Sentence stress and rhythm
6 In and out of fashion	*used to* (review) + *would* Adverbs and adverbial phrases	Common adverbial phrases Everyday English	/æ/ <u>a</u>pple and /e/ l<u>e</u>mon
7 Kindness matters	Dummy *it* Modal verbs review	Making an effort	Connecting sounds (intrusive /w/ and /j/)
8 Peacemakers	Past perfect passive Past perfect continuous	Conflicts and solutions	Linking sounds
Module 2 Check your progress			
Module 3 — Making a difference			
9 Get involved	Conditionals review Mixed conditionals	Ways of getting involved	Contractions in 3rd conditionals
10 SOS Earth	Future continuous Future perfect Future time expressions	Global issues Conserving energy Everyday English	Contracted forms of *will have*
11 When stars step in	Reduced relative clauses (omission of relative pronouns) Question tags review	Fame Expressing opinions	Intonation in question tags
12 The global village	Phrasal verbs review	Phrasal verbs	Shifting stress
Module 3 Check your progress			
Module 4 — Around the world			
13 Language	Passive report structures	Understanding language	Words ending in *-ough*
14 The wonders of the world	Participle clauses *didn't need to / needn't have*	Geographical features Travel verbs Everyday English	/ɪ/ s<u>i</u>t and /iː/ s<u>ee</u>
15 Movie magic	Clauses of purpose with *to / in order to / so as to* Result clauses with *so / such (that)*	Reacting to films	Word stress in multi-syllabic words
16 Music in the air	Indirect questions	Making comparisons stronger Listening to Music	Word stress affecting meaning: *record* (noun) vs. *record* (verb)
Module 4 Check your progress			

Projects • Pronunciation • Speaking: extra material • Wordlist • Phonetic chart

Speaking & functions	Listening	Reading	Writing
Talking about special talents	Interview with a psychologist about autistic savants	Blind Tom and Stephen Wiltshire Literature: *The Curious Incident of the Dog in the Night-time*	Narrative (1)
Talking about people's problems and feelings	Discussion about flower remedies	Placebos Prove Powerful Remedies from the Rainforest Story: *Eyes open*	Article for a school magazine
Talking about the way our brains work Discussing sport Discussing the nature of intelligence	Interview with two sportswomen	They Just Can't Help It Culture: Intelligence Across Cultures	Discursive essay (1)
Talking about time	Interview about Doctor Who Song: *If I Could Turn Back Time*	Quiz about Doctor Who Letter giving advice	Informal letter
Discussing shyness Talking about personal qualities	Interview with an expert on shyness	Questionnaire: How confident are you? Literature: *Pride and Prejudice*	Description of a person
Organising a flash mob	Interview with someone who organises flash mobs	Text about crazes from the past Story: *Sorry!*	Letter to a newspaper
Talking about acts of kindness Asking questions using modals Talking about birthdays	People talking about special objects they have inherited	Hit-and-Run Kindness Culture: Birthday Traditions	A summary
Resolving conflicts	Interview about Wangari Maathai Song: *Peace, Love and Understanding*	Alfred Nobel Rests in Peace	Appreciation of a Nobel Prize winner
Discussing age limits in the UK / your country	A radio phone-in programme about giving the vote to 16-year-olds	Weblog about a trip to Mount Everest Literature: *Lord of the Flies*	Letter raising money for charity
Discussing global issues Discussing ways of conserving energy	Radio programme about alternative energy	Time's Running Out Story: *The factory*	Write a magazine article about the future
Expressing opinions Discussing the role of music concerts in raising awareness of global issues	People's views on famous people getting involved in politics	Celebrity Ambassadors Culture: Can Music Make a Difference?	Discursive essay (2)
Discussing Fair Trade products	The Village Earth Song: *I'd Like to Teach the World to Sing*	Young People Leading the Way on Fair Trade	Report on a class survey
Discussing language and accents	TV programme about regional accents	Near-Extinct Language Returns Literature: *The World According to Garp*	Narrative (2)
Describing an interesting trip	Account of a trip to the Grand Canyon	Three texts about wonderful places in the world Story: *Round the world*	Description of a place
Discussing films and 'film therapy'	Conversation about films	Movie Therapy Culture: Planet Bollywood	Film synopsis
Discussing the effect music has on you Discussing which music you like/dislike	Radio programme about musical instruments from round the world Song: *Lost in Music*	A World of Music	Haikus/limericks/mini-sagas

Introduction

> *'If you can teach teenagers, you can teach anyone.'* Michael Grinder

Teaching teenagers is an interesting and challenging task. A group of adolescents can be highly motivated, cooperative and fun to teach on one day, and the next day the whole group or individual students might turn out to be truly 'difficult' – the teacher might, for example, be faced with discipline problems, disruptive or provocative behaviour, a lack of motivation, or unwillingness on the students' part to do homework assigned to them.

The roots of these problems frequently lie in the fact that adolescents are going through a period of significant changes in their lives. The key challenge in the transition period between being a child and becoming an adult is the adolescent's struggle for identity – a process that requires the development of a distinct sense of who they are. A consequence of this process is that adolescents can feel threatened, and at the same time experience overwhelming emotions. They frequently try to compensate for the perceived threats with extremely rude behaviour, and try to 'hide' their emotions behind a wall of extreme outward conformity. The more individual students manage to look, talk, act and behave like the other members of their peer group, the less threatened and insecure they feel.

Insights into the causes underlying the problems might help us to understand better the complex situation our students are in. However, such insights do not automatically lead to more success in teaching. We need to react to the challenges in a professional way.[1] This includes the need to:
- select content and organise the students' learning according to their psychological needs;
- create a positive learning atmosphere;
- cater for differences in students' learning styles and intelligence(s), and facilitate the development of our students' study skills.

English in Mind has been written taking all these points into account. They have significantly influenced the choice of texts, artwork and design, the structure of the units, the typology of exercises, and the means by which students' study skills are facilitated and extended.

The importance of the content for success

There are a number of reasons why the choice of the right content has a crucial influence over success or failure in the teaching of adolescents. Teachers frequently observe that teenagers are reluctant to 'talk about themselves'. This has to do with the adolescent's need for psychological security. Consequently, the 'further away' from their own world the content of the teaching is, the more motivating and stimulating it will be for the students. The preference for psychologically remote content goes hand in hand with a fascination with extremes and realistic details. Furthermore, students love identifying with heroes and heroines, because these idols are perceived to embody the qualities needed in order to survive in a threatening world: qualities such as courage, genius, creativity and love. In the foreign language class, students can become fascinated with stories about heroes and heroines to which they can ascribe such qualities. *English in Mind* treats students as young adults, offering them a range of interesting topics and a balance between educational value and teenage interest and fun.

As Kieran Egan[1] stresses, learning in the adolescent classroom can be successfully organised by starting with something far from the students' experience, but also connected to it by some quality with which they can associate. This process of starting far from the students makes it easier for the students to become interested in the topic, and also enables the teacher finally to relate the content to the students' own world.

A positive learning atmosphere

The creation of a positive learning atmosphere largely depends on the rapport between teacher and students, and the one which students have among themselves. It requires the teacher to be a genuine, empathetic listener, and to have a number of other psychological skills. *English in Mind* supports the teacher's task of creating positive learning experiences through: clear tasks; a large number of carefully designed exercises; regular opportunities for the students to check their own work; and a learning process designed to guarantee that the students will learn to express themselves both in speaking and in writing.

Learning styles and multiple intelligences

There is significant evidence that students will be better motivated, and learn more successfully, if differences in learning styles and intelligences are taken into account in the teaching-learning process.[2] The development of a number of activities in *English in Mind* have been

---

[1] An excellent analysis of teenage development and consequences for our teaching in general can be found in Kieran Egan: *Romantic Understanding*, Routledge and Kegan Paul, New York and London, 1990. This book has had a significant influence on the thinking behind *English in Mind*, and the development of the concept of the course.

[2] See for example Eric Jensen: *Brain-Based Learning and Teaching*, Turning Point Publishing, Del Mar, CA, USA, 1995, on learning styles. An overview of the theory of multiple intelligences can be found in Howard Gardner: *Multiple Intelligences: The Theory in Practice*, Basic Books, New York 1993.

influenced by such insights, and students find frequent study tips that show them how they can better utilise their own resources.[3]

The methodology used in *English in Mind*

Skills: *English in Mind* uses a communicative, multi-skills approach to develop the students' foreign language abilities in an interesting and motivational way. A wide range of interesting text types is used to present authentic use of language, including magazine and newspaper clippings, interviews, narratives, songs and extracts from English literature.

Grammar: *English in Mind* is based on a strong grammatical syllabus and takes into account students' mixed abilities by dealing with grammar in a carefully graded way, and offering additional teaching support (see below).

Vocabulary: *English in Mind* offers a systematic vocabulary syllabus, including important lexical chunks for conversation.

Culture: *English in Mind* gives students insights into a number of important cross-cultural and intercultural themes. Significant cultural features of English-speaking countries are presented, and students are involved in actively reflecting on the similarities and differences between other cultures and their own.

Consolidation: Four Check your progress revision units per level will give teachers a clear picture of their students' progress and make students aware of what they have learned. Each revision unit is also accompanied by a project which gives students the opportunity to use new language in a less controlled context and allows for learner independence.

Teacher support: *English in Mind* is clearly structured and easy to teach. The Teacher's Book offers step-by-step lesson notes, background information on content, culture and language, additional teaching ideas and the tapescripts. The accompanying Teacher's Resource Pack contains photocopiable materials for further practice and extra lessons, taking into consideration the needs of mixed-ability groups by providing extra material for fast finishers or students who need more support, as well as formal tests.

Student support: *English in Mind* offers systematic support to students through: Study help sections and Skills tips; classroom language; guidance in units to help with the development of classroom discourse and the students' writing; a wordlist including phonetic transcriptions and lists of irregular verbs and phonetics (at the back of the Student's Book); and a Grammar reference (at the back of the Workbook).

English in Mind: components

Each level of the *English in Mind* series contains the following components:
- Student's Book
- Class CDs or Class Cassettes
- Workbook with accompanying Audio CD / CD-ROM
- Teacher's Book
- Teacher's Resource Pack
- Website resources

The Student's Book

Modular structure: The *English in Mind* Student's Books are organised on a modular basis – each contains four modules of four units per module. The modules have broad themes and are organised as follows: a) a two-page module opener; b) four units of six pages each; c) a two-page Check your progress section.

Module openers are two pages which allow teachers to 'set the scene' for their students, concerning both the informational content and the language content of what is to come in the module itself. This helps both to motivate the students and to provide the important 'signposting' which allows them to see where their learning is going next. The pages contain: a) a visual task in which students match topics to a selection of photographs taken from the coming units; b) a list of skills learning objectives for the module; c) a short matching task which previews the main grammar content of the coming module; and d) a simple vocabulary task, again previewing the coming content.

The **units** contain the following:
- an opening **reading** text
- one or two **grammar** sections
- one or two sets of **vocabulary**, sometimes followed by **pronunciation**
- **speaking** and **listening skills** work
- either a **Literature in mind** text, a **Culture in mind** text, a **dialogue** or a **song**, followed by **writing skills** work

The **reading texts** aim to engage and motivate the students with interesting and relevant content, and to provide contextualised examples of target grammar and lexis. The texts have 'lead-in' tasks and are followed by comprehension tasks of various kinds. All the opening texts are also recorded on the Class CD/Cassette, which allows teachers to follow the initial reading with a 'read and listen' phase, giving the students the invaluable opportunity of connecting the written word with the spoken version, which is especially useful for auditory learners. Alternatively, with stronger classes, teachers may decide to do one of the exercises as a listening task, with books closed.

---

[3] See Marion Williams and Robert L. Burden: *Psychology for Language Teachers*, Cambridge University Press, 1997 (pp. 143–162), on how the learner deals with the process of learning.

There are one or two **Grammar** sections per unit. The emphasis is on active involvement in the learning process. Examples from the texts are isolated and used as a basis for tasks, which focus on both concept and form of the target grammar area. Students are encouraged to find other examples and work out rules for themselves. Occasionally there are also Look boxes which highlight an important connected issue concerning the grammar area, for example, in Unit 3, work on relative clauses has a Look box showing the use of *which* to refer to the whole of the previous clause. This is followed by a number of graded exercises, both receptive and productive, which allow students to begin to employ the target language in different contexts and to produce realistic language. Next, there is usually a speaking activity, aiming at further personalisation of the language.

Each unit has at least one **Vocabulary** section, with specific word fields. Again, examples from the initial text are focused on, and a lexical set is developed, with exercises for students to put the vocabulary into use. Vocabulary is frequently recycled in later texts in the unit (e.g. photo stories or Culture in mind texts), and also in later units.

Pronunciation is included in every unit. There are exercises on common phoneme problems and also aspects of stress (within words, and across sentences), intonation, elision and links between sounds.

Language skills are present in every unit. There is always at least one **listening skills** activity, with listening texts of various genres; at least one (but usually several) **speaking skills** activity for fluency development; **reading skills** are taught through the opening texts and also later texts in some units, as well as the Culture in mind sections. There is always a **writing skills** task, at the end of each unit.

In level 4 of the course, each unit includes one of the following: a **Literature in mind** section (Units 1, 5, 9 and 13), a **dialogue** (Units 2, 6, 10 and 14), a **Culture in mind** section (Units 3, 7, 11 and 15) or a **song** (Units 4, 8, 12, 16). The **Literature in mind** sections each present an extract from a novel in English as an opportunity for students to access and appreciate some fine writing from different periods and in different styles. The **dialogues** are conversations between teenagers in everyday situations, allowing students to read and listen for interest and also to experience the use of common everyday language expressions. These Everyday English expressions are worked on in exercises following the dialogue. The **Culture in mind** texts are reading texts which provide further reading practice, and an opportunity for students to develop their knowledge and understanding of the world at large and in particular the English-speaking world. They include a wide variety of stimulating topics, for example, concepts of 'intelligence' in different cultures, unusual birthday celebrations, the Live Aid and Live 8 concerts and the success of the Indian film industry.

The final activity in each unit is a **writing skills** task. These are an opportunity for students to further their control of language and to experiment in the production of tasks in a variety of genres (e.g. letters, emails, postcards, etc.). There are model texts for the students to aid their own writing, and exercises providing guidance in terms of content and organisation. Through the completion of the writing tasks, students, if they wish, can also build up a bank of materials, or 'portfolio', during their period of learning: this can be very useful to them as the source of a sense of clear progress and as a means of self-assessment. A 'portfolio' of work can also be shown to other people (exam bodies, parents, even future employers) as evidence of achievement in language learning. Many of the writing tasks also provide useful and relevant practice for examinations such as Cambridge ESOL PET and FCE.

When a module of four units closes, the module ends with a two-page **Check your progress** section. Here the teacher will find exercises in the Grammar, Vocabulary and Everyday English expressions that were presented in the module. The purpose of these (as opposed to the more formal tests offered in the Teacher's Resource Pack) is for teachers and students alike to check quickly the learning and progress made during the module just covered; they can be done in class or at home. Every exercise has a marking scheme, and students can use the marks they gain to do some simple self-assessment of their progress (a light 'task' is offered for this).

Beyond the modules and units themselves, *English in Mind* offers at the **end of the Student's Book** a further set of materials for teachers and students. These consist of:

- **Projects**: activities (one per module) which students can do in pairs or groups (or even individually if desired), for students to put the language they have so far learned into practical and enjoyable use. They are especially useful for mixed-ability classes, as they allow students to work at their own pace. The projects produced could also be part of the 'portfolio' of material mentioned earlier.
- An **irregular verb** list for students to refer to when they need.
- A listing of **phonetic symbols**, again for student reference.
- A **wordlist** with the core lexis of the Student's Book, with phonetic transcriptions. This is organised by unit, and within each unit heading there are the major word-fields, divided into parts of speech (verbs, nouns, adjectives, etc.). The wordlists are a feature that teachers can use in classrooms, for example, to develop students' reference skills, or to indicate ways in which they themselves might organise vocabulary notebooks, and by students at home, as a useful reference and also to prepare for tests or progress checks.

The Workbook

The Workbook is a resource for both teachers and students, providing further practice in the language and skills covered in the Student's Book. It is organised unit-by-unit, following the Student's Book. Each Workbook unit has six pages, and the following contents:

Remember and check: this initial exercise encourages students to remember the content of the initial reading text in the Student's Book unit.

Exercises: an extensive range of supporting exercises in the grammatical, lexical and phonological areas of the Student's Book unit, following the progression of the unit, so that teachers can use the exercises either during or at the end of the Student's Book unit.

Literature in mind and **Culture in mind:** extra exercises on these sections following up material in the Student's Book.

Study help: these sections follow a syllabus of study skills areas, to develop the students' capacities as independent and successful learners. After a brief description of the skill, there are exercises for the students to begin to practise it.

Skills in mind page: these pages contain a separate skills development syllabus, which focuses on one or two main skill areas in each unit. There is also a skill tip relating to the main skill area, which the students can immediately put into action when doing the skills task(s).

Unit check page: this is a one-page check of knowledge of the key language of the unit, integrating both grammar and vocabulary in the three exercise types. The exercise types are: a) a cloze text to be completed using items given in a box; b) a sentence-level multiple choice exercise; c) a guided error correction exercise.

At the end of the Workbook, there is a **Grammar reference** section. Here, there are explanations of the main grammar topics of each unit, with examples. It can be used for reference by students at home, or the teacher might wish to refer to it in class if the students appreciate grammatical explanations.

The Workbook includes an **Audio CD / CD-ROM**, which contains both the listening material for the Workbook (listening texts and pronunciation exercises) and a CD-ROM element, containing definitions for the wordlist items with a spoken model for each one. A range of carefully graded grammar and vocabulary exercises provide further practice of language presented in each module.

The Teacher's Book

The Teacher's Book contains:

- clear, simple, practical teaching **notes** on each unit and how to implement the exercises as effectively as possible
- complete **tapescripts** for all listening and pronunciation activities
- complete **answers** to all exercises (grammar, vocabulary, comprehension questions, etc.)
- **optional further activities**, for stronger or weaker classes, to facilitate the use of the material in mixed-ability classes
- **background notes** relating to the information content (where appropriate) of reading texts and Culture in mind pages
- **language notes** relating to grammatical areas, to assist less-experienced teachers who might have concerns about the target language and how it operates (these can also be used to refer to the Workbook Grammar reference section)
- a complete **answer key** and **tapescripts** for the **Workbook**.

The Teacher's Resource Pack

This extra component, spiral bound for easy photocopying, contains the following photocopiable resources:

- an **Entry** test which can be used for diagnostic testing or also used for remedial work
- **module tests** containing separate sections for: Grammar, Vocabulary, Everyday English, Reading, Listening (the recordings for which are on the Class Cassettes/CDs), Speaking and Writing. A key for the Tests is also provided
- **photocopiable communicative activities**: one page for each unit reflecting the core grammar and/or vocabulary of the unit
- **photocopiable extra grammar exercises**: one page of four exercises for each unit, reflecting the key grammar areas of the unit
- **teaching notes** for the above.

Web resources

In addition to information about the series, the *English in Mind* website contains downloadable pages of further activities and exercises for students as well as other resources. It can be found at this part of the Cambridge University Press website:

www.cambridge.org/elt/englishinmind

Module 1
The wonders of the mind

YOU WILL LEARN ABOUT ...

Ask students to look at the pictures on the page. Ask them to read through the topics in the box and check that they understand each item.
You can ask them the following questions, in L1 if appropriate:

1 *What's the woman's job?*
2 *What's unusual about this group of students?*
3 *What special talent has this young man got?*
4 *What can you see in the jars?*
5 *What kind of TV programme is this?*
6 *Why do you think people collect these plants?*

In pairs or small groups, students discuss which topic area they think each picture matches. Check the answers.

Answers
1 Women in 'male' sports
2 Differences in male and female brains
3 'Autistic savants' – people of unique talent
4 The powerful healing effects of the human mind
5 A cult BBC TV programme called *Doctor Who*
6 Plants from the Amazon used for medical purposes

YOU WILL LEARN HOW TO ...

Use grammar

Students read through the grammar points and the examples. Go through the first item with them as an example. In pairs, students now match the grammar items in their book. Check the answers.

Answers
Past tense: He began to realise that Stephen was communicating through drawings.
Present perfect tense: Since then he has published a number of books.
Passive: Biological mechanisms have been discovered through new techniques.
Passive continuous: A new generation of painkillers is being developed.
Relative clause: I love reading, which is why I buy so many books.
Reported speech: He said that his health was getting worse.

Use vocabulary

Write the headings on the board. Go through the items in the Student's Book and check understanding. Ask students if they can think of one more item for the *Expressions with mind* heading. Elicit some responses and add them to the list on the board. Students now do the same for the other headings. Some possibilities are:

Expressions with *mind*: play mind games, keep in mind, blow (your) mind

Operations and illness: surgery, scalpel, ward

Sports: basketball, golf, athletics

Expressions with *time*: at the same time, a race against time, for the time being

1 Super brains

Unit overview

TOPIC: The mind – autism and people with extraordinary mental abilities

TEXTS
Reading and listening: two articles about autistic people with outstanding abilities
Listening: a radio interview with a psychologist
Reading: an extract from *The Curious Incident of the Dog in the Night-time* by Mark Haddon
Writing: a story that begins with a given sentence

SPEAKING AND FUNCTIONS
Talking about people with special talents
Discussing ways of using the mind
Discussing a character in an extract from a novel

LANGUAGE
Grammar: Present tense review: present simple, present continuous, present perfect simple, present perfect continuous; Past tense review: past simple, past continuous, past perfect
Vocabulary: Expressions with *mind*; Expressions with *brain*
Pronunciation: /ð/ *the* and /θ/ *thing*

1 Read and listen

If you set the background information as a homework research task, ask the students to tell the class what they found out.

BACKGROUND INFORMATION

Autistic savants: Autism is a neurological disorder, the cause of which is unknown. People suffering from this condition tend to be socially isolated, as they have great difficulty interacting and communicating with others. They often have obsessive, repetitive routines and are extremely disturbed by change. Some autistic people develop an intense preoccupation with a single subject of interest. Of these, some have exceptional abilities in a particular area and are known as *autistic savants*. Their abilities may include doing lightning-fast mental calculations and memorising facts, statistics or musical sequences. Famous films based on autistic savants are *Rain Man* with Dustin Hoffman and *Forrest Gump* with Tom Hanks.

The BBC: The BBC (British Broadcasting Corporation) is the most popular television company in Britain, famous for producing drama, comedy, news programmes and documentaries. The BBC is funded by an obligatory licence fee, paid annually by everybody who owns a TV. It is illegal to watch TV if you do not have this licence.

Warm up

Books closed. Write the title of the unit on the board and ask students what they understand by it. Who would they describe as *super brains*? Ask if they have seen *Rain Man* or *Forrest Gump* and if so, what is special about the lead characters. You could pre-teach the words *autistic* and *autism* at this point, giving an explanation in L1 if necessary.

a Ask students to look at the pictures and discuss what the two boys might have in common. Students read the texts quickly to check their predictions.

Answer
They both grew up with autism (and other disabilities), and they both had an extraordinary artistic talent.

b Check understanding of questions 1–4. Elicit answers but do not comment at this stage. Pre-teach difficult vocabulary: *slave, reproduce, memorise, challenge, landmark*. Play the recording. Students read and listen to the texts and complete the table. Ask them to compare their answers in pairs before feedback. Play the recording again, pausing as necessary to clarify any problems.

TAPESCRIPT
See the reading texts on page 6 of the Student's Book.

Answers
Blind Tom
1 Playing the piano.
2 James N. Bethune.
3 He was taken on a tour of the US.
4 He played at the White House; he performed all over the US and in other countries.

Stephen Wiltshire
1 Drawing.
2 His teacher, Chris Marris.
3 He appeared in a BBC TV programme.
4 He has published books of his drawings and paintings.

OPTIONAL ACTIVITY

These two readings could be done as a jigsaw reading. Split the class into two groups – group A students read about Blind Tom and group B students read about Stephen Wiltshire. They find answers to the comprehension questions for their text. Organise the class in A–B pairs. Students give a description of the person in their text and help their partner with the answers to the comprehension questions. This type of activity can be used whenever students are confronted with two short texts.

---

2 Speak

To introduce this activity, write the list of words on the board and ask the class as a whole whether any of the students have a special talent in these areas. Listen to some of their comments and discuss any interesting points further. Go through the questions to check that students understand, and ask them to discuss in small groups. After a short period, ask some students to tell the class about their group's answers.

OPTIONAL ACTIVITY

As a follow-up to the final question, you could group students according to which special talent they would most like to have and ask them to work together with a partner to plan what they would do with that talent. They then regroup to explain their plans to other students.

---

3 Grammar
Present tense review

a) Weaker classes: Books closed. Write on the board:
1 *She plays the piano.*
2 *She's playing the piano.*
3 *She's written three letters.*
4 *She's been writing letters all morning.*

Check that students know the names of the four tenses and how they are constructed. Ask them to briefly explain the differences in meaning (*sentence 1 is in the present simple and talks about a regular habit; sentence 2 is in the present continuous and talks about an action happening at the moment of speaking; sentence 3 is in the present perfect and talks about a finished action which took place in an unspecified time period; sentence 4 is in the present perfect continuous and talks about an action, which may or may not be completed, in an unfinished time period*). Students open their books and follow the procedure for stronger classes.

Stronger classes: Ask students to underline examples of the four tenses in the text about Stephen Wiltshire. Students then identify the reason why each tense is used in the underlined examples.

Answers
Present simple: has, is
Present continuous: are starting
Present perfect: has become, has published
Present perfect continuous: has been creating

b) Students complete the sentences using the tenses in Exercise 3a. Check the answers and ask students to explain why each tense is used, referring back to previous explanations.

Answers
2 has written   3 is ... drawing
4 has been developing   5 have become   6 has

Language notes

1 Students should now be quite familiar with the present simple and continuous tenses, but may still have difficulty with the present perfect simple and continuous. Remind them that the present perfect simple is often used to describe actions which are completed, while the present perfect continuous is used when the speaker wants to focus on the action, not whether it is complete or not. Compare these sentences:
- *I've been running.*
  I've run ten kilometres.
- *I've been making cakes.*
  I've made 30 cakes.

2 Students are often confused by sentences with the verbs *work* and *live*. For example, compare these sentences:
- *I've lived/worked here for ten years.*
  I've been living/working here for ten years.
The meaning here is essentially the same, but the choice of tense changes the emphasis, with the present perfect simple stressing the period of time and the present perfect continuous stressing the action of working or living.

OPTIONAL ACTIVITY

If your students need practice in the use of the present perfect simple and continuous, write these sentences on the board:
1 *I feel sick. I _____ (eat) four cakes this afternoon.* (**'ve eaten**)
2 A: *You look tired.*
  B: *I am. I _____ (decorate) since seven o'clock this morning.* (**'ve been decorating**)
3 *I _____ (try) to contact Sarah for days, but she's never in.* (**'ve been trying**)
4 *The government _____ (ban) smoking in all public places.* (**has banned**)
5 *My grandfather _____ (smoke) for seventy years.* (**has been smoking**)
6 *The school football team _____ (win) the cup seven times.* (**has won**)

Go through the first sentence with the class. Ask students why the verb is in the present perfect rather than the present perfect continuous (*the speaker mentions the number of cakes and focuses on a completed action, therefore the present perfect* have eaten *is used*). Students complete the sentences with the verbs. Check their answers and encourage them to give reasons for their use of each tense.

Past tense review

c) Weaker classes: Books closed. Write on the board:
1 They met in 1989.
2 They were living in London when they met.
3 When John arrived, the film had started.

Check that students can name the tenses of the underlined verbs and know how they are constructed. Ask them to briefly explain the difference in meaning (*verb 1 is in the past simple and talks about a completed action at a specific time; verb 2 is in the past continuous and gives background information to another past action; verb 3 is in the past perfect and talks about a past action which took place before another past event*).

Students open their books and follow the procedure for stronger classes.

Stronger classes: Students underline examples of the three tenses in the text about Blind Tom. Ask them to say why each tense is used in the underlined examples.

Answers
1 bought, had, was, heard, went, found, realised, hired, reproduced, confirmed, took part, were, took, performed, featured, played, had to, failed, died
2 was walking
3 had heard

d) Elicit the answer to question 1. Students complete the sentences, choosing the correct tense. Encourage them to look at time expressions to help them decide which tense to use. When giving feedback, draw attention to the way different tenses are used together. If students are struggling with past tenses, this exercise can be done in open class. Use the sentences to explain how different tenses work together.

Answers
1 learned   2 was playing   3 wrote   4 said
5 had learned

> **Language note**
> It is possible to use *always* with the present or past continuous to talk about a persistently repeated action, usually an annoying one, e.g. *You're always complaining. He was always shouting at people.* However, the past continuous cannot be used in Exercise 3d sentence 4 because of the word order.

e) Students complete the paragraph, choosing the correct tense. Check the answers in open class.

Answers
1 hadn't learned   2 began   3 was listening
4 has learned   5 finds   6 has been working
7 plays

Grammar notebook
Remind students to write down the rules for the tenses and to write a few examples of their own.

4 Vocabulary
Expressions with *mind*

a) 🔊 Remind students that idioms do not have a literal meaning and often have no direct translation in another language. They should be learned as one piece of vocabulary and not broken down to individual words. Introduce the concept of *mind* and contrast this with the meaning of *brain*. Refer to the title of the book – ask what *English in Mind* means. It may be a good idea for students to think of idioms in their own language which include the word for *mind*. Then ask students to match the definitions with the expressions. This can be done in pairs. Play the recording, pausing as necessary for students to check their answers and repeat the expressions.

Stronger students: If students finish early, ask them to think of example sentences using the expressions.

TAPESCRIPT/ANSWERS
2 i   take (your) mind off something
3 f   keep (something) in mind
4 a   make up (your) mind
5 j   slip (your) mind
6 d   be out of (your) mind
7 c   be in two minds
8 g   speak (your) mind
9 h   read (someone's) mind
10 e   have got (something) on (your) mind

> **OPTIONAL ACTIVITY**
> Describe or act out various situations and ask students to explain what you are doing or have done. For example, pretend you can't decide between two films at the cinema (*be in two minds*), then choose a film (*make up your mind*), and then choose a different one (*change your mind*). This is an opportunity to practise tenses from Exercise 3: *What am I doing? What did I do? What was I doing? What have I just done?* Students describe the situations using expressions from Exercise 4a.

b) Draw students' attention to the two pictures. Ask them to say what is happening in each picture and to match them with two of the dialogues. Students then complete the dialogues. Check their answers and encourage them to write an example of their own for each expression in their vocabulary notebook.

Unit 1   13

Answers
2 make up your mind
3 changed my mind
4 'm in two minds
5 slipped my mind
6 take my mind
7 keep it in mind
8 speak your mind
9 read your mind
10 out of your mind

OPTIONAL ACTIVITY
Weaker classes: Students can act out the dialogues. Make sure they are saying them with the correct stress and intonation.
Stronger classes: Students can write their own short dialogues using the expressions. They can then act them out in front of the class. Make sure they are using the expressions in an appropriate context and saying them with the correct stress and intonation. With very creative classes, students can mime situations, while other students think of the dialogue that is being mimed.

Language notes
1 The expressions in sentences 2, 3, 4 and 8 in Exercise 4b are often followed by *about*.
2 Note that the expressions *take your mind off something* and *slip your mind* are a bit different from the others: here something affects the person's mind – the person is not the subject. Students may produce statements like **I've taken my mind off the problem* or **I've slipped my mind*.

Vocabulary notebook
Encourage students to add the vocabulary from this exercise to their notebook. They may find it useful to note down translations of the expressions.

5 Speak
Read through the four questions with the class to check understanding. It is a good idea to answer a couple of questions yourself to give an example of the type of answers they might produce. Students ask and answer in pairs. Invite some students to express their ideas to the class and encourage discussion.

Weaker classes: Students can write their answers before speaking. Encourage them to look at their notes as little as possible.

6 Listen
If you set the background information as a homework research task, ask the students to tell the class what they found out.

BACKGROUND INFORMATION
Prime numbers: A prime number is a number which can be divided only by 1 and itself. Prime numbers are always odd as even numbers can always be divided by 2.

Square roots: A square root is a number which is multiplied by itself to give a certain number. For example, 7 is the square root of 49 (7 x 7 = 49). 49 is the square of 7.

Warm up
To introduce the topic of numbers, write three numbers which are relevant to you on the board. Invite students to ask you questions, the answer to which must be *yes* or *no* (with a clue or two if they are finding it difficult), until they discover what the numbers represent. For example, *3 = the day of my birthday*; *84 = the number of my house*. Then get students to do the same in pairs or small groups.

a) Books closed. Write the number sequences on the board and elicit answers from the class.

Answers
A 29, 31, 37
B 10, 12, 25

b) Ask which of the sequences are prime numbers and which are square roots and write the words next to the sequences. Elicit the meaning of *square root* and *prime number*.

Answers
A: prime numbers B: square roots

c) Tell students that they are going to listen to an interview with a psychologist about autistic savants. Refer students back to Exercise 1 and ask what they think autistic savants might be good at remembering.

d) Students listen to the recording and check their ideas. Tell them not to worry about any unknown vocabulary at this stage, but just to try to get a general understanding of the conversation. Play the recording again, with pauses if necessary.

TAPESCRIPT
Interviewer Good evening, and welcome to *Psychology Today*. Our topic today is 'autistic savants' – people who are not only autistic, but also have an exceptional, extraordinary ability of some kind. And here to talk to us is Dr Margaret Sellers. Hello, Dr Sellers.
Expert Good evening.
Interviewer Perhaps you could give us one or two examples of the special abilities that autistic savants can have?

Expert OK. Well, the most common forms involve things like mathematical calculations, exceptional memory, artistic abilities and musical abilities. To start with mathematics – there's a very special mathematical ability that many autistic individuals display. You ask them a question like: 'What day of the week was the 22nd of May, 1961?' and they can give you the correct answer very, very quickly, within seconds – Monday. And of course they're always right! It's what we call *calendar memory*. Other autistic people can multiply and divide very large numbers in their head, and they can calculate square roots and prime numbers, things like that, with almost no hesitation.

Interviewer And memory?

Expert Yes, just to give you a couple of examples ... err, well, there are autistic savants who can memorise the complete road systems of their countries – you know, the names and numbers of all the roads and where they all go to – and there are others who can remember the birthday of everyone they meet, even after meeting someone once and not seeing them again for 20 years or more. Sports statistics are another example. Some savants can tell you everything, everything about a sports team or a player.

Interviewer Is this a male phenomenon, by the way? It seems there are more boys or men among autistic savants than girls or women.

Expert No, not exclusively. But it's interesting that boys are four times more likely to be autistic savants than girls.

Interviewer Yes, that is interesting. Do we know why?

Expert No – and to be honest, there's not much that we do know for sure about this. Erm, autistic savants are like other autistic people in most ways, for example, routine is very important for them; things must always happen in the same way and at the same time and so on, routine is very important for autistic people – but only about 10 per cent of autistics also have this extra, special ability that makes them 'savant'.

Interviewer 10 per cent? I see. So it's quite rare.

Expert Oh yes. It's usually recognised in a person quite early, in their childhood, but the autistic savant cannot tell us how they do the things they do, so it's hard to research. And surprisingly, it seems that there is nothing different about the brains of autistic savants, their brains are just like ours. And this means perhaps that all of us have the potential to be savants, all of us could be savants, but it is autism that brings the talents out.

Interviewer So, is it only autistic people who ...

Answers
dates, road systems, birthdays, sports statistics

(e) 🔊 Read through the questions to ensure that students understand the meaning. Explain difficult vocabulary: *common, ratio, percentage, significance*. Encourage students to think of the type of answer they are looking for. Is it a number, a word, a group of words? Play the recording again. Students listen and answer the questions.

Weaker classes: Help students to understand the listening by pre-teaching *memory, memorise, calculate, multiply, divide, more likely, routine*.

Answers
1 Things like mathematical calculations, exceptional memory, artistic abilities and musical abilities.
2 Some autistic savants can calculate square roots and prime numbers almost without hesitation.
3 The ratio of boys to girls is 4:1.
4 About 10%.
5 Perhaps all of us could be savants, but it is autism that brings the talents out.

OPTIONAL ACTIVITY
Give students two minutes to continue the prime number sequence as far as possible. They should work in pairs – and in English!

7 Vocabulary
Expressions with *brain*

(a) Books closed. Draw a picture of a brain on the board and ask students what they do with their brain. Write their ideas on the board. Examples might include *think, have ideas, remember, calculate, dream, invent, fantasise, analyse* and so on. Tell students to open their books and draw their attention to the expressions around the picture. Ask them to read the dialogues to work out the meanings of the expressions in context. Students work in pairs to match the expressions with the definitions.

Answers
2 pick your sister's brains
3 brainwave
4 brainchild
5 the brains
6 You've got boys on the brain.

(b) Before students complete the exercise, ask check questions to make sure they have understood the meaning of the expressions. For example:
Have we brainstormed ideas in this lesson?
If you want help with your homework, whose brains do you pick?
Have you had a brainwave recently?
Whose brainchild was Microsoft?
Who is the brains in your family?
What have you got on the brain?

Students complete the sentences using the expressions in Exercise 7a. Check the answers and encourage students to write an example of their own for each expression in their vocabulary notebook.

Unit 1 15

Answers
1 got ... on the brain   2 the brains   3 brainwave
4 brainchild   5 pick ... brains   6 brainstorm

OPTIONAL ACTIVITY

In pairs, students write a short dialogue which contains one or more of the expressions with *brain*. You could ask pairs to act out the dialogue to the class and vote on the most interesting.

---

8 Pronunciation
/ð/ *the* and /θ/ *thing*

a 🔊 Students turn to page 120 and read through the words. Play the recording, pausing after each word for students to repeat. Ask them to write the words in the correct column according to the pronunciation of *th*. Go through the first few with them if necessary.

Answers

ð	θ
these	three
that	think
them	thanks
this	thirty
therefore	thief

b 🔊 Before playing the recording, ask students to read the sentences and think about how to pronounce them. Play the recording, pausing after each sentence for students to check and repeat. Encourage them to pronounce the *th* sounds correctly and to use correct intonation.

Literature in mind

9 Read

If you set the background information as a homework research task, ask the students to tell the class what they found out.

BACKGROUND INFORMATION

The Curious Incident of the Dog in the Night-time: This novel was written by Mark Haddon and published in 2003. The narrator, Christopher, has Asperger's Syndrome, which is a milder form of autism. He has difficulties relating to other people and a very literal understanding of language, but at the same time he is a mathematical genius with a remarkable photographic memory. The novel is both a murder mystery and an exploration of how the world is experienced by someone with Asperger's Syndrome. It was extremely popular with teenagers and adults and won the 2003 Whitbread Book of the Year.

Warm up

To introduce the topic of literature, ask students which books they have read recently and which are the most popular books with teenagers in their country. Encourage them to recommend a book to the class and to say why they liked it.

a Students read the cover of the book and the short summary of the story. Ask them whether they would be interested in reading the book and why or why not.

b Students read the text quickly to find out what the police have come to investigate. Tell them it is not important to understand every word.

Answer
They've come to investigate a dog which has been killed.

c The descriptions in the extract are important to understanding how the mind of the main character works, but they contain some quite difficult vocabulary, so it is a good idea to pre-teach some key words. Pre-teach *tights, stuck, poking out, squatted, stacking up, loaves, slicing, blockage, groaning, white noise*. Weaker classes may find the text difficult and may need more guidance. Ask students to read the text again and answer the questions. Students check their answers with a partner before feedback.

Answers
1 Because they have uniforms and numbers and you know what they are meant to be doing.
2 He notices small details which most people would not see.
3 He is 15 years and 3 months and 2 days. Most people would not be so exact, or would not even know their exact age.
4 He was confused and upset because the policeman was asking too many questions and asking them too quickly.
5 He starts groaning to shut out all other sounds.
6 By making him the narrator and letting us see things through his eyes.

Discussion box
Weaker classes: Students can choose one question to discuss.
Stronger classes: In pairs or small groups, students go through the questions in the box and discuss them.
Monitor and help as necessary, encouraging students to express themselves in English and to use any vocabulary they have learned from the text. Ask pairs or groups to feedback to the class and discuss any interesting points further.

OPTIONAL ACTIVITY

As a fun activity, students could write a short description of another member of the class, focusing on a tiny detail of their appearance, as Christopher does in the first paragraph of the text. Ask students to read their descriptions to the class and see if other students can guess who is being described.

10 Write

The planning for this exercise can be done in class and the writing can be set as homework.

a) Students look at the picture. Ask them to describe what is happening and to guess why. Ask how the people are feeling. Students read the story quickly and answer questions 1 and 2.

Answers
1 She felt worried and anxious.
2 She felt extremely embarrassed.

b) Students look for time expressions in the story. Get feedback and write the expressions in a column on the board. To check understanding, ask students to think of sentences including the expressions. Write some examples on the board.

Answers
all day, All morning, At first, that morning, Two hours later, By now, A few seconds later, immediately

c) Students look at the questions and plan their story. Make sure they spend a lot of time on this – emphasise the importance of organising some basic ideas and a general framework for the story at the outset. Ask them to use their plan to write a story of three or four paragraphs. In a subsequent lesson, encourage students to read each other's stories and decide which they think would win the writing competition.

OPTIONAL ACTIVITY

A more interactive activity is known as process writing. After a planning session, students write their first draft. This is written quickly with more emphasis on fluency than accuracy. This first draft is then read by another student who gives the writer ideas on how to improve it. At this first reading, they should concentrate on content and clarity and on how to make the story more interesting, rather than correcting grammar.
The writer then rewrites the story to include the new ideas, with more emphasis on accuracy. This is then read again, either by the first partner or by another. This time, the reader focuses on accuracy. The teacher may read the story at this stage to give further corrections. The story is then rewritten again to include these corrections. After so much work it is a good idea to put the stories on the wall, so that the whole class can circulate and read them.

2 Mind over matter

Unit overview

TOPIC: Health and medicine

TEXTS
Reading and listening: an article about placebos
Reading: an article about rainforest remedies used by tribal healers in South America
Listening: a conversation about flower remedies
Writing: an article for a school magazine

SPEAKING AND FUNCTIONS
Discussing placebos and the use of humans and animals to test medicines
Discussing problems and remedies

LANGUAGE
Grammar: Passive review: present simple, present perfect, past simple, past perfect and future forms of the passive; Passive continuous tenses
Vocabulary: Health and medicine; Adjectives to describe feelings
Pronunciation: Consonant clusters

1 Read and listen

If you set the background information as a homework research task, ask the students to tell the class what they found out.

BACKGROUND INFORMATION

Placebos: A placebo (originally a Latin word meaning *I will please*) is a substance that a doctor may prescribe, telling the patient that it is a therapeutic treatment, when in fact it has no active ingredients at all. In many cases, patients' belief in the treatment makes them feel better. Most studies into the effects of placebos have found that they do have a positive effect, not only mentally, but also in a physical improvement in the condition. Experimenters use placebos in clinical trials of new medicines. A 'test group' of patients receives the therapy being tested and a 'control group' receives the placebo. It can then be determined if positive results from the test group exceed those due to the 'placebo effect'. If they do, the therapy given to the test group is assumed to be effective.

Warm up

Ask students what makes them feel better when they are ill or in pain. Brainstorm ideas. Explain the expression in the unit title, *mind over matter* (the power of the mind to control or overcome physical problems). Have students ever experienced something like this? A familiar example might be when they were small children and their mother gave them a kiss on a cut or bruise to make it better – an example of the placebo effect!

a Students read the text quickly to answer the question. Tell them not to try to understand every word but to get a general idea of what the text is about. When you discuss the answer with the class, allow students to make their explanation in L1.

Answer
A placebo is something that looks like a medical treatment for an illness but actually hasn't got any healing ingredients.

b 🔊 Check that students understand the questions. You may want to pre-teach the following key words: *cancer, tumour, fake, worthless, ignore, heal*. Play the recording while students read. You could pause as necessary to check understanding and clarify any difficulties. Students answer the questions and compare answers with a partner before feedback.

TAPESCRIPT
See the reading text on page 12 of the Student's Book.

Answers
1 His tumours disappeared within two days.
2 An official report saying that Krebiozen was worthless.
3 Doctors have ignored the story because it is too strange and they can't explain it.
4 Doctors are discovering that the placebo effect is powerful. They have found that if patients believe they will get better, this can cause a chemical reaction in the brain which affects the body. Body reactions can be caused by what the brain expects to happen.

OPTIONAL ACTIVITY

If you would like your students to do more close comprehension work on the text, you can use the following *true / false / don't know* exercise. The statements are in the order of the text. To make the exercise more challenging, you could write them on the board in a different order.
1 *At first, Mr Wright didn't want an injection.* **(false)**
2 *Mr Wright lived for two years after his second injection.* **(false)**
3 *Reactions to placebos are caused by the brain predicting what is going to happen.* **(true)**
4 *Placebos can cure diseases completely.* **(don't know)**
5 *Doctors do not use placebos any more.* **(false)**

Discussion box
Weaker classes: Students can choose one question to discuss.
Stronger classes: In pairs or small groups, students go through the questions in the box and discuss them.
Monitor and help as necessary, encouraging students to express themselves in English and to use any vocabulary they have learned from the text. Ask pairs or groups to feedback to the class and discuss any interesting points further.

2 Grammar
Passive forms review

Students covered the passive in SB2, Units 6 and 9, and SB3, Unit 7.

a) Weaker classes: Books closed. Write on the board:
Doctors often use placebos.
Placebos ...

Ask students to complete the second sentence to mean the same as the first one (*Placebos are often used by doctors.*). Ask students to find the subject (*Doctors*) and object (*placebos*) of the first sentence. Then ask why we sometimes change the order and use the passive. Explain that the passive is used to place importance on the 'receiver' of the action – we are more interested in the placebos than the doctors. Write the following sentences on the board and elicit the names of the tenses used. Then help the students to make passive versions.

1. *They teach Spanish in many English schools.*
   (*Spanish is taught in many English schools.*)
2. *A policeman has arrested my brother.*
   (*My brother has been arrested.*)
3. *Yesterday a man in London discovered a new painting by Picasso.*
   (*A new painting by Picasso was discovered in London yesterday.*)
4. *Somebody had stolen my bag.*
   (*My bag had been stolen.*)
5. *A man will open the new theatre next week.*
   (*The new theatre will be opened next week.*)

Continue with the procedure for stronger classes.

Stronger classes: Students underline examples of the five passive tenses in the text. If they underline each tense in a different colour, it will stand out clearly. As you get feedback, write examples on the board. Draw attention to the word order and ask who the 'doer' of the action is in each case. Then ask students to complete the rule in the box. This can be done as a whole class activity or individually, depending on the level of the class.

Answers
Present simple passive: are achieved, are not caused
Present perfect passive: has been ignored, has been thought of
Past simple passive: was diagnosed, was given
Past perfect passive: had been given
Future passive: will be used
Rule: be, past participle; perfect, be; perfect, be; will, won't, past participle; by

Language note
The text also has an example of the passive with *can*: *it can be shown* (paragraph 3). You may want to tell students that other modals can be used in this way, e.g. *This medicine **should be taken** once a day. Your parcel **might be delivered** tomorrow.*

b) Ask students to read through sentences 1–6 and pre-teach the words *mild* and *appendicitis*. Students complete the sentences.

Answers
2 was diagnosed   3 was discovered, was tested
4 will be done   5 are caused   6 had been given

--- OPTIONAL ACTIVITY ---
Write the following sentences on the board.
In 1910, the Eiffel Tower was being built in Paris. (False. It was built in 1889.)
In 1910, the aeroplane hadn't been invented. (False. The Wright Brothers made the first flights in 1903.)
In 1910, contact lenses had been invented. (True. The first lens was fitted in 1887 by German physiologist Adolf Fick.)
In 1910, the helicopter had been invented. (True. The first helicopter was flown in Buenos Aires in 1916 by Raul Pateras de Pescara.)
Ask students to discuss whether the sentences are true or false. Encourage them to use passive forms in their discussion. Check the answers. Have a competition to see which student can get closest to the actual dates.

Grammar notebook
Remind students to note down the rules for the passive and to write a few examples of their own.

3 Vocabulary
Health and medicine

Warm up

Draw a sick-looking man on the left-hand side of the board and a well man on the right. Elicit from students some of the steps the man may have to take to be cured. Try to elicit as much of the vocabulary for the matching exercise as possible and write notes on the board.

a) 🔊 Ask students to match the definitions with the expressions. Play the recording for students to listen and check their answers.

Unit 2   19

TAPESCRIPT/ANSWERS
1 c to operate on someone
2 h local anaesthetic
3 j to recover from
4 g general anaesthetic
5 b operating theatre
6 f diagnosis
7 i to suffer from
8 a surgeon
9 e symptom
10 d a check-up

b) Students complete the sentences using expressions a–j from Exercise 3a. Remind them that they should write the correct form of the words. Students compare answers with a partner before feedback. As you check the answers, draw attention to the useful medical expressions in the sentences: *a thorough check-up, in great shape, bad flu, seriously ill, a high temperature, terrible headaches.*

Answers
1 check-up   2 operated on   3 surgeon
4 a general anaesthetic, a local anaesthetic
5 recover from   6 diagnosis   7 operating theatre
8 symptoms   9 's suffering from

> **Language note**
> Students may be surprised at the term *operating theatre*. Explain that in the 19th century, operations took place in auditoriums and were watched by large groups of medical students, making the room resemble a theatre.

Vocabulary notebook
Encourage students to start a new section *Health and medicine* in their notebook and add these words. They may find it useful to note down translations of the words too.

── **OPTIONAL ACTIVITY** ──
For more medical vocabulary, write the following sentences on the board and ask students to put the verbs in the correct places.
took   took   wrote   saw   felt   got
1 Barbara .... the medicine. (**took**)
2 The doctor .... her a prescription. (**wrote**)
3 Barbara .... better. (**got/felt**)
4 Barbara .... ill. (**felt**)
5 She .... a doctor. (**saw**)
6 The doctor .... her temperature and blood pressure. (**took**)
Check the answers. Then ask students to put the six sentences into the order in which the events happened (4, 5, 6, 2, 1, 3).

4 Pronunciation
Consonant clusters

a) 🔊 Students turn to page 120 and read through the sentences. Play the recording. Students listen, focusing specifically on the underlined consonants.

b) 🔊 Play the recording again, pausing after each sentence. Students repeat the featured word on its own and then the whole sentence.

5 Read
If you set the background information as a homework research task, ask students to tell the class what they have found out.

> **BACKGROUND INFORMATION**
> **Shamans:** A Shaman is a healer in tribal societies – a mixture of medical practitioner and spiritual guide. Both spiritual and physical methods are used to heal. It is believed that the Shaman, often in a trance state, is able to communicate with the spirit world to predict and control the future, to protect the tribe and to cure illness. Many Shamans have expert knowledge of the plant life in their area and often prescribe herbs as treatment. Each healing is tailored to the needs of the individual patient. Western medicine seeks to find one cure that works for many – if the number it helps is too small it isn't offered at all. The Shaman provides unique treatment, which holistically addresses what a person needs at this time.
>
> **Parkinson's Disease:** This disorder affects the nervous system, disrupting communication between the brain and the muscles in the body. Sufferers endure poor balance and lack of movement and they often shake uncontrollably. Famous sufferers include the actor Michael J. Fox and the boxer Muhammad Ali.

Warm up
Ask students how they think people would cure illness if we did not have chemists and hospitals. Listen to a few ideas in open class.

a) Ask students to look at the picture and use it to pre-teach *healers, remedies* and *herbs*. Read through the questions and help with other new vocabulary. Students read the text quickly to find the answers. Tell them not to try to understand every word but to look for the specific information required by the questions.

b) Read through the text with the class, pausing where necessary to help with vocabulary and comprehension. Check understanding of the two questions. Students answer the questions and check their answers with a partner before feedback.

Answers
1 Quinine, Curare.
2 They are very powerful and they are non-addictive.

6 Grammar
Passive continuous tenses

a) Ask students to find the sentences in the text and focus on the passive continuous verbs. Explain that these are the passive forms of the present continuous and past continuous tenses. To make this clear, write the following on the board:

Active	Passive
They're building six new houses in Pitt Street.	Six new houses are being built in Pitt Street.
Someone was cleaning the hall for the concert.	The hall was being cleaned for the concert.

To reinforce the point, you could ask students to change the examples in the exercise into the active form. (*Every day people are discovering more and more plants. People are developing a new generation of painkillers. Native Indians were using these plants long before the Europeans arrived.*) Focus on the form of the passive continuous verbs and ask students to complete the rule. Emphasise the use of *being*.

Answers
1 are being 2 is being 3 were being
Rule: be; past participle

Language notes
1 Students may be confused about the difference between the present/past simple passive and the present/past continuous passive. Emphasise that the rules they know for active verbs apply also to passive ones. If they are not sure which tense to use, advise them to change the sentence into the active form – this will help them to recognise whether the simple or continuous form is needed.
2 Sentences 1 and 3 in Exercise 6a could be written in the simple passive form: *Every day, more and more plants are discovered. These plants were used by native Indians …* However, the use of the continuous form stresses the idea of an ongoing process continuing over a period of time, either in the present or in the past.
3 Pay close attention to pronunciation, especially for the present continuous passive. In rapid speech, the initial *am*, *is* or *are* may not be heard, and *being* may be heard as *been*, resulting in errors such as **I being asked to work very hard.* or **Our exams been marked at the moment.*

---

b) Students complete sentences 1–6 using the correct form of the passive continuous. Go through the first sentence as an example. Ask students to compare answers with a partner before checking in class.

Answers
2 are being used by many people because they are often cheaper.
3 the size of Belgium was being destroyed
4 was being made
5 are now being advertised on TV by holiday companies in Britain.
6 types of plants are being found (by scientists)

OPTIONAL ACTIVITY
For further practice of the present continuous passive, ask students to think of changes that are currently taking place in their school, town or country. Write examples on the board, e.g. *A new hotel is being built in Park Street.*

---

7 Listen

If you set the background information as a homework research task, ask students to tell the class what they have found out.

BACKGROUND INFORMATION

Flower remedies: The most popular flower remedies in the UK are Bach flower remedies – dilutions of flower essences discovered and developed by Dr Edward Bach in the 1930s. Practitioners claim that the energy of the flower is transmitted to the user, but some researchers say that any success is an example of the placebo effect. There are 38 original Bach remedies, each prescribed for certain mental and emotional problems, including depression, anxiety, insomnia and stress. Remedies can be used alone or in conjunction with other remedies, and some say each flower gives specific qualities to the remedy. Up to six or seven remedies are typically mixed together by a naturopath or other healer for each patient to meet his/her individual needs. The best-known Bach flower remedy is Rescue Remedy™, which is believed to relieve acute stress, anxiety and panic attacks, especially in emergencies. It has been claimed that this remedy has been effective in calming domestic animals and in the treatment of diseased plants.

a) Tell students they are going to listen to two people talking about flower remedies. Draw attention to the six pictures and ask them to identify the plants in L1. Read out the plant names in English and ask students to repeat. Look at the list of problems (a–f) and check understanding of the vocabulary. You can also pre-teach *envy* and *envious*. Play the recording.

Unit 2

Students listen and match the remedies with the problems. Ask them to compare answers with a partner before checking in class.

TAPESCRIPT

Girl What's the matter, Andy? You really don't seem your usual self these days.
Boy Me? Oh, I'm OK, I guess. I mean ... oh, I don't know. I'm just really, really tired. I think it's because of those exams. You know, I worked and studied so hard for weeks and weeks, and now the exams are over, but I'm still just exhausted.
Girl And what are you doing about it?
Boy Sorry?
Girl I mean, are you taking anything?
Boy Medicine, you mean?
Girl Uh huh.
Boy Well, no. I haven't fallen ill. I'm just tired. I'm not going to see a doctor for that.
Girl Sure. But do you know what you should do? You should get some olive flower remedy and take that.
Boy Flower remedy? Oh please!
Girl What?
Boy Come on, Cathy! That stuff doesn't work. Olive flower remedy!
Girl It certainly does! I took it when I was very tired and I felt so much better. Flower remedies are excellent!
Boy Right. Show me a flower remedy that can heal a broken leg.
Girl Well, of course, there isn't one. You're just being stupid now. And anyway, flower remedies are much more about curing the mind, not just the body.
Boy Oh, I see. So if I'm feeling depressed, there's a flower remedy that will cheer me up and help me get over it.
Girl Well, in actual fact – yes. It's mustard. And before you laugh, my aunt was in a really bad way last year, really depressed, and she took mustard and it helped a lot.
Boy So what is this stuff? I mean, do you eat it?
Girl No, it's drops of liquid extracted from flowers. You put the drops in water and drink it, and after a few days, it starts working.
Boy So what other problems can it help?
Girl Well, any psychological problem, really. Like, sometimes people feel really sorry for themselves all the time, and that's not a very positive feeling, it brings you down – but there's a flower remedy for that. It's willow.
Boy So these flower remedies can cure just about anything.
Girl Well, I don't know about that. But they can cure all kinds of psychological problems. I heard of someone who was always envious of other people, and he took the holly remedy, and it helped.
Boy So they work even for things like envy?
Girl Yes. There are almost 40 remedies. If you're feeling guilty about something, you can take pine. If you don't have a lot of self-confidence, the flower remedy larch is supposed to help.
Boy OK, well I suppose anything's worth a try. Olive remedy, you say, for tiredness?
Girl Yes, that's right. Good luck!

Answers
1 f   2 d   3 b   4 e   5 c   6 a

b 🔊 Read through the statements with the class. Students listen to the recording again to decide if the statements are true or false. Remind them to correct the false statements.

Answers
1 F (He isn't taking any medicine.)   2 T   3 T   4 T
5 F (There are almost 40 flower remedies.)

8 Vocabulary
Feelings

Warm up

Books closed. Write the words *feeling sorry for yourself, depressed, guilty, having no confidence, exhausted, jealous* on the board. Ask students if they can think of any other words for negative emotional states.

a Write the following sentences on the board and ask students how they feel in these situations. Elicit or explain the six adjectives from the list 1–6.

1 *You are going to a concert and you can't find your ticket.* (panicky)
2 *You are on a school trip and want to go home and see your friends and family.* (homesick)
3 *You aren't listening to what people are saying to you.* (inattentive)
4 *You always forget where you put your keys.* (absent-minded)
5 *You have two exams tomorrow that you must pass. You can't sleep.* (over-anxious)
6 *You are looking at photographs of happy times ten years ago.* (nostalgic)

Students match adjectives 1–6 with definitions a–f.

Answers
1 c   2 d   3 a   4 e   5 f   6 b

b Ask students to read through the sentences and check any difficult words. Students complete the sentences with adjectives. Ask them to compare answers with a partner before checking with the whole class.

Answers
1 guilty   2 absent-minded   3 exhausted
4 jealous   5 panicky   6 homesick   7 inattentive
8 nostalgic

Module 1

OPTIONAL ACTIVITY

Ask students to think of a situation when they have felt bad for some reason. In pairs, they describe the situation to their partner, without mentioning their feelings. The other person guesses how their partner felt, using one or more of the adjectives in Exercises 7 and 8.

Vocabulary notebook

Encourage students to start a new section *Feelings* in their notebook and add these words. They may find it useful to note down translations of the words too.

9 Speak

a In pairs, students discuss the questions.

b Pairs join up to form groups of four and discuss again. Then ask some students to offer examples of problems and possible remedies to the class.

Eyes open

10 Read and listen

If you set the background information as a homework research task, ask students to tell the class what they have found out.

> **BACKGROUND INFORMATION**
>
> **The driving test:** has existed in the UK since 1935. Nowadays, more than one million people take their test every year. Around 40% pass on their first attempt, but it is not uncommon for people to take the test several times before passing. To take the test, you must be over 17 and you must have received training from a licensed driver, usually around 25 hours of lessons.
> The UK driving test includes a 40-minute practical test in which you have to drive correctly under the watchful eye of an examiner and a 40-minute theory test of 35 multiple choice questions, of which 30 have to be answered correctly.

Warm up

Ask students how old they want to be when they take their driving test. Do they think it is difficult to pass? Why / Why not?

a 🔊 If students have used previous levels of *English in Mind*, ask them what they can remember about Caroline, Joanne and Matt from the photo story. Look at the photo and introduce them to the new character, Ash. Ask who they think the woman is (*a driving test examiner*). Students read the questions and predict the answers. Play the recording while students read and check their predictions. Check the answers.

TAPESCRIPT
See the dialogue on page 16 of the Student's Book.
Answers
He's got his driving test. He fails the test.

b Students answer the questions. Encourage them to answer from memory before reading the text again to check. Check the answers and ask students to give reasons.

Weaker classes: Before students look at the questions, you may want to play the recording again, pausing as necessary to clarify any problems.

Answers
1 He expects to fail.
2 She says that he should try positive thinking.
3 Six.
4 He's going to Manchester for a meal with a girl he met after his driving test.

11 Everyday English

a Students look back at the text in Exercise 10 and find out who said the expressions. Then ask them to study the context and decide what the expressions mean. Get them to repeat the full sentences from the text, giving attention to the intonation.

Answers
1 Matt   2 Matt   3 Ash   4 Caroline   5 Matt
a 4   b 1   c 5   d 2   e 3

b In pairs, students read and complete the dialogues. Check the answers and then ask students to practise the dialogues with their partner.

Answers
1 How come
2 Easier said than done.
3 How on earth
4 You're well on your way

c Students look back at the text to find two examples of someone interrupting and the reaction of the other speaker.

Answers
Matt: You're off your trolley.
Caroline: Matt – let me finish, will you?

Joanne: But Ash, what's this test got to do with …
Ash: Hang on a minute – I haven't finished.

> **OPTIONAL ACTIVITIES**
>
> These optional activities can be used after every Everyday English exercise in the Student's Book.
> **Weaker classes:** Students can act out the dialogues. Make sure they are saying them with the correct stress and intonation.
> **Stronger classes:** Students can write their own short dialogues using the expressions. They can then act them out in front of the class. Make sure they are using the expressions in an appropriate context and saying them with the correct stress and intonation.

12 Write

The planning for this exercise can be done in class and the writing can be set as homework.

a) Read through the poster and the list with students. Ask which of the ideas are shown in the pictures. Ask students what else they would do to improve the quality of their life. Brainstorm ideas and write them up on the board.

b) Students read the paragraphs quickly and identify the topic from the list in Exercise 12a.

Answer
think positively about yourself

c) Explain that the text contains two topic sentences that introduce the ideas in each paragraph. Ask students to read the text again to find the two topic sentences.

Answers
People often don't do what they really want to because of a fear of failure.
The secret to overcoming this problem is learning to believe in yourself.

--- OPTIONAL ACTIVITY ---
Write the following sentences on the board. Tell students that these are topic sentences and ask them to decide which of the brainstorming ideas in Exercise 12a they correspond to. Students check their answers with a partner before feedback.
1 *People these days have too much to do and not enough time to do it.* (learn how to use your time well)
2 *A happy mind needs a healthy body.* (watch what you eat)
3 *They say that a problem shared is a problem halved.* (talk about your problems)

d) Point out that a paragraph should go on to develop the idea expressed in the topic sentence. One way to do this is to give examples. Ask students to look back at the text and find the examples used.

Answers
- You don't apply for a job in case you don't get it. You don't perform at the school concert because others might laugh at you.
- Talk about your problem with a friend.
  Look for advice on the internet.
  Visualise yourself being successful.
  Practise breathing techniques.

--- OPTIONAL ACTIVITY ---
Write the following sentences on the board:
1 *Watch what you eat.*
2 *Learn how to do something well.*
3 *Laugh a lot.*
Read through the three ideas and ask students to write some examples for each one. Students compare ideas with a partner before you take a few examples in class feedback.

e) Students write the paragraphs. This may be an opportunity for them to create a poster with drawings to illustrate their paragraphs. These can be displayed around the room and students can vote on the best one.

Module 1

3 Brainwaves

Unit overview

TOPIC: Differences between men and women and between cultures

TEXTS
Reading and listening: an article about the differences between male and female brains
Listening: an interview and a news report featuring two sportswomen
Reading: different concepts of intelligence in different cultures
Writing: a composition expressing opinions on a sport

SPEAKING AND FUNCTIONS
Discussing different brain types
Discussing women and men in sport
Discussing different types of intelligence

LANGUAGE
Grammar: Relative clauses review: defining and non-defining relative clauses; Relative clauses with *which* referring to a previous clause
Vocabulary: Sports
Pronunciation: Intonation in questions

1 Read and listen

If you set the background information as a homework research task, ask the students to tell the class what they found out.

BACKGROUND INFORMATION

DIY: stands for *do it yourself*. It is very popular in the UK for people to do home improvements like painting, decorating or carpentry themselves rather than paying a professional to do it for them.

Cambridge University: was founded in 1209 and is the second oldest university in the world. It is made up of 31 colleges and has around 25,000 students. 54% of students are female and 46% are male. Famous former students include Charles Darwin, Isaac Newton and Prince Charles.

Warm up

Books closed. Write two headings on the board, *Men's jobs* and *Women's jobs*, and ask students to give you examples of each. Ask them whether men or women make better psychologists, teachers, scientists, taxi drivers, etc. Ask whether boys or girls are more intelligent, and encourage students to give reasons for their answer. Use this discussion to pre-teach *gender* and *gender stereotype*.

a) Read through the questions with the class and elicit the meaning of *newborn*. Ask students to guess the answers to the questions. They then read the text to check their answers.

Answers
1 new-born girls   2 women

b) 🔊 Read through the questions with the class, checking for any difficulties. Play the recording while students read and listen. Students answer the questions and compare answers with a partner before feedback. Play the recording again, pausing as necessary to clarify any problems.

TAPESCRIPT
See the reading text on page 18 of the Student's Book.

Possible answers
1 The ability to understand other people, sensitivity to facial expressions, noticing changes in other people's feelings, judging a person's character.
2 Boys love putting things together and building things. Girls are more interested in character and feelings. The reason is that there are biological differences between male and female brains.
3 Because they think it suggests that one gender is better than the other or creates gender stereotypes.
4 A scientific study shows that boys and girls respond to things differently even when they are newborn or very young babies.
5 Students' own answers.

OPTIONAL ACTIVITY

Write the following statements on the board:
For biological reasons, women often go into the helping professions while men become scientists and engineers.
Because men are more interested in cars, they are likely to be better drivers than women.
Divide the class into four groups and ask each group to prepare a short presentation in favour of or against one of the statements. There should be one group in favour of each statement and one group against. Tell students to think of arguments and examples to support their position – they may have to suppress their real opinions to do this. After some planning time, reorganise the class so that the *before* and *against* groups for each statement are facing each other. Students from each group give their presentation and then go on to debate the topic.

2 Grammar
Relative clauses review

Students covered relative clauses in SB2, Unit 13 and SB3, Unit 15.

a) Weaker classes: Write the following sentences on the board:
1. *That's the house _____ I was born.* (where)
2. *I've got a friend _____ plays the guitar.* (who)
3. *We met a boy _____ mother is a film director.* (whose)
4. *I like stories _____ have a happy ending.* (which/that)

Ask students to complete the sentences, and write the correct answers on the board. Remind students that these words are called *relative pronouns*. They link together two clauses and they refer back to someone or something mentioned earlier in the sentence. Now follow the procedure for stronger students.

Stronger classes: Ask students to complete the sentences. They then find the sentences in the text to check their answers. Point out that in sentences 1 and 4 the relative pronoun can be either *which* or *that*. Ask students to say what or who the relative pronoun refers to in each sentence (1 *magazines*; 2 *friends*; 3 *the lab*; 4 *toys*; 5 *people*).

Answers
1 that (or which)   2 who   3 where
4 which (or that)   5 whose

> **Language notes**
> 1 All the examples in Exercise 2a are defining relative clauses – they give information that is essential to the meaning of the sentence. For this type of clause, *that* is commonly used instead of *which* to refer to things. We also sometimes use *that* to refer to people, especially in conversation.
> 2 In defining relative clauses, we often leave out *who*, *which* or *that* if it is not the subject of the clause, for example:
> *Helena is the girl I met in Greece.* (subject = *I*)
> *Here's the book you lent me.* (subject = *you*)

b) Students complete the rule.

Answers
who; which, that; where; whose

c) Weaker classes: To clarify the use of non-defining relative clauses, write the following sentence on the board:

John is a doctor.

Then add information:

John, who speaks German and Russian, is a doctor.

Point out that the information between the commas is additional and that the sentence makes sense without it. Now follow the procedure for stronger classes.

Stronger classes: Read through the explanation of defining (D) and non-defining (A) relative clauses and check understanding. Ask students to look back at the sentences in Exercise 2a and to say whether the information following the relative pronoun is defining or additional (*it is defining in all the sentences*). In pairs, students decide whether the sentences in 2c are D or A. Point out the use of commas around non-defining clauses.

Answers
1 D   2 A   3 A   4 D   5 A

> **Language note**
> In sentence 1, with its defining relative clause, the pronoun *that* could be used instead of *which*. However, in sentence 3, the relative clause is non-defining. Here the relative pronoun is *which* – we don't normally use *that*. Students may produce sentences like **I've had this jacket, that wasn't very expensive, for five years.* or **John, that works with me, used to be a teacher.*

Look
Read the information in the Look box with the class. Ask students to say what the pronoun *which* refers to in the example (*Jo couldn't get a ticket*). Tell them that this use of *which* is particularly common in spoken English. We often express our feelings about something by ending a sentence with *which* + *be* + adjective, e.g. *I don't have to go to school next week, which is great! I had three exams last week, which was terrible!*

d) Read the examples from the text and ask students to say what the pronoun *which* refers to in each case.

Answers
new-born girls look longer at a face, and new-born boys look longer at a mechanical mobile
the theory creates gender stereotypes

e) Read through the example with the class. Students use *which* to complete the sentences in 2–6. Let students compare answers in pairs before getting feedback. Point out that all the relative clauses in this exercise offer additional information.

Answers
2 Some men and boys can be very aggressive, which isn't true of so many girls and women.
3 The research is about male and female brains, which makes it controversial.
4 Girls often notice people's problems, which means female brains may be built more for empathy.
5 Maths requires a lot of systems-thinking, which is why a lot of men choose it.
6 The author says that both genders have strengths and weaknesses, which makes a lot of sense.

Grammar notebook
Remind students to note down the rules for relative clauses and to write a few examples of their own.

OPTIONAL ACTIVITY

For further practice of relative clauses, write the following sentences on the board. Ask students to make the two sentences into one using a relative pronoun. Students have to decide whether the extra information is defining (D) or additional (A). Let students compare answers with a partner before feedback.
1 *Charlotte is a singer in a band. She lives next door to me.*
 (Charlotte, who lives next door to me, is a singer in a band. A)
2 *That's the club. I met my wife there.*
 (That's the club where I met my wife. D)
3 *I know a man. He has a collection of football boots.*
 (I know a man who has a collection of football boots. D)
4 *Neil can speak four languages. His daughter works with my sister.*
 (Neil, whose daughter works with my sister, can speak four languages. A)

---

3 Speak and listen

If you set the background information as a homework research task, ask the students to tell the class what they found out.

> **BACKGROUND INFORMATION**
>
> **Kart racing:** is a motor sport using small, simple vehicles called *karts* or *go-karts* which are raced on a variety of different circuits. Some karts can go as fast as 250 kph. The sport originated in the 1950s in the USA, but is now internationally popular.
>
> **Danica Patrick:** was born in Wisconsin, USA in 1982. She began karting at the age of ten and went on to win several national championships in karting. She is now a professional racing car driver in the Indy Racing League. She was only the fourth woman to race in the Indianapolis 500 and she was named Newcomer of the Year in 2005.
>
> **Maribel Dominguez:** is the captain and all-time leading scorer in the Mexican women's national football team. After scoring 42 goals in 43 games for the national women's team, she was signed by Celaya, a men's team in the Mexican second division. However, football's governing body FIFA (Fédération Internationale de Football Association) refused to let her play for the club, saying that there must be a clear separation between men's and women's football.

Warm up

In pairs, students have two minutes to think of as many different sports as possible. Then go round the class asking different students to say the name of a sport without repeating any of those previously mentioned. Write any new vocabulary on the board.

> **Language note**
> The English words for many sports (*football, volleyball, surfing, tennis,* etc.) are in international use, but the pronunciation has been adapted to suit different languages. Take this opportunity to show students how the English pronunciation differs from foreign versions of these words.

(**a**) Students look at the photos. Ask them to list the sports in the three categories.

(**b**) Students add other sports to their three lists, perhaps referring back to the list they wrote in the warm-up. Monitor and help students with any new vocabulary. Check that students are spelling and pronouncing words properly.

(**c**) In pairs, students discuss their lists. Encourage them to offer information and opinions about the sports they have tried and to give reasons explaining why they would/wouldn't like to try others. You may like to give them some examples of your own to get them started. For feedback, ask students to give some examples for each category. Find out which class member has done the most unusual sport.

(**d**) Tell students they are going to hear about two sportswomen: a racing car driver and a footballer. Read the sentences with the class and pre-teach difficult vocabulary: *go-karts, amateur league, flipped, knock on wood, tournament, accomplish, beyond words.* Ask students to predict which of the two sportswomen says each of the sentences.

(**e**) 🔊 Play the recording. Students listen and check their answers. Tell them to listen specifically for sentences 1–7 and not to worry if they don't understand every word.

TAPESCRIPT
Danica Patrick
My name's Danica Patrick. I am 22 years old and I race in the Indy Racing League. I've been racing for 14 years. I started out in go-karts and climbed a progressive ladder to where I'm at now. I've been in various accidents through my career. I flipped a few go-karts when I was young. I haven't flipped a race car yet, though. Knock on wood, I haven't broken a bone. I've never really liked to go fast. I just like to go faster than everyone else. So if that's 25 miles per hour, so be it. Or 225 miles per hour, so be that. I just really like to accomplish things. I like to iron because I like to watch a shirt go from wrinkly to flat. I just like to see things improve.

Unit 3

Maribel Dominguez

Mexico's top female football player, Maribel Dominguez, recently caused controversy in the international world of football when she accepted a two-year contract to play alongside men in a second-division Mexican football club, Celaya. Since there isn't a decent amateur league for women in Mexico, Dominguez was forced to look for other options.

Unfortunately for Dominguez, FIFA decided that the male and female game should most definitely be kept apart and she was told she could not join the club. This wasn't the first time that Dominguez had run into trouble because she was a girl wanting to play football. As a young child, she had to keep her hair cut short so that the local boys wouldn't know she was a girl and would let her play with them. They only found out she wasn't a boy when they saw her picture in the paper because she'd got into the national women's team. They went to her house and asked her mother if she was really a girl. When they found out the truth, they got quite a shock.

As for the future, Dominguez hopes to go to Europe, where women's football is taken more seriously, and play for a club in Italy or Spain. She's already represented her country in both the Women's World Cup and the Olympics. At 26 she just wants the chance to do this again. In her words, 'To play in one of those tournaments feels just incredible. To play with a team, to all play at your very best, to score a goal when everybody, the whole world, is watching. There is nothing like it. It is beyond words. It is the best thing that can ever happen to a footballer.'

Answers
1 Danica Patrick   2 Maribel Dominguez
3 Danica Patrick   4 Danica Patrick
5 Maribel Dominguez   6 Danica Patrick
7 Maribel Dominguez

(f) 🔊 Read the questions with the class and pre-teach *philosophy*, *speed*, *ironing* and *motivation*. Play the recording.

Weaker classes: Pause after the third sentence and give students time to do the calculation for question 1. Play the recording again while students listen and complete the exercise. Check the answers, playing and pausing the recording as necessary to clarify any vocabulary problems.

Stronger classes: Ask students try to answer the questions from memory, based on the first listening. Play the recording again for them to check their answers.

Answers
1 Eight.
2 She doesn't really like to go fast, she just likes to go faster than everybody else.
3 She likes to watch the shirt go from wrinkly to flat. / She likes to see things improve.
4 She's got a lot of motivation to improve her performance.

(g) Follow the procedure for weaker or stronger classes as in Exercise 3f.

Answers
1 Because she accepted a contract to join a men's football team.
2 Because she had cut her hair short and they didn't know she was a girl.
3 She hopes to go to Europe and play for a club in Italy or Spain.
4 Playing in a big tournament.

Discussion box
Weaker classes: Students can choose one question to discuss.
Stronger classes: In pairs or small groups, students go through the questions in the box and discuss them. Monitor and help as necessary, encouraging students to express themselves in English and to use any vocabulary they have learned from the text. Ask pairs or groups to feedback to the class and discuss any interesting points further. You may like to expand the discussion on question 2 into an open class debate.

4 Vocabulary and speaking
Sports

Warm up
Books closed. Refer back to the sports mentioned in the previous exercise and ask students to give any names they know for equipment needed to play them. Write the vocabulary on the board. Students open their books and look at the picture on page 21. Ask them to name the sports equipment. If they don't know all the names, don't give them the answers at this stage.

(a) 🔊 Students read texts 1–6 and decide which of the sports in Exercise 4b they refer to. Play the recording. Students listen and check their answers. Ask them if they can now name all of the sports equipment in the picture.

Answers
2 football   3 ice hockey   4 boxing   5 tennis
6 swimming

(b) Students use vocabulary from the texts in Exercise 4a to complete the table. Encourage them to try to complete the table from memory, before looking back at the texts. Check the answers. Ask students if they can think of any other words to add to the table.

Answers

	Equipment needed	Place where it is done
tennis	ball, net, racket	court
football	ball, net	pitch
ice-hockey	skates, puck, sticks	rink
boxing	gloves, helmet	ring
surfing	board	sea
swimming	cap, goggles	pool

> **Language note**
> Students are often confused by the different names used to describe sports venues. You may like to show them the following table:
>
> | Sport | Place where it is done |
> |---|---|
> | football | pitch |
> | cricket | pitch |
> | hockey | pitch |
> | rugby | pitch |
> | tennis | court |
> | basketball | court |
> | badminton | court |
> | golf | course |

(c) In pairs, students choose a sport and their partner asks *yes/no* questions to guess what it is. Do an example with the whole class first, and encourage students to use as many words from Exercise 4b as possible. At the end, you could choose a few students to think of a sport for the whole class to guess.

Weaker classes: Before the pairwork stage, elicit possible questions and write them on the board for students to refer to during the activity.

(d) Write a football score on the board, for example *England 3 – Scotland 1*. Elicit sentences using the verbs *win, score, beat, lose*, e.g. *England won. Scotland scored one goal. England beat Scotland. Scotland lost 3–1*. Check understanding of *medal* and *referee*. Students complete the sentences and compare answers with a partner before feedback.

> **Language note**
> There are several different words for *0* in English. For football scores we say *nil*, as in *three–nil* (3–0) or a *nil–nil draw* (0–0). For tennis scores we say *love*, as in *forty–love* (40–0). When we are saying phone numbers we say *o*, as in *two seven six five o four* (276504).

(e) In groups, students discuss the questions in Exercise 4d. Encourage them to use the words from the box. Ask some students to say their opinions to the class and invite discussion.

Weaker classes: Students can write their ideas before speaking. Encourage them to look at their notes as little as possible.

Answers
1 wins/loses/draws 2 won 3 beats 4 score
5 gets sent off 6 draw

Vocabulary notebook
Encourage students to start a new section *Sport* in their notebook and add these words. They may find it useful to note down translations of the words too.

5 Pronunciation
Intonation in questions

(a) 🔊 Students turn to page 120 and read the sentences. Play the recording several times and ask students to decide whether the intonation rises or falls at the end of each question.

Answers
1 ↓ 2 ↑ 3 ↓ 4 ↓ 5 ↑ 6 ↓ 7 ↓

(b) Ask students to look at the sentences and help them to work out this rule: *Intonation usually falls in questions that begin with a question word. Intonation usually rises in questions that have no question word and require a yes/no answer.* However, warn students that this rule is not invariable. The intonation can vary, depending on the context and the speaker's feelings.

(c) 🔊 Play the recording, pausing after each sentence for students to repeat. Encourage them to produce the same intonation patterns as on the recording.

Culture in mind
6 Read

> **BACKGROUND INFORMATION**
>
> **Intelligence types:** Psychologist Howard Gardner identified the following distinct types of intelligence found in children.
>
> 1 **Linguistic:** Children with this kind of intelligence like writing, reading, telling stories or doing crossword puzzles.
>
> 2 **Logical–Mathematical:** These children like patterns, categories and relationships. They are good at arithmetic problems and strategy games.
>
> 3 **Bodily–Kinaesthetic:** These children process knowledge through bodily sensations. They are often athletic, dancers or good at crafts.
>
> 4 **Spatial:** These children think in images and pictures. They may be fascinated with mazes or jigsaw puzzles, or spend free time drawing, building with Lego or daydreaming.
>
> 5 **Musical:** Musical children are always singing or drumming to themselves. They are usually quite aware of sounds others may miss.

6 **Interpersonal:** These children are leaders among their peers, are good at communicating and seem to understand others' feelings and motives.

7 **Intrapersonal:** These children may be shy. They are very aware of their own feelings and are self-motivated.

(a) Write the word *intelligence* on the board and ask students what they understand by the word. Does it mean the same as *clever*? Focus on the pictures on page 22. Ask students which of the photos they associate the most and the least with *intelligence* and to give reasons for their answers.

(b) Students read through the questions. Check that they understand the difference between *Western* and *non-Western*. Pre-teach difficult key words in the text: *rational debate, hierarchies, academic skills, interpersonal skills, wisdom*. Ask students to read the text. As the language and concepts are quite difficult, you may want to read through the text with them a second time, helping with vocabulary and comprehension. Students answer the questions and compare answers with a partner before feedback.

Answers
1 In Western cultures intelligence is seen as the ability to solve problems and engage in rational debate. In non-Western cultures it is seen as the ability to play your roles in society.
2 Taiwanese-Chinese culture.
3 Interpersonal skills and introspective abilities.

Discussion box
Weaker classes: Students can choose one question to discuss.
Stronger classes: In pairs or small groups, students go through both questions in the box and discuss them. Monitor and help as necessary, encouraging students to express themselves in English and to use any vocabulary they have learned from the text. Ask pairs or groups to feedback to the class and discuss any interesting points further.

— OPTIONAL ACTIVITY —
Make photocopies of the list of seven types of intelligence outlined above in the Background information and hand them out. Ask students to work in small groups and discuss which type of intelligence they have. As feedback, ask some groups to describe their conclusions and see if the rest of the class agree.

7 Write

(a) Ask students if they have ever seen a boxing match (either live or on television). Invite them to discuss briefly what happens at a boxing match and whether or not they think boxing is a good sport to watch. Students read the composition and decide whether it was written by a boy or a girl. Ask them to give reasons for their choice.

(b) Write the words in the box on the board. Ask students which is used to give extra information (*moreover*), which is used for contrast (*however*), which introduces an example (*for example*) and which introduces the ending of a composition (*to conclude*). Students read the composition again and add the words in the box.

Stronger classes: Ask students to use the words in the box to make sentences. Write some examples on the board and ask students what the purpose of the words is.

Answers
1 for example   2 However   3 Moreover
4 To conclude

Language note
You may want to make students aware of some more expressions used to give extra information (*furthermore, in addition, what's more*), to make a contrast (*on the other hand*), to introduce an example (*for instance*) and to introduce the end of a composition (*finally, in conclusion, to summarise*).

(c) Read through the paragraph titles with the students and ask them to decide which paragraph they refer to.

Answers
A Para 4   B Para 2   C Para 1   D Para 3

(d) Draw students' attention to the construction of the composition. Point out that it has a clear introduction and conclusion and that the writer's opinions are backed up by examples. Emphasise that it is important to plan a composition carefully before writing. Look at the mind map and ask students to think of more negatives, positives and opinions. They then prepare a similar mind map for a sport of their choice, and use this to organise their four paragraphs. The writing and checking stages could be set for homework.

4 Time travellers

Unit overview

TOPIC: Time

TEXTS
Reading: an extract from a TV guide
Listening: a radio interview about a cult television series
Reading: a letter from a daughter to her father expressing concern and giving advice
Speaking and listening: song: *If I Could Turn Back Time*
Writing: an informal letter to a friend

SPEAKING AND FUNCTIONS
Asking and answering questions using expressions with *time*
Discussing a letter of advice and possible reactions to it

LANGUAGE
Grammar: Reported speech review: changes in verb tenses; Reporting verbs review: verb patterns
Vocabulary: Expressions with *time*
Pronunciation: Schwa /ə/ teach<u>er</u>

1 Listen

If you set the background information as a homework research task, ask the students to tell the class what they found out.

BACKGROUND INFORMATION

Doctor Who: is an extremely popular BBC science fiction series which originally ran in the UK between 1963 and 1989. The Doctor travels through time and space in a time machine, accompanied by a human helper. He fights a variety of monsters and evil beings, the most famous of which are the Daleks. From time to time the Doctor 'regenerates' and takes on a new body (so that the part can be played by a different actor). The show was successfully re-launched in 2005 and remains popular with children and adults alike.

Warm up

Write *science fiction* on the board and ask students to think of as many science fiction films or TV programmes as possible. Make a list of their suggestions on the board. Ask students each to choose a particular favourite. They then find somebody in the class who has not seen the programme/film and explain it to them. Monitor and help with vocabulary if necessary.

a) Look at the photo. If students are familiar with *Doctor Who*, ask them to say a little about the series. If not, ask them to imagine the type of things that might happen in this show. Read through the extract from a TV guide with the class and check difficult vocabulary: *charismatic, enthusiastic, sidekick, cult.* Students answer questions 1–4.

Answers
1 1989   2 Time Lord   3 with an assistant
4 TV series

b) 🔊 Read through the questions and check for any difficulties with vocabulary. Ask students to try to guess some of the answers, but do not comment on them at this stage. Play the recording. It is a long dialogue, so you will probably need to play it several times. Students listen for the answers to the questions and then compare answers with a partner. Check the answers with the class. You may want to play the recording again, pausing and asking questions to clarify other content in the dialogue.

TAPESCRIPT
Presenter And, just in case you need reminding, *Doctor Who* returns to BBC on Saturday. And I, for one, am very excited. Now obviously, not all of you are as old as me, so just in case you've no idea what *Doctor Who* is all about, I've got Dana Littleton with me here in the studio. Now Dana is an expert on *Doctor Who*. She's an MA student in Media Studies at Warwick University. She's been studying the programme as part of her course. And she's here to tell you all you ever needed to know about it. Dana, hello and welcome.
Dana Thank you, it's nice to be here.
Presenter Now Dana, believe it or not, I was talking to a young woman the other day and she said that she'd never heard of *Doctor Who*. When I told her that *Doctor Who* was a classic cult TV series, she just looked at me as if I was mad. So, come on, tell us: what's it all about?
Dana Well, *Doctor Who* is a BBC TV series, which features the adventures of a time-travelling character called the Doctor. It was first broadcast in 1963, and became extremely popular and, as you say, a bit of a cult programme.
Presenter And it comes into the category of a science fiction series, is that right?
Dana Well, yes and no. Although the basic idea behind the programme is very sci-fi, one of the things that has made the show so popular is the way it changes genre so often. So, for example, umm one show might be comedy and the next might be real horror. You always get something different. But, as a cult show, you just hum the

Unit 4

first few lines of the theme tune and everyone knows what you're talking about.

Presenter So who exactly is the Doctor?

Dana OK, the Doctor is a member of an alien race called the Time Lords, who live on the planet Gallifrey. These Time Lords have the ability to travel through space and time and change the ways of the universe. Now the Time Lords said that they would never change anything in the universe, but Doctor Who doesn't agree with that, so he does travel about and changes things.

Presenter So, he's a bad guy?

Dana Well, not really. He only does this because he wants to fight evil and help people.

Presenter And how does he get about the universe?

Dana The Doctor has a time travel machine called the Tardis. From the outside this looks like a tiny old-fashioned blue Police telephone box. But of course, inside it's huge. And that's because the Tardis is dimensionally transcendental.

Presenter Wow! You'll have to explain what that means.

Dana Well, there isn't really a definition. I asked a scientist once and he said that it was a fancy way of saying it's bigger on the inside than the outside.

Presenter OK, I get it. A bit like my house! Some people say it's like a Tardis because it's bigger inside than it looks from the street.

Dana Yes, and that's an example of the cult language of *Doctor Who* which has entered into everyday English. The show is so popular that people started to say the word *Tardis* and everyone knew what you were talking about.

Presenter Now tell us about some of the nasty monsters in the programme.

Dana Well, of course, one of the best things about the show are the wonderful monsters who the Doctor has to fight on his travels. There's the Ice-men and the sea monsters and the Cybermen and of course the Daleks.

Presenter Ah yes, the Daleks. Those metallic things on wheels with those funny stick-like arms and all those circles all over their bodies. And for anyone who doesn't know what a Dalek sounds like, listen carefully now.

Dana Now when I was a kid and I heard that, I used to hide behind my sofa. I think we all did. The Daleks were pretty scary.

Presenter Now another thing that I think you should mention is how the Doctor can change his appearance.

Dana Well, the original Doctor was played by William Hartnell but one day he told the show's producers that his health was getting worse and that he couldn't play the Doctor any more. Now they didn't want to lose their show, so they came up with the great idea that every time a Time Lord gets old or wounded in a battle, his body transforms so that he looks like a new person. This meant they could change the actor and continue with the series.

Presenter And how many Doctors have there been?

Dana Since William Hartnell there have been eight other official Doctors.

Presenter And Doctor Who has an assistant, right?

Dana Yes, that's right. The Doctor almost always has an assistant and most of these are young women from present-day Earth, although there have been a few assistants from the past and the future too.

Presenter Well, it's all very exciting and I must say that I for one will be glued to my TV set this Saturday evening. Dana, thank you so much for sharing all this with us. Will you be watching the new series too?

Dana I've already seen it at a preview and I will tell you, it is fabulous. Don't miss it.

Presenter Well, Dana says the show's fabulous, so it must be, because she knows what she's talking …

Answers

1 c   2 d   3 b   4 a   5 d   6 d   7 c   8 c

OPTIONAL ACTIVITY

Doctor Who is capable of travelling back through time. Ask students which era they would like to visit and why. In pairs, students discuss what different things they would find if they visited another period of time.

---

2 Grammar
Reported speech review

Students covered reported speech in SB2, Unit 16 and SB3, Unit 13.

a) Weaker classes: If students need to be reminded of the rules of reported speech, write the following sentences on the board:

I live in London.
I'm playing football this evening.
I've been to France three times.
I'll go to the shop.

Say the sentences and ask students to report what you said. Help them as much as necessary and write the answers on the board:

You said (that) you lived in London.
You said (that) you were playing football this evening.
You said (that) you'd been to France three times.
You said (that) you would go to the shop.

Remind students how tenses change when we are reporting speech. Then follow the procedure for stronger classes.

Stronger classes: Students read the sentences from the text and write down what was actually said in each case. Check their answers.

Answers
2 I can't play the Doctor anymore.
3 I've never heard of Doctor Who.
4 We'll never change anything in the universe.

OPTIONAL ACTIVITY
To remind students of the rules of reported speech, ask them to write down answers to three questions:
What did you do yesterday?
What are you going to do at the weekend?
Have you ever met a famous person?
Two of their answers should be true and the other false. Choose different students to say one of their answers. Other students report what was said and decide if the answer was true or not. Encourage students to correct any errors in reported speech themselves.

b Ask students to complete the table. They can compare answers with a partner before getting feedback.
Stronger classes: If students are confident with the structures, ask them to think of an example for each of the tenses in reported speech.

Answers

present continuous	past continuous
present perfect	past perfect
past simple	past perfect
can/can't	could/couldn't
will/won't	would/wouldn't
must	had to

c Ask students if they remember which other words often change when we use reported speech. Give them some time to discuss this with a partner before asking them for examples.

Answers
pronouns (e.g. *I, you, mine, ours*); possessive adjectives (e.g. *my, your*); some time expressions (e.g. *now, tomorrow, this afternoon*)

Language notes
1 Remind students that in some cases we don't have to change the tense or the time expression when reporting speech. If the statement is still true when we report it, we can leave it in the original tense, e.g. *David told me he can't swim. Kate said she's going to Italy this summer.*
2 If we are reporting something that has just been said, the reporting verb can be in the present simple and the reported statement can be left in its original tense, e.g. *That was Sarah on the phone. She says she doesn't want to go to the cinema.*

d Students write the reported speech for each sentence. Remind them that quotation marks are not used in reported speech and *that* is optional after the reporting verbs *say* and *tell*. Check the answers and ensure that students are using the correct tenses.

Answers
2 The Doctor said (that) they had to get to the Tardis before it was too late.
3 The Doctor said (that) they would only know what year it was outside when they arrived.
4 The Doctor said (that) he had a plan and he knew how they could kill the Ice-Men.
5 Romana told the Doctor (that) he was getting the time wrong.
6 Chronotis told the Doctor (that) he had heard so much about him.
7 The Doctor said that they didn't know what was going on.
8 The Doctor announced that there wouldn't be enough time.

Language note
If we are reporting what was said by an unknown speaker, we use the impersonal *they*, e.g. *Somebody telephoned about the car. They said we could pick it up tomorrow.*

Grammar notebook
Remind students to note down the rules for reported speech and to write a few examples of their own.

3 Vocabulary
Expressions with *time*

🔊 Explain to students that there are many English idioms connected to time. Ask them to give you any examples they may already know and write these on the board. Then ask them to circle the correct words in sentences 1–10. They should guess the ones they don't know, or look them up in a dictionary if they have time. Play the recording for students to check their answers.

TAPESCRIPT/ANSWERS
1 Come on! Quickly! We're running out of time!
2 My father's always busy. He never has time to relax.
3 I'm not in a hurry. Take your time.
4 Our Maths teacher often complains that we give him a hard time.
5 I got home just in time to miss the rain.
6 I'm not late. I'm exactly on time. Look at the clock.
7 Come on, let's get started – we've wasted a lot of time already.
8 I think you should take time off and go on holiday. You've worked too hard.
9 Annie's a very relaxed person. She spends a lot of time meditating.

Unit 4 33

Language note
Students may have difficulty distinguishing between *on time* and *in time*. Explain that we use *on time* if something happens exactly at the expected time (*The 2:30 train arrived on time* = at 2:30). We use *in time* if something happens before the expected time (*We arrived in time for the film* = we arrived before the start of the film). *Just in time* refers to something happening very close to the expected time.

Vocabulary notebook
Encourage students to start a section called *Time* and to note down the phrases from this exercise. They may find it useful to note down translations too.

––– OPTIONAL ACTIVITY –––
Write the following sentences on the board. In pairs, students complete the sentences with the correct time expression.
1 If we don't leave now, we won't be .... time to meet the others at the cinema. **(in)**
2 Read the question carefully and .... your time. Then you will make fewer mistakes. **(take)**
3 Rajeev is very healthy. He .... a lot of time doing sport and playing games. **(spends)**
4 Come on, stop shopping! The plane leaves soon. We're .... out of time. **(running)**
5 What a surprise! You're usually late, but today you're exactly .... time. **(on)**
6 You can't work all weekend! You need some time .... **(off)**

4 Pronunciation

Schwa /ə/ *teacher*

a 🔊 Tell students that the schwa is the most common vowel sound in the English language. Students turn to page 120 and read the sentences. Play the recording, pausing after each sentence. Point out that the /ə/ sound is often used to shorten longer vowel sounds in natural speech (*was* /wɒz/ becomes /wəz/, *can* /kæn/ becomes /kən/, etc.) and is not stressed. Encourage students to concentrate on how the underlined words are pronounced. Draw attention to the same /ə/ sound for the unstressed syllable in *lesson*.

b 🔊 Play the recording again, pausing after each sentence for students to repeat. Make sure they are following the intonation patterns on the recording and that they are not stressing the schwa.

5 Speak

Divide the class into pairs and give each student a letter A or B. Ask A students to look at questions 1–4, while B students turn to page 122 and read their questions. They then ask each other their questions. Monitor and encourage students to answer in full sentences using the time expressions, and to expand on their answers. Ask a few pairs to tell the class about their partner's answers.

Weaker classes: Weaker students may benefit from having some time to practise saying the sentences to themselves to work on pronunciation and intonation before asking their partner.

6 Read

If you set the background information as a homework research task, ask the students to tell the class what they found out.

BACKGROUND INFORMATION

Time Shifting: Published in 1997, this self-help book by Stephan Rechtschaffen warns that people spend too much time thinking about the past and future and not enough time thinking about the present. The book offers exercises that demonstrate how to focus on the present while finding time for everyday happiness. Stephan Rechtschaffen is a physician and leader of workshops on health and personal growth. He is the author of several other books including *Vitality and Wellness* and *The Complete Book of Energy Medicines*. He lives in New York.

a Show students the picture of the book cover and ask them to guess what the book might be about. Tell them they are going to read a letter from a teenage girl to her father. Ask them to read the letter quickly to find out as much as they can about her father. Discuss the question with the class and write notes on the board.

Possible answers
He's a manager with a lot of responsibility at work, and he works too hard. He finds it difficult to relax. He's always busy and is always in a hurry, so he doesn't have much free time for himself or his family. He loves his daughter but he missed her birthday. He drives fast and often feels stressed and angry.

b Check that students understand the meaning of the items in the list. They read the text again to find an example of each one. Let students check their answers in pairs before asking for feedback.

Answers
1 Paragraph 2 (You warned me that I'd probably regret it later.)
2 Paragraph 6 (He recommends 'shifting time' on a regular basis.)
3 Paragraph 5 (He advises managers not to think about making money all the time.)
4 Paragraph 7 (The book encourages people to try something completely different.)
5 Paragraph 4 (He claims they're often trying to avoid their real feelings.)

> **Discussion box**
> **Weaker classes:** Students can choose one question to discuss.
> **Stronger classes:** In pairs or small groups, students go through the questions in the box and discuss them.
> Monitor and help as necessary, encouraging students to express themselves in English and to use any vocabulary they have learned from the text. Ask pairs or groups to feedback to the class and exchange opinions about the ideas in Cathy's letter.

7 Grammar
Reporting verbs review

Students covered reporting verbs in SB3, Unit 13.

a Write the verbs *say* and *tell* on the board. Then ask students to look through the text in Exercise 6 and find some more reporting verbs (*complain, warn, encourage, persuade, claim, advise, recommend, suggest, promise*). Draw attention to the other verbs in the tables and check that all the meanings are clear. Tell students that different reporting verbs have different patterns; for example, *tell* is followed by an object, but *say* is not. Ask students to complete the tables, referring to the text to help them. Check the answers and elicit some example sentences for each of the verb patterns. Point out the importance of learning not only the verbs themselves, but the grammatical forms that follow them.

Answers

say *claim* state emphasise *warn*	that …
recommend *suggest*	that you do …
recommend *suggest* deny	doing …
encourage convince recommend persuade *advise* *warn*	someone (not) to do …
promise (not) refuse	to do …

Look
Point out that *promise* can also be followed by *that*, e.g. *Sam promised that he would send us a postcard.* Also note that *deny* can be followed by *that*, e.g. *They denied that they had stolen the money.* Ask students to add these to the first section of the table. Remind students that when the verbs in this section are followed by *that*, the tense rules for reported speech apply.

b Check that students understand the meaning of speech types a–h. Ask them to match the sentences with the speech types.

Answers
2 b 3 a 4 c 5 e 6 g 7 h 8 f

c Students rewrite the sentences using the reporting verbs in Exercise 7a. Their answers for 7b will help them to choose the appropriate verb, and they should then look back to the tables in 7a to check the pattern. Explain that more than one answer is possible in some cases. Circulate to check that students are creating sentences correctly. Check the answers with the class.

Answers
1. She refused to help me.
2. He promised not to be late. / He promised that he wouldn't be late.
3. He claimed that his father had won over fifty golf competitions.
4. The doctor warned him/her that he/she was going to get ill if he/she didn't eat more healthily.
5. She denied working too hard. / She denied that she worked too hard.
6. They recommended trying the new French restaurant. / They recommended that I/we try the new French restaurant.
7. The doctor advised me to take a break sometimes.
8. She encouraged Steve to jump.

Grammar notebook
Remind students to note down the patterns for reporting verbs and to write a few examples of their own. They could also record these verbs and their patterns in their vocabulary notebook.

8 Speak and listen

If you set the background information as a homework research task, ask the students to tell the class what they found out.

> **BACKGROUND INFORMATION**
> **Cher:** /ʃɜː/ is a singer and actress who was born in California on 20 May 1946. She became famous as a singer in the 1960s, had her own TV show in the USA in the 70s and became known as a serious actress in the 80s. Her films include *Mask, Suspect, The Witches of Eastwick* and *Mermaids.* Her hit songs include *Gypsies, Tramps and Thieves, I Found Someone* and *Believe* (the biggest-selling UK hit ever by a female singer). *If I Could Turn Back Time*, written by Diane Warren, first appeared on Cher's 1989 *Heart of Stone* album. As a single, it reached number 6 in the UK and number 3 in the USA.

a) Tell students that they are going to listen to a song called *If I could Turn Back Time*. Ask them to think about the title and say what they think the song is about.

Answer
1 Someone who regrets what they did.

b) 🔊 Students read the lyrics of the song. Check difficult words, e.g. *pride, weapons, wound, shattered, torn apart*. Play the recording while students listen and fill the gaps with the words in the box. Students compare answers with a partner. Play the recording again.

TAPESCRIPT
See the song on page 28 of the Student's Book.

Answers
1 knife 2 weapons 3 hurt 4 reach 5 used
6 world 7 care 8 strong 9 proud 10 blind

c) Students match the words in the song with the definitions. Check the answers.
1 d 2 e 3 a 4 b 5 c

d) Write a common simile on the board, e.g. *He ran like the wind*. Elicit the meaning of the sentence (*He ran very fast*). Explain that if we want to describe something in a clear and interesting way, we can use similes /ˈsɪmɪliːz/. Ask students to read through the words of the song to find three similes using the word *like*. During feedback ask students to explain what the writer of the song is trying to say.

Answers
Pride's like a knife.
Words are like weapons.
I was torn apart, like someone took a knife and drove it deep into my heart.

> **Language note**
> A **simile** is a figure of speech in which the subject is compared to something else. Tell students that many similes are formed with *like*, as in the examples from the song. Another common type of simile uses *as*, e.g. *as busy as a bee, as cold as ice*.

e) Ask students to think of similes of their own, either completing the sentences or using their own ideas. Let students work in pairs and encourage them to use their imagination. Ask different pairs to read out their most interesting similes. You could write these on the board and take a class vote to decide which one students like best.

Answers
Students' own answers.

OPTIONAL ACTIVITY
Students choose their best similes and make a poster with drawings illustrating them. These can be displayed in the classroom.

Did you know …?
Read the information in the box with the class. Invite students to say anything else they know about Cher.

9 Write

a) As an introduction to this exercise, tell students to imagine that they are going to write a letter to a friend. Write the following on the board:
You haven't written for a very long time.
You want to go and visit your friend.
You want an answer soon.
Ask students for some ideas about what they could write to express these three ideas in a letter. Also ask them how they would end the letter. Elicit some suggestions from students but do not comment at this stage. Students read the questions and then read the letter quickly to find the answers.

Answers
1 Because she's been very busy with exams.
2 The summer holidays.
3 The week of the 10th to the 15th of August.
4 Reply to her request as soon as possible.

b) Remind students that this is an informal letter. Explain that the underlined expressions are not incorrect, but they are too formal for a letter to a friend. Ask students to replace them with the less formal expressions.

Answers
Para 1: 2
Para 2: 4; 5
Para 3: 1
Para 4: 3

c) Tell students they are going to write a reply to Sally. Before they write, ask them to choose the most suitable expressions from 1–5.

Answers
1 b 2 a 3 a 4 b 5 a

d) Read through the information with students. Ask them to write a reply to Sally's letter. After planning, they could complete the writing at home. In a subsequent lesson, encourage students to read each other's letters.

Weaker classes: Work with the class to build up a list of possible sentence openings to help students with the main body of their letter. For example:
Para 1 It was great to get your letter …
         I'd love to see you …
Para 2 Of course you can stay …
         The problem is …
         I can't change these plans because …
         How about …?
Para 3 I hope …
         Let me know …

36 Module 1

OPTIONAL ACTIVITY

Write the following on the board. Ask students to write the words in their notebook in the correct order. They should also decide if the sentences are formal or informal.
1 *pleasure give would see me it to great you*
   (It would give me great pleasure to see you. Formal)
2 *love you I'd see to* (I'd love to see you. Informal)
3 *decision me please your of inform* (Please inform me of your decision. Formal)
4 *think me let know what you* (Let me know what you think. Informal)

✱ Module 1 Check your progress

1 Grammar

(a) 2 has painted   3 show   4 has … created
   5 have studied   6 loves

(b) 2 loved   3 was … singing   4 started   5 saw, wanted   6 impressed   7 had happened, was

(c) 2 Many rainforest plants have been tested for a cure for cancer.
   3 Huge areas of rainforest are being destroyed every day.
   4 Medication is being developed from frog poison.
   5 Fascinating insights have been gained into some of the rainforests' secrets.
   6 Lots of new medications will be developed in the future to help people with cancer.
   7 Aspirin was made into a modern medicine in 1897 by a German scientist.

(d) 2 My friend, who loves helping people, wants to become a psychologist.
   3 This is the book which our teacher was talking about.
   4 Many experts will attend the conference, where new theories will be presented.
   5 I have recently read a theory which claims that differences between male and female brains can be explained through differences in their genes.
   6 Our neighbour, whose daughter lives in Portsmouth, is going to the UK soon.

(e) 2 The aliens claimed that they could destroy our planet.
   3 The commander warned that their spaceship would land soon.
   4 My friend promised to be / that he would be at the club by five o'clock.
   5 Steve denied breaking / that he had broken my mobile.
   6 Our teacher recommended repeating / that we repeat the phrases twice a day before the test.

2 Vocabulary

(a) 2 mind   3 mind   4 brains   5 minds   6 time
   7 time   8 brain

(b) 2 diagnosed with   3 inattentive   4 jealous
   5 guilty   6 's recovering / recovered / 's recovered from   7 operating theatre   8 doctor

(c) 1 d   2 a   3 f   4 e   5 b   6 c

How did you do?
Students work out their scores. Check how they have done and follow up any problem areas with revision work.

Unit 4 | 37

Module 2
The way we are

YOU WILL LEARN ABOUT ...

Ask students to look at the pictures on the page. Ask them to read through the topics in the box and check that they understand each item. You can ask them the following questions, in L1 if appropriate:

1 *What do you think these children are celebrating?*
2 *Where do you think this woman is from?*
3 *What are these people doing?*
4 *What are these toys called?*
5 *Do you know why this man is famous?*
6 *Who is this actress?*

In pairs or small groups, students discuss which topic area they think each picture matches. Check the answers.

Answers
1 Birthday traditions in different countries
2 Nobel Peace Prize winner Wangari Maathai
3 Flash mobs
4 Objects that were all the rage for a while
5 Alfred Nobel and why he started an international award for peace
6 Famous people who had to live with shyness

YOU WILL LEARN HOW TO ...

Use grammar

Students read through the grammar points and the examples. Go through the first item with them as an example. In pairs, students now match the grammar items in their book. Check the answers.

Answers
What clauses: What I like about her is that she's really kind.
Verbs with gerund or infinitive: I remembered to phone her.
Talk about past habits: I would walk 3 miles to school every day.
Adverbial phrases: He talked to me in a friendly way.
Dummy *it*: It's hard to say you're sorry sometimes.
Past perfect passive: He had been shot three times.
Past perfect continuous: They had been waiting for three days.
Modal review: I couldn't see a thing.

Use vocabulary

Write the headings on the board. Go through the items in the Student's Book and check understanding. Ask students if they can think of one more item for the *Personality adjectives* heading. Elicit some responses and add them to the list on the board. Students now do the same for the other headings. Some possibilities are:

Personality adjectives: *tactless, big-headed, interesting, brainy*

Verbs to do with conflicts: *fight, disagree, dispute*

Childhood toys: *train set, doll's house, kite*

5 Personalities

Unit overview

TOPIC: Personality characteristics

TEXTS
Reading: a questionnaire about confidence
Listening: an interview with an expert on shyness
Listening: people describing themselves and others
Reading: an extract from *Pride and Prejudice* by Jane Austen
Writing: a description of a person

SPEAKING AND FUNCTIONS
Discussing important personal qualities
Talking about shyness

LANGUAGE
Grammar: *what* clauses; Verbs + gerund/infinitive review
Vocabulary: Personality
Pronunciation: Sentence stress and rhythm

1 Read

Warm up

Ask students to draw a horizontal line in their notebook with *shy* at one end and *confident* at the other. Ask students to write their name somewhere on the line to indicate how confident they are. Then they do the same for the students nearest to them in the class. Students then compare their lines with the students whose names they have written. Do they have the same ideas of how confident they are? Ask students what makes a person seem confident or shy and write ideas on the board.

a Tell students they are going to complete a questionnaire to find out how confident they are. Tell them to skim through the questionnaire very quickly, and ask them what they have to do to complete it (*choose one answer for each situation*). Then read through the questionnaire with them, checking difficult vocabulary: *make a good impression, spill, stain, awkward, give up on something, tell off, heated, overhear, blush*. Students complete the questionnaire.

b Students turn to page 122, count up their score and read the comment. Give them time to compare scores with a partner and to discuss the answers they made to the questions. Ask students if they agree with the comment, and if they think questionnaires are a good way of finding out about your personality.

Students then write a description of another situation with three multiple-choice answers for their partner. Encourage them to discuss their answers briefly. If there is time, ask students to form new pairs to read and respond to each other's questionnaire.

Weaker classes: Students work together in pairs to write the description and the alternative answers for the questionnaire.

Stronger classes: Students could listen to each other's questionnaire item rather than reading it. You could organise this as a mingle activity, with students standing up and circulating, asking as many people as possible in a given time period.

OPTIONAL ACTIVITY

Tell students that they are going to write a new questionnaire. In small groups, students choose a different adjective for their topic, e.g. *Are you depressed/optimistic/pessimistic/friendly?* Ask groups to think of five *yes/no* questions for their questionnaire, e.g. *Are you friendly? Do you like going to parties? Do you smile and say hello to your teacher in the mornings?* Students read out their questions to students from other groups and record their answers. They then re-assemble in their original group and compare results. Encourage them to draw some general conclusions (e.g. *Most students we interviewed are quite optimistic ...*) and to present them to the class.

---

2 Grammar

what clauses

a Look at the three examples with the class. Explain that in these sentences *what* means *the thing that*. Give a few more simple examples for the first type of sentence: *What's nice about this T-shirt is its colour. What surprised me was that the door was locked.* Ask students to work out why *that* is used in some examples but not others. If they can't decide, write this pair of examples on the board:

What I love about Kim is her sense of humour.
What I love about Kim is that she always makes you laugh.

Elicit the point that in the second example the *what* clause is followed not by a noun, but by a new clause, with its own subject and verb. This new clause must be introduced by *that*.

Unit 5   39

> **Language notes**
> 1 In the first type of example above, the sentence can be inverted: *Kim's sense of humour is what I love about her.* In the second type, with a *that* clause, we don't make this inversion.
> 2 *What* cannot be used as a relative pronoun after a noun. Students might produce sentences like **Here are the tickets what you wanted.* Remind them that we use *that* or *which*, not *what*, in this type of sentence.

b Read through the sentences with the class. Ask students to join the sentences using *what*.

Answers
2 I don't remember what she told me.
3 What makes him seem rude is that he never says 'please' or 'thank you'.
4 What you should remember is that everyone makes mistakes.
5 What I find really annoying is that he never stops talking.
6 I always forget what I should do in formal situations.

Grammar notebook
Remind students to note down the rules for this structure and to write a few examples of their own.

3 Vocabulary
Personality

Warm up

Ask students to think about the types of personalities their friends have. Elicit adjectives to describe the characteristics that students look for in their friends. Write the adjectives on the board. You could also ask for adjectives describing characteristics they don't like.

a Students read the descriptions and decide which of the characters Bob considers to be his friends. In some cases there will probably be some debate about the answers. Monitor and help with any difficult vocabulary. Students compare answers with a partner before feedback. Ask if they agree about the personality types, e.g. do they like bubbly people / intellectual people? Can careless or scatty people make good friends?

Weaker classes: You may want to ask students to translate the adjectives into their own language to check that they have understood the meanings.

Possible answers
Probable friends: Sue, Charles, Wendy, Barbara
Possible friends: Ian, Chuck, Steve

b Pre-teach *scruffy*. Ask students to read through the sentences and choose the correct adjectives. Play the recording. Pause to check the answers and ask students to repeat the adjectives.

Answers
1 sympathetic 2 charming 3 intellectual
4 smug 5 cheeky 6 shallow 7 careless
8 bubbly 9 witty 10 pretentious 11 pushy
12 scatty 13 hypocritical

> **OPTIONAL ACTIVITY**
> Depending on the sensitivity of the class, you may like to ask students to work in pairs and use the adjectives to describe each other and other students in the class. Ask students which of the attributes they would look for in their ideal friend. Listen to some of their ideas in open class and try to build up a description of the perfect friend.

Vocabulary notebook
Encourage students to add these words to their notebook under the heading *Personality*. They may find it useful to note down translations of the words too.

4 Pronunciation
Sentence stress and rhythm

a Students turn to page 120 and read through the sentences. Play the recording and ask students to focus on the rhythm of the sentences. You could ask them to underline the stressed syllables.

b Play the recording again, pausing for students to repeat each sentence. Encourage students to mimic the recording.

5 Speak

Read through the questions with the class and check understanding. In small groups, students respond to the questions, exchanging opinions and telling each other about their experiences. Encourage them to use adjectives from Exercise 3. Ask some groups to report back and invite class discussion.

6 Listen

If you set the background information as a homework research task, ask the students to tell the class what they found out.

> **BACKGROUND INFORMATION**
> **Kim Basinger** (pronounced /ˈbeɪsɪŋgə/): was born in 1953 in Georgia, USA. She became an actress after great success as a model. Her most famous films include *9½ Weeks* (1986), *Batman* (1989), and *LA Confidential* (1997) for which she received an Oscar for Best Supporting Actress.
> **Susie O'Neill** (pronounced /əʊˈniːl/): is a former competitive swimmer from Australia who won eight Olympic medals, including the gold for the

200 metres butterfly in 1996 and for the 200 metres freestyle in 2000. She is now a TV commentator in Australia.

Bob Dylan (pronounced /ˈdɪlən/): was born as Robert Zimmerman in 1941 and is an American singer and guitarist. He has been popular since the 1960s and has released over 50 albums. His songs include *Blowin' in the Wind*, *Like a Rolling Stone* and *The Times They are A-changin'*. He still plays over 100 concerts every year.

Eric Clapton: is an English guitarist who became famous in the 1960s when he played with The Yardbirds, Cream and Blind Faith. He has had a very successful solo career ever since. His hits include *Wonderful Tonight* and *Layla*. His nickname is *Slowhand*, a reference to his relaxed style of playing.

a Ask students if they recognise any of the people in the photographs. If they don't know who the people are, ask them to guess what they do and what they are like. Tell them that the four people have something in common and ask them to guess what this could be. Elicit suggestions but don't comment on them at this stage.

b Tell students they are going to listen to an interview with the organiser of a self-help group. Play the recording while students listen to check their ideas in Exercise 6a.

TAPESCRIPT

Woman And welcome back to *Early Morning*, the best breakfast show on TV. It's 7.45 on a bright winter morning here in London, where the temperature is 8 degrees Celsius. It's Monday the 12th of November.

Man Now, our next guest this morning is here to talk to us about something that a lot of people experience, and that's shyness.

Woman Not everyone finds it easy to talk to other people or enjoys being in the spotlight, and some people try very hard not to be the centre of attention.

Man That's right – although breakfast television presenters are perhaps not amongst them! Anyway, a new group has been set up recently here in London to help people who are shy to overcome it. Here to talk to us is one of the people who set the group up, Monica Hargreaves. Good morning, Monica.

Monica Good morning, Nigel.

Man Now, shyness is quite a common problem for many people, isn't it?

Monica Well, yes, it is. It's very common, actually. Even some quite famous people are very shy indeed.

Woman Really?

Monica Yes – and even people in professions where you'd think that shyness would make it almost impossible to succeed. Erm, like acting or singing.

Man Right. I heard once that Kim Basinger, the American actress, has had a problem with shyness.

Monica Absolutely. Apparently, when she was at school, she hated having to read aloud in class, it was her worst fear. And some years ago, erm, I don't remember which year, she was nominated for an Oscar and so she was really worried and anxious, because of course she had to make a speech if she won. So she tried practising her Oscar acceptance speech for days in advance, but it didn't work – when she won the Oscar, she still found it almost impossible to speak.

Woman And yet she's so good in front of a camera.

Monica Well, there you are. There's a big difference. Cameras don't think and don't form opinions about you. They don't talk to you. Only people do that – and that's what shy people are anxious about. They think that other people always have a low opinion of them. It's actually social anxiety, and it can have really, really powerful effects.

Man Such as?

Monica Well, one example is an Australian swimmer, a woman called Susie O'Neill. She was a fantastic swimmer, but she herself said that her shyness was so bad when she was young that sometimes she almost tried not to win.

Man Not to win? Why?

Monica Well, because if she won, she'd have to go up and get a medal, then she'd be the centre of attention, everyone would be looking at her, and she couldn't stand that. And she also preferred not to be chosen for team events, because then she'd have to talk to people she didn't know. Her anxiety was so bad, she nearly stopped swimming altogether.

Woman That's amazing. Did she overcome it?

Monica Yes, she did. Thank goodness!

Man You mentioned singers too.

Monica Yes. Look at Bob Dylan. A successful singer, and very famous, but he couldn't stand going on stage. Once, for example, he was playing in front of a huge crowd, and he was so nervous, that he didn't notice that there was something wrong with his guitar – and it sounded awful. And Eric Clapton was a very shy person too. He had to work very hard when he was younger to deal with his shyness.

Woman Anyway, it *is* something that people can overcome.

Monica Oh, yes. A lot of people do. The thing is, of course, that we only realise someone is shy when they can't deal with it.

Woman Sorry, I don't quite follow you.

Monica Well, I mean, some shy people learn to overcome their shyness, they refuse to give in to it and they find ways of dealing with it. So when you or I meet them, we don't see them as shy people.

Man Oh, right. I'd never thought of that.

Woman So, that's the point of your group – to help people get over shyness.

Monica Exactly. And we start by making sure they know that in most ways it's OK to be shy! But sometimes it gives the wrong impression.

Man How's that?

Monica Well, other people can easily think that they're a bit rude, or uninterested. Because when they're anxious, or shy, sometimes they forget to talk to people, to ask them about themselves, and they come across as self-centred. So what we try to convince them of is that it's OK to be shy, so that they can forget about how they feel, and think about other people more than themselves all the time.

Woman Interesting – shy people can come across as rude? So what …

Answers
1 Kim Basinger, actress
2 Susie O'Neill, swimmer
3 Bob Dylan, singer and guitarist
4 Eric Clapton, guitarist
They all suffered from shyness.

c) 🔊 Students read through the summary of Monica's interview and try to fill in the gaps, using a pencil so that they can change answers later if necessary. Ask them to compare answers with a partner. Then play the recording again, pausing if necessary to help students fill in the missing words.

Weaker classes: If students find the listening difficult, write the answers on the board in random order after the first listening and let them choose the correct answers as they listen again.

Answers
1 spotlight 2 attention 3 class 4 Oscar
5 social 6 low 7 overcome 8 meet 9 rude
10 uninterested

Discussion box
Weaker classes: Students can choose one or two questions to discuss.
Stronger classes: In pairs or small groups, students go through the questions in the box and discuss them. Monitor and help as necessary, encouraging students to express themselves in English and to use any vocabulary they have learned from the text. Ask pairs or groups to feedback to the class and discuss any interesting points further.

---

7 Grammar
Verbs + gerund/infinitive review

Students covered verbs + gerund/infinitive in SB3, Unit 9.

a) Weaker classes: Write these sentence openings on the board:

I want …
I don't enjoy …

Give students a minute to make as many sentences as possible using these openings. Ask some students to read out their sentences. Make sure that when they want to add another verb, they are using *to* + infinitive after *want*, and the gerund after *don't enjoy*. Then follow the procedure for stronger classes.

Stronger classes: Ask students to circle the correct words to complete the sentences from the interview. Remind students that verbs of liking/disliking are usually followed by the gerund form. Other verbs, like *want* or *decide*, take *to* + infinitive. During feedback, ask students if any of the verbs could be followed by an infinitive or a gerund. If necessary, explain that both *hate* and *prefer* are verbs like this. In sentence 2 we could say *Kim Basinger hated to have to read …* and in sentence 3 we could say *Susie O'Neill preferred not being chosen …* Ask students if they know any other verbs that can be followed by both infinitives and gerunds.

Answers
1 being 2 having 3 not to be chosen
4 swimming 5 going 6 to give in

b) Read through the rules with the class and check that students understand the meanings of the verbs. Ask them to circle the correct words. If students need further practice, ask them to make example sentences using some verbs of each type in the box.

Answers
a gerund, an infinitive
a gerund
an infinitive

c) Ask students to discuss the differences in meaning with a partner. Feedback in open class.

Answers
1a = I stopped doing something else in order to drink my coffee.
1b = I was drinking my coffee and then I stopped doing it.
2a I bought the book in the past – I remember that I did this.
2b I remembered what I had to do so I bought the book (I didn't forget).

d) Students choose the correct word in the rule.

Answer
different

try with infinitive or gerund

e Read the sentences with the class and ask students to complete the rule.

Answer
gerund, infinitive

> **Language note**
> Students may have difficulty distinguishing between the different meanings of *try*. Encourage them to translate the sentences, as they may use different verbs in their own language. To help them see the difference, ask them to think of cures for a headache (*Try drinking water. Try taking an aspirin.*), then ask them to try to do difficult things (*Try to say the alphabet backwards. Try to say 'bottle of beer' without moving your lips.*).

f Ask students to look at the pictures and tell you what they can see. Students match the sentences with the pictures. Clarify the difference between the two forms. Point out that sentence 1 means 'We opened the window in an attempt to make the room cooler, but it didn't work.' Sentence 2 means 'I wanted to open the window. I tried to do it, but it wasn't possible.'

Answers
1 b   2 a

g Read through the sentences and check understanding of *self-centred*. Students complete the sentences and compare answers with a partner before feedback. If necessary, go through the first sentence as an example. Check the answers.

Answers
1 watching   2 to help   3 to invite   4 seeing
5 surfing   6 to talk   7 being   8 going
9 to phone   10 to give

Grammar notebook
Remind students to note down the rules for these structures and to write a few examples of their own. You may like to ask them to write the verbs from the exercise into the following table.

Verb + gerund	Verb + *to* + infinitive	Verb + gerund OR + infinitive	
		Same meaning	*Different meaning*

8 Literature in mind

Read

If you set the background information as a homework research task, ask the students to tell the class what they found out.

BACKGROUND INFORMATION

Jane Austen: (1775–1817) was born in Hampshire, England. She wrote six classic novels between 1811 and 1817: *Sense and Sensibility, Pride and Prejudice, Mansfield Park, Emma, Northanger Abbey* and *Persuasion*. Her work is recognised for its definition of character and the insights it offers into the 18th century middle and upper classes. Her books are still extremely popular throughout the world. In a major BBC poll in 2005, *Pride and Prejudice* was voted the second most popular British novel (first was *The Lord of the Rings* by J.R.R. Tolkien). The photo on this page is from the 2005 film of *Pride and Prejudice* starring Keira Knightley and Matthew Macfadyen.

a Ask students if they have heard of Jane Austen. Tell them they are going to read an extract from one of her novels, *Pride and Prejudice*. Students look at the cover of the book and read the summary of the story to decide if they think they would like to read the book. Discuss students' ideas and help with vocabulary if necessary.

b Explain that a *ball* is a big formal party, especially for dancing. Ask students to look at the photo and suggest some ways in which a ball in the early 19th century might be different from a modern dance party. Ask students to read through the extract to find the answers to questions 1 and 2, and also to find out how things were different in the time of Jane Austen. Tell them not to worry about difficult vocabulary, but just to concentrate on the task. Check the answers with the class.

Answers
1 It takes place at a dance/ball.
2 They're friends.

c Read through the text with the class, pausing where necessary to check comprehension and help with difficult vocabulary: *unreserved, decline, lady, sharpen, offend, insupportable, choosy, tolerable*. Check understanding of the questions. Students answer the questions and compare answers with a partner before feedback.

Possible answers
1 Because he wasn't friendly. He didn't dance or try to mix with other people. He was proud and disagreeable.
2 Because he had offended one of her daughters.
3 He refused to dance. He said he hated dancing unless he knew his partner well, and he didn't like any of the women in the room.
4 Because nobody had asked her to dance and she was sitting near them.

5 He said she was not pretty enough for him and that he didn't want to dance with a girl that nobody else wanted to dance with.
6 Because she found the situation ridiculous and enjoyed laughing about it.

— OPTIONAL ACTIVITY —
Write these definitions on the board. Ask students to find words in the text that match them.
1 not shy (**unreserved**)
2 a difference (**contrast**)
3 to be forced to do something (**obliged**)
4 a gathering of people (**assembly**)
5 personality, way of being (**disposition**)

9 Write

Students can do the preparation for this in class and the writing can be set for homework.

(a) Refer students to the box and ask them to write the adjectives in the two lists. Allow them to use a dictionary for help.

Answers
Personality: sensible, disorganised, cheerful, honest, lazy
Appearance: smart, tall, handsome, wavy, plump, slim, scruffy

(b) Encourage students to add another four words to each list and then compare their lists with a partner. Ask some pairs to give you their examples and write them on the board.

(c) Tell students they are going to read an email in which a girl gives a description of someone she has just met at a party. Students read to identify the topic of the first four paragraphs. During feedback, deal with difficult vocabulary in the email: *gossip, caught my attention, exaggerating*.

Possible answers
First paragraph: a general description of the party
Second paragraph: basic facts about Bob
Third paragraph: Bob's appearance
Fourth paragraph: Bob's personality

(d) Point out to students that the third paragraph contains unnecessary information and ask them to decide which sentences could be left out.

Answers
He's average height too. His nose is quite small.

(e) Students look at the descriptions of Bob's eyes and smile in paragraph 3. Draw attention to the simile (*like the colour of the ocean you see in those holiday postcards*) and the use of adjectives (*gorgeous, bright blue, warm, friendly*). Students write their own descriptions of someone's hair and mouth. Ask different students to read out their descriptions.

(f) Students find the examples of behaviour in paragraph 4. Check the answers and explain that these details, like the descriptions in Exercise 9e, are very important if we want to make a description interesting.

Answers
He said loads of nice things about Jean. He listened to her problems and he gave her some good advice.

(g) Ask students to write three or four sentences describing someone (real or imaginary) who is generous and imaginative. Remind them to give examples of the person's behaviour to illustrate his/her qualities. Ask some students to read out their description, and ask the class to say whether they would like to meet this person.

(h) Introduce the writing task and ask students to plan their email, using Jean's email as a model. Encourage them to:
- organise their writing as outlined in Exercise 9c.
- use interesting descriptions of appearance.
- include examples of the person's behaviour to show their character.
- make sure their writing is informal.

Students could do the writing for homework. In a subsequent lesson, give them the opportunity to read each other's descriptions and decide which is the most interesting.

— OPTIONAL ACTIVITY —
As an extension of Exercise 9b, write the words *Personality* and *Appearance* on the board and ask students to add as many adjectives as possible to the two lists in two minutes. Ask for their suggestions and write them under the headings on the board.

Vocabulary notebook
Encourage students to add the adjectives from Exercise 9a words to their notebook under the headings *Personality* and *Appearance*. They may find it useful to note down translations of the words too.

6 In and out of fashion

Unit overview

TOPIC: Fashions and crazes

TEXTS
Reading and listening: an article about crazes
Listening: a news item on flash mobs
Listening: an interview with someone who organises flash mobs
Listening and reading: a conversation about a favourite toy
Writing: a formal letter to a newspaper

SPEAKING AND FUNCTIONS
Discussing crazes
Presenting a marketing plan
Talking about past habits
Discussing flash mobs and organising a flash mob event

LANGUAGE
Grammar: *would* and *used to*; Adverbs and adverbial phrases
Vocabulary: Common adverbial phrases
Pronunciation: /æ/ *apple* and /e/ *lemon*

Warm up

Ask students if anyone has a hobby which they have become addicted to – something they do every day, often several times, or for hours without stopping. Perhaps give an example of your own. Discuss interesting comments in class, helping with vocabulary if necessary.

a) Ask students to describe what they can see in the photos. Ask if any of the students have played with any of the things in the photos. Use the photos to pre-teach the words *hoop* and *cube*.

b) Read through the three topics and explain the meaning of *swept the world*. Students read the texts quickly to identify the main topic. When you check the answer, ask them to say the word that means 'a fashion that sweeps the world' (*craze*).

Answer
3 Each of the objects was, at some time, the latest fashion and swept the world.

c) 🔊 Play the recording while students read and listen. Students answer the questions and compare answers with a partner before feedback. Play the recording again, pausing as necessary to clarify any problems.

TAPESCRIPT
See the reading texts on page 40 of the Student's Book.

Answers
1 Rubik's Cube   2 Tamagotchi   3 Tamagotchi
4 Hula Hoop

d) Read through the definitions with the class and help with any vocabulary difficulties. Give students time to read the texts closely and to check their answers with a partner before feedback.

Answers
1 a craze   2 caught on   3 got caught up in
4 compulsive   5 addictive   6 the latest
7 overwhelming   8 on the black market

Discussion box
Weaker classes: Students can choose one question to discuss.
Stronger classes: In pairs or small groups, students go through the questions in the box and discuss them.
Monitor and help as necessary, encouraging students to express themselves in English and to use any vocabulary they have learned from the text. Ask pairs or groups to feedback to the class and discuss any interesting points further.

1 Read and listen

If you set the background information as a homework research task, ask the students to tell the class what they found out.

BACKGROUND INFORMATION

The hula hoop: remains a popular toy with children and is also used as an exercise tool to flatten stomachs.

Frisbees: are plastic discs, 20 to 25 centimetres in diameter, with a lip. The basic use is a game of throwing and catching.

Rubik's Cube: Invented by Hungarian Ernö Rubik, a Rubik's Cube can have over 43 trillion different positions. Financially, the Cube was so successful that Rubik became the first self-made millionaire in a communist country.

Tamagotchi: may be translated as *egg-friend*. The object is to keep your digital pet alive, well fed and happy for as long as possible. By pressing the three buttons on the toy, you can play games and win points which can then be transferred into food, to be given to the little animal on the screen. The owner must also clean up when the tamagotchi uses the toilet!

2 Speak

a In open class, elicit possible ways of marketing a product (TV advertisements, paying famous people to use it, giving away free samples, etc.). Tell students that they are going to re-market one of the three products in Exercise 1 to modern teenagers. Ask them to work together in pairs or small groups to answer the questions and decide what they would do to make the object popular again. Students work together to create a short presentation (no more than about three minutes) for the rest of the class.

b Groups present their ideas to the rest of the class. Ask them to come to the front of the class and encourage them to use the board to help present their main arguments. Take a class vote on which was the best presentation.

3 Grammar

would and used to

Students covered *used to* in SB2, Unit 13 and SB3, Unit 16.

a To revise *used to*, ask students to think back to when they were eight years old. How were their lives different? Write the following on the board:

1 (music) I used to like ... , but now I like ...
2 (reading) I used to read ... , but now I read ...
3 (TV) I used to watch ... , but now I watch ...
4 (personality) I used to be ... , but now I'm ...

Ask students to complete the sentences and elicit answers in open class. Ask students to think of another example of their own. Now focus on the three sentences in the book. Students look back at the text and complete the sentences.

Answers
1 would   2 used to   3 used to

b Students look back at the examples in Exercise 3a and complete the rule. Clarify the difference between *habits* or *repeated actions* and *states*, drawing attention to the verbs that are used to describe a state or situation. Go back to the four examples on the board and ask students in which of the four sentences we could replace *used to* with *would* (sentences 2 and 3).

Answers
used to, would; used to

c Look at the example with the class. Students read the sentences and cross out *would* when it is not possible to use it.

Answers
would should be crossed out in these sentences:
2, 5, 7

d Ask students to think of things they used to play with when they were young children. Write some examples on the board. In pairs, students talk about the toys they played with in their childhood. Encourage them to use *would* and *used to*. Ask a few pairs to give some examples as feedback, and allow discussion on any interesting points.

Grammar notebook
Remind students to note down the rules for these structures and to write a few examples of their own.

4 Listen

If you set the background information as a homework research task, ask the students to tell the class what they found out.

> **BACKGROUND INFORMATION**
>
> **Flash mobs:** The first flash mob was organised in Manhattan in 2003 by Bill Wasik, senior editor of *Harper's Magazine*. They have since taken place all over the world. They are usually organised over the internet or by sending text messages on mobile phones. Flash mobs started as a bit of fun, but have since been used to make political statements, with people appearing suddenly in large groups to make protests.

a Students look at the photos. Ask for their ideas about what might be happening in each photo and what they might have in common. Introduce the term *flash mob*, but don't explain it at this stage.

b 🔊 Tell the students that they are going to listen to an interview with a woman who is connected with the photos. Play the recording. Students listen and check their ideas from Exercise 4a. Ask them to give any information they can about flash mobs.

TAPESCRIPT
Presenter   Good morning, and welcome to today's edition of *People and Places*. Today we're going to talk about a rather strange phenomenon known as 'flash mobs'. Sally Jameson was present at the very first flash mob. Here's her report.
Reporter   Flash mobs are an American phenomenon. The first one took place in June 2003, when about a hundred people suddenly appeared in the carpet department of a large store in New York, and they all began to ask the shop assistants, at the same time, about a $10,000 rug. As you can imagine, the shop assistants reacted with surprise and more than a little confusion. Ten minutes later, the crowd left as quickly and quietly as they had arrived.

46   Module 2

A flash mob can be described as a gathering of a large number of strangers, a mob, who get organised in secret by email or by text messaging, and who meet together for no apparent reason and for a short time (which is why we have the word 'flash'), to do something that is both unusual and pointless.

After the carpet store flash mob, other flash mob events followed in quick succession. In New York, two hundred people, complete strangers to each other, lay down silently in a square. Then they got up and went their separate ways. In San Francisco, a group of people put a red carpet down in front of a busy subway station during the rush-hour, and for five minutes and with great enthusiasm, they loudly applauded the travellers who were coming out of the station.

So who started this craze? An American known only as 'Bill'. We managed to track him down and he agreed to talk to us, as long as we did not divulge his real name. Here is what he had to say.

c 🔊 Read through the sentences with the class and check that students understand *rug* and *clapped*. Play the recording again. Students listen again to decide if the sentences are true or false.

Answers
1 T   2 F (They were surprised and confused.)
3 F (They stayed for ten minutes.)   4 T   5 T
6 T   7 F (He's American.)

d Ask students who Bill is (*the man who started flash mobs*). Ask them to think about what they would like to ask him and to write down at least two questions.

e Students compare questions with a partner. Ask some students to say their questions, and write them on the board.

f 🔊 Tell students that they are going to hear Bill talking about flash mobs. Play the recording once or twice. Students listen to hear which questions Bill answers. Tick off these questions on the board and elicit any information students heard in answer to them.

TAPESCRIPT
It was just an idea I got for a bit of fun, you know? I used to walk past places, ordinary places, and one day I just thought: 'Wouldn't it be funny if all of a sudden, a hundred people turned up here?' And a few days later I wrote an email, forwarded it to myself and then sent it on to lots of people I knew. They sent it to other people that *they* knew, and the thing took on a life of its own.

I always wanted this thing to be anonymous – I didn't want people to know it was me who had the idea or what my name was. No, not because I felt scared or guilty, no – just because I didn't want the idea to have a leader, I wanted people to do it for themselves and for fun. I didn't want them to wait for me every time.

There are all kinds of different things that flash mobs can do. Erm, a lot take place in shops. One of my favourite examples was actually in Rome, when two or three hundred people turned up in the same bookshop for about five minutes and started asking the owner for the same book! And another favourite one of mine was in London – erm, at a subway station a lot of people arrived and sang part of an opera in harmony, then they disappeared again. And a really strange one, again in a shop and again in London, was when a crowd turned up at a shop that sells sofas. They spoke English for seven minutes without using the letter 'o' – can you believe that? – then applauded the owner of the shop and left!

The key things about flash mobs are: a) they're pointless but also harmless – no one gets hurt, everything is done in a friendly way. And b) it's for a very short period of time. People are busy and if something's going to take a lot of time they might not show up, but if it's only for ten minutes they might think 'Oh, that's OK, I can find time for that.'

I read somewhere that a British sociologist, I can't remember his name, talked a bit about flash mobs and he said something about how flash mobs are quite a healthy thing, they get people together in an interesting and playful way. I like that.

Are flash mobs just a fad? I don't know. Will there be more? Again, I don't know, but I hope so. I hope people do more of them, and do them with pleasure and in a fun way.

g 🔊 Read through the questions. Explain difficult vocabulary: *anonymous* and *sociologist*. Then play the recording again. Students listen and write notes in answer to the questions.

Answers
1 Because he didn't want the idea to have a leader. He wanted people to do it themselves for fun.
2 Two or three hundred people went to a bookstore and asked for the same book.
3 A group of people sang part of an opera in a subway station.
4 They are pointless but harmless, and they are very quick.
5 They are healthy as people get together and have fun.
6 He doesn't know if they will continue, but he hopes so.

Discussion box
Weaker classes: Students can choose one question to discuss.
Stronger classes: In pairs or small groups, students go through the questions in the box and discuss them. Monitor and help as necessary, encouraging students to express themselves in English and to use any vocabulary they have learned from the text. Ask pairs or groups to feedback to the class and discuss any interesting points further.

Unit 6

5 Speak

a Students work in small groups and think of a fun flash mob event. Monitor to help with any difficult vocabulary as they discuss their ideas.

b Ask each group to describe their event. Make a note of each one on the board. Students discuss the events and decide which they think is the best.

6 Grammar
Adverbs and adverbial phrases

Students covered adverbs in SB2, Unit 3.

a Ask students to complete the sentences from the listening text. Ask which word is an adjective (*sudden*) and which is an adverb (*suddenly*).

Answers
suddenly; sudden

b Students complete the sentences in the rule.

Answers
adjectives; adverbs

c Explain that instead of adverbs, we can use *adverbial phrases* of three or four words to say how someone does something. Students look at the adverbial phrases in Exercise 6d and decide which types of words are used to complete them.

Answers
We use adjectives with expressions in A.
We use nouns with expressions in B.

d Students complete the lists using the words in the box. Elicit example sentences with some of the phrases from each list.

Answers
A: in an *exciting* way, in a *horrible* way, in a *different* way
B: with *difficulty*, with *excitement*, with *interest*

e Students work individually or in pairs, choosing suitable words to complete the sentences. Point out that there is often more than one possibility.

Answers
2 a friendly way
3 difficulty
4 interest/enthusiasm
5 fear
6 a fun way / an interesting/exciting way
7 a different way
8 enthusiasm/excitement

Grammar notebook
Remind students to note down the rules for this structure and to write a few examples of their own.

7 Vocabulary
Common adverbial phrases

a Check that students know the meaning of *intentionally*. Ask them to match the phrases with the definitions. Tell them to guess the meaning of unknown phrases and to use a dictionary to check if they have time. They could work on this in pairs. After checking the answers, say the phrases and ask students to repeat them.

Answers
1 e 2 f 3 a 4 h 5 d 6 b 7 c 8 g

b Read through the sentences with the class and check any difficult vocabulary: *surprise party, broke out*. Students complete the sentences with the phrases in Exercise 7a.

Answers
1 on purpose 2 in secret 3 in a row
4 in private 5 by accident 6 in a hurry
7 in public 8 in a panic

--- OPTIONAL ACTIVITY ---
Write the following questions on the board:
1 *Have you ever broken anything by accident?*
2 *Have you ever broken anything on purpose?*
3 *When did you last react to something in a panic?*
4 *Do you like speaking in public?*
5 *When did you last do something in a hurry?*
In pairs, students discuss the questions. You may like to give them an example of your own to get them started. Encourage students to use the adverbial phrases from Exercise 7 in their answers. Listen to some of their answers in open class.

Vocabulary notebook
Encourage students to start a new section *Adverbial phrases* in their notebook and add these words. They may find it useful to note down translations.

8 Pronunciation
/æ/ *apple* and /e/ *lemon*

a 🔊 Say the words *apple* and *lemon*, exaggerating the difference between the two vowel sounds. Students turn to page 120 and read quickly through the words. Play the recording twice. Students tick the words they hear and then listen again to check. Play the recording once again and ask students to repeat.

Answers
1 sat 2 pet 3 bat 4 ten 5 pen 6 bend
7 man 8 sad

--- OPTIONAL ACTIVITY ---
For further practice of the difference between these sounds, put students in pairs and ask them to say the words to each other. Their partner has to tell them which of the words they are saying.

48 Module 2

b) 🔊 Ask students to read through the sentences. Play the recording, pausing after each sentence for students to repeat, first all together and then individually.

Sorry!

9 Read and listen

Warm up

Write these questions on the board: *Did you use to have a favourite toy when you were small? Why did you like it? Have you still got it?* Students ask and answer the questions in pairs. Ask some pairs to report back to the class.

a) 🔊 Students look at the photo, identify the people and describe what they are doing. Ask them to guess the answers to the questions, but don't comment on their answers at this stage. Play the recording. Students read and listen to check their answers.

TAPESCRIPT
See the dialogue on page 44 of the Student's Book.

Answers
They're giving her a teddy bear. They want to apologise for making fun of her yesterday.

b) Students read the text again and find the answers to the questions.

Weaker classes: Before students look at the questions, you may want to play the recording again, pausing as necessary to clarify any problems. Then read through the questions with the class and check that the meaning is clear.

Answers
1 She thinks her friends will think she's being silly.
2 She said it was taking up space and getting dirty.
3 She thinks they were childish and unsympathetic, because they made jokes when they weren't wanted and didn't help their friend.
4 Because she'd rather have her old bear back, but she appreciates their concern.

10 Everyday English

a) Students look back to the text in Exercise 9 and find out who said the expressions. Ask them to look at the expressions in their context to match them with meanings a–d. Ask students to repeat the full sentences from the text, giving attention to the intonation.

Answers
1 Caroline   2 Caroline   3 Matt   4 Joanne
a besides   b for a start   c real   d out of order

b) Students read through the dialogues and complete the replies.

Answers
1 Besides   2 out of order   3 for a start   4 real

┌─ OPTIONAL ACTIVITIES ─────────────
│ See Unit 2, Exercise 11 Everyday English,
│ Optional activities.

11 Write

The planning for this exercise can be done in class and the letter can be set as homework.

a) Tell students they are going to read a letter to a newspaper. Pre-teach *over-reacts, mini-riot, misleading*. Ask students to read the letter quickly and then look at the notes which another person has made on this letter. Students answer the questions.

Possible answers
1 He hates it. He thinks it's a waste of time and potentially dangerous.
2 He/She disagrees strongly. He/She thinks Mr Hill's arguments are weak, his opinions are intolerant and his letter is potentially misleading.

b) Make it clear that letter b is written by the person who made the notes on letter a. Students read letter b to find out which of the notes the writer has included.

Answers
Notes 1, 2, 4 and 5 are included.

c) Students read letter c and underline the main points. Check these in open class. Students look at each point and decide whether they agree or disagree. Ask them to write notes on each point.

Answers
Young people buy whatever companies want them to buy.
(The things people buy) are just crazes that cost a lot of money and are bad for young people.
The only things young people are interested in are fads and electronic communication.
(In the past) things used to be different (better).

Tell students they are going to write a letter to the editor of the newspaper giving their point of view about letter c. Encourage them to:
- start with *Dear Sir* and finish with *Yours sincerely*.
- use their notes from Exercise 11c.
- give examples to support their opinions.

Unit 6   49

7 Kindness matters

Unit overview

TOPIC: Acts of kindness

TEXTS
Reading and listening: an article about an organisation whose members do good deeds
Listening and speaking: people talking about inherited possessions
Reading: a website about birthday customs in different countries
Writing: a summary

SPEAKING AND FUNCTIONS
Discussing acts of kindness
Talking about special presents
Talking about future possibilities
Discussing traditions for birthdays and other occasions

LANGUAGE
Grammar: Dummy *it*; Modal verbs review
Vocabulary: Making an effort
Pronunciation: Linking sounds (intrusive /w/ and /j/)

1 Read and listen

If you set the background information as a homework research task, ask the students to tell the class what they found out.

BACKGROUND INFORMATION

Danny Wallace: (also referred to as Leader and King Danny I of Lovely) is a writer and comedian, born in 1976. His books include *Yes Man, 365 Ways to Make the World a Better Place* and *Join Me*. Besides being leader of the *Join Me* collective, he also started his own country, calling it *Lovely*, from his flat in North London in 2005. His goal is to make as many people happy as he can.

Join Me: has over 10,000 members, all carrying out 'Random Acts of Kindness on Fridays'. A similar concept is seen in the film *Pay It Forward*, starring Haley Joel Osment as a young boy who has the idea of being kind to three people, who must then each be kind to three more people, and so on.

Warm up

Books closed. Ask students to write down the names of two people they know who are kind – people who always try to help others and make other people happy. Ask them to think of examples of kind actions that these people have done. They could discuss their answers in pairs or small groups. Listen to a few examples in open class.

a Ask students to look at the photo on page 46 and answer the questions, guessing what the situation might be. Students read through the text quickly to check their answers. Tell them not to worry about the meaning of every word, but to concentrate on the task.

b 🔊 Read the paragraph topics with the class. Play the recording. Students read and listen to the text and then match the topics with the paragraphs.

TAPESCRIPT
See the reading text on page 46 of the Student's Book.

Answers
1 C   2 B   3 A   4 D

c 🔊 Play the recording again while students read and listen. Pause as necessary to clarify vocabulary and help with comprehension. Students answer the questions and compare answers with a partner before feedback.

Answers
1 He put an advertisement on the internet because he was bored.
2 They often walk away.
3 They do an act of kindness every Friday.
4 They are all over the world.
5 They like doing something nice for someone. It makes them more confident and able to ignore social barriers.

OPTIONAL ACTIVITY

Students work in pairs and think of a random act of kindness that they can do at some point over the next few days. In a subsequent lesson, ask students if they have done their act of kindness and how it was received.

Discussion box
Weaker classes: Students can choose one question to discuss.
Stronger classes: In pairs or small groups, students go through the questions in the box and discuss them.
Monitor and help as necessary, encouraging students to express themselves in English and to use any vocabulary they have learned from the text. Ask pairs or groups to feedback to the class and discuss any interesting points further.

2 Grammar
Dummy *it*

a) Ask students to look back at the text in Exercise 1 to complete the sentences. During feedback, write the sentences on the board and ask students what *it* refers to in each one. Point out that *it* in these sentences refers to something which comes later in the sentence. We usually use *it* to refer to something which has come before.

Answers
1. It's, to
2. It's, to
3. it is, to

b) Students match the two parts of the sentences to make statements that they agree with. Give students an example of your own to get them started and make it clear that many different answers are possible. Let students compare answers with a partner and listen to a few examples in open class as feedback.

Answers
Students' own answers

c) Look at the example with the class and point out the structure of the sentence (*It's / It isn't* + adjective + *to* + infinitive). Ask students to transform the other sentences using the same structure. Check the answers.

Answers
2. It's fun to be kind to people.
3. It's important to help other people.
4. It's crazy to give money away to people on a bus.
5. It's normal to get nervous sometimes.
6. It isn't hard to remember to say nice things.

d) Weaker classes: To help students think of examples, write the following words on the board: *transport, restaurants, people, clubs, sport, cinemas, music, shops*. Ask students questions about the facilities in the town where they live (e.g. *Is it easy to find a good restaurant? Is it difficult to find a music shop? Is it normal to travel by bus?*). Then follow the procedure for stronger classes.

Stronger classes: Ask students to write some sentences describing the place where they live using the structure *It ... to ...* Ask them to read their answers to a partner before listening to some examples in open class and comparing opinions. If students dislike certain things, they may enjoy discussing possible ways of improving them.

Grammar notebook
Remind students to note down the rules for this structure and to write a few examples of their own.

3 Vocabulary
Making an effort

a) Ask students to find the expressions in the text which match the definitions. As you check the answers, ask students questions to ensure they are clear about the meaning of the expressions, e.g. *When do you go to great lengths? How do you know if someone is doing something half-heartedly?* Say the expressions and ask students to repeat them.

Answers
1. struggling
2. half-heartedly
3. go to great lengths
4. trial and error
5. find it easy
6. get a lot out of it
7. do it properly
8. doing something wrong

b) Students complete the text with the expressions from Exercise 3a. Point out that they may need to change the form of some verbs to make them grammatically correct.

Answers
1. struggled
2. half-heartedly
3. went to great lengths
4. find it easy
5. trial and error
6. did ... properly
7. get a lot out of
8. done something wrong

c) Students discuss their learning experiences using the expressions in Exercise 3b. To get them started, you may like to give an example of the way you learned something. Encourage students to correct each other's sentences if necessary. Ask a few pairs to tell the class about their partner's answers.

OPTIONAL ACTIVITY

It is a very useful activity to carry out a needs analysis on your students. To find out how they feel about various aspects of the language, write the following on the board: *grammar, vocabulary, spelling, pronunciation*. To find out how they feel about classroom activities, write the following: *listen to recordings, read texts, speak to partners, repeat words*, etc. Ask students to use the structure *It ... to ...* and the vocabulary from Exercise 3 to make sentences, e.g. *It's hard to learn phrasal verbs. I struggle to understand listening texts.* When students have thought of some sentences, ask them to discuss their opinions in small groups, then expand into an open class discussion.

Vocabulary notebook
Encourage students to start a new section *Making an effort* in their notebook and add the expressions from Exercise 3. They may find it useful to note down translations of the expressions too.

4 Pronunciation
Connecting sounds (intrusive /w/ and /j/)

a 🔊 Write this sentence on the board: *Hello, I am ...* (your name). Explain to students that when we speak, words are often joined together and different sounds are sometimes created as our mouths move to form the next word. This is especially true when a vowel sound at the end of one word is followed by another at the beginning of the next. Say the words *hello, I, am* separately and then join them together in natural speech, showing students that a /w/ is created between *Hello* and *I* and a /j/ between *I* and *am*. Students turn to page 120 and read through the sentences. Play the recording. Ask students to note down which sound they hear between the underlined words. Go through the first one with them if necessary.

Answers
1 y   2 w   3 w   4 y   5 w   6 y

b 🔊 Play the recording again, pausing after each sentence for students to repeat. Encourage them to link the sounds as on the recording.

5 Listen and speak

a Ask students to describe what they can see in the photos. Pre-teach difficult vocabulary in sentences 1–6: *shiny, scholarship, precise*. Students complete the sentences with the verbs in the box. Then ask them to match two sentences with each photo. Don't check the answers yet.

Answers
1 did – Ceri Chamberlain
2 did – Guy Jowett
3 left – Ceri Chamberlain
4 won – Guy Jowett
5 takes – Paula Cocozza
6 bring – Paula Cocozza

b 🔊 Explain the meaning of *inherited*. Tell students they are going to listen to three people talking about something they have inherited from a relative. Students listen and check their answers from Exercise 5a.

TAPESCRIPT
Ceri Chamberlain
Presents in our house were always books. My dad was an English teacher and he loved to read. He taught me to read before I went to school. He was my hero and I always wanted to impress him. On holiday we used to read the same book, we used to read aloud to each other. When I was ten we went to Switzerland and read *The Tenant of Wildfell Hall*. We had a rule. You couldn't start reading it before the other person was there. I remember coming down to breakfast and seeing my father desperately trying not to open the book. I think my mother and brother found it a bit annoying but sometimes they would be hanging around, listening, wanting to find out what happened next. My father and I communicated through books. When I grew up there was never any fear of words with me. I did English Literature at university because of this passion. My dad was such an inspiration to me. A few years later, he and Mum got divorced and he moved down to Somerset with his new girlfriend. Then he got really sick – he had cancer – he couldn't read any more. I used to visit him at the weekends and read to him – simple books because, at this stage in his illness, he didn't want to concentrate so much. After he died his girlfriend phoned me to say that he had left his collection of books to me. We've always had a tradition in my family: 'If you find something good, pass it on.' I must carry on that tradition with my family.

Guy Jowett
My grandfather's qualification from the Royal College of Organists 1923 used to hang proudly beside his piano. At 13 he played the organ at the local cinema and later he won a scholarship to Cambridge to study music. But his father wouldn't let him go – he said he had to go out there and earn some money. And that's how my grandfather became a bank manager instead of a pianist. But he always wanted a special piano. He was 76 when he finally found it – an old Steinway. It wasn't in great condition but because of this it was cheap and he could afford to buy it. He took it home and did it up until it looked shiny and beautiful again. We all had piano lessons on it when we were young, but my memories are more of my grandfather playing the piano and us being transfixed. How could anybody play it so beautifully? His fingers hardly seemed to touch the keys. One day my grandfather said he was going to give up playing the piano and sell it. I told him that I'd rather it stayed in the family and I asked him if I could buy it from him. At that point he wrote a note saying 'This Steinway piano belongs to Guy Jowett and was given to him by me, signed Ronald P. Jowett, December 30 1988.' I'm very proud to have this piano. It encourages me to play. I may even get lessons on it again. And maybe one day I'll write someone else a note and leave it to them.

Paula Cocozza
Under the desk in my bedroom is a brown leather suitcase, where I keep all my treasured possessions and in that suitcase is a small blue box. Inside the box are three everyday items: a small pair of scissors, a ring with a turquoise sapphire and a stone with a hole in it. They have no real value themselves but I wouldn't sell them for all the money in the world. They live together in this blue box for no other reason than this is how they were returned to me after my grandmother died. The scissors and ring came as no surprise. I had given both to my grandmother as a young teenager at different Christmases. I think they were meant to

remind me that she used to make me beautiful dresses when I was younger and that she had eyes the colour of the sea on a sunny day. But the stone with a hole in it – that I had not been expecting. We had found it, the two of us, on one of those sunny days by the sea. Only we weren't looking at the sea or the sky. We were looking at the oceans of stones underneath our feet. I was eight and I had a serious mission that day. I had to find a stone with a hole in it. My grandmother told me we should look for one because it would always bring us good luck. I found one, small and dark with a nice big hole running right through it. My grandmother put it into her purse. Then, 25 years later, when she finally passed away and we were clearing out her house, I found that stone in her handbag. She must have kept it in her purse and carried it with her wherever she went for the last quarter of a century. Now this stone, like the other objects in that box, is my reminder of the past and takes me back to a precise moment when my grandmother and I were together.

c 🔊 Give students time to read through the sentences and deal with any problem vocabulary: *originally, passion, approve, remind*. Play the recording again while students choose the correct answers. Students compare answers with a partner before feedback.

Answers
1 b   2 b   3 c   4 a   5 a   6 a

d Give students an example by describing in some detail a present which was special for you. Students think of the best present they have received and answer the three questions, making notes in preparation for the next exercise.

e In small groups, students talk about the best present they have received. Encourage students to describe their present without referring to their notes. Discuss any interesting answers in class.

6 Grammar
Modal verbs review

Students covered modal verbs in SB2, Units 4 and 11, and SB3, Units 8, 11 and 12.

a Students read the sentences from the listening text. Draw attention to the pronouns in italics and ask students to try to remember which of the three presents they refer to. Remind students of the importance of using pronouns in sentences to avoid repetition of nouns.

Answers
2 P   3 P   4 S   5 B   6 P   7 P

b Write a few sentences with modal verbs on the board, e.g. *You must be tired. We should buy a new car. He couldn't speak English*. Ask students to identify the modal verbs and to think of some other examples. Remind students that a modal is always followed by the infinitive of another verb and that its form doesn't change. Ask students to circle the modal verbs in sentences 1–8.

Answers
1 must   2 could   3 may   4 should   5 couldn't
6 must   7 'll (will)   8 could

Language note
Students may think that forms of *be*, *have* and *do* are modal verbs. These are auxiliary verbs and are used to form tenses. Modal verbs like *can, may, should*, etc. have no infinitive, no continuous form, no passive form, no -s ending for the third person singular. Questions are formed by inverting the modal and the subject (*Must I ...? Can we ...?*). Students often make errors with modal verbs, so you may like to write the following on the board and ask students to tell you why they are wrong.
1   *I must to go.*
2   *I don't can come this evening.*
3   *Do I must do my homework now?*
4   *He cans play the piano.*

c Students work in pairs to match the sentences in Exercise 6a with the uses of the modal verb. Give them time to discuss their answers. Check the answers and elicit other examples for some of the modals.

Answers
b 8   c 3   d 5   e 2   f 6   g 1   h 4

d Students choose the correct modal verb for each sentence. Ask them to compare answers with a partner. During feedback, encourage students to explain why the second option is not correct.

Answers
1 should   2 won't   3 can't   4 can   5 May
6 might   7 would   8 must

Grammar notebook
Remind students to note down the rules for this structure and to write a few examples of their own.

7 Speak

a Students complete the questions with a modal verb and check their answers with a partner before feedback in open class.

Answers
1 would   2 will   3 would/could/might   4 will

b Students work with a different partner and discuss the questions. In feedback discuss the questions further with the whole class.

Unit 7   53

Culture in mind

8 Read

a) As an introduction to this exercise, write the names of the nine countries on the board and ask students to brainstorm information about each one. Look at the pictures with the class and ask students to describe what they can see. Use the pictures to pre-teach *blindfold* and *waltz*. Then ask students to read the text quickly and write the names of the countries under the pictures. Tell them not to worry about understanding every word, but to focus on the task. Check the answers.

Answers
a Mexico   b Argentina   c Denmark   d India
e The Netherlands

b) Read through the text with the class, pausing where necessary to check comprehension and help with difficult vocabulary: *noodles, streamers, corresponding to, shrine, hollow, papier mâché, goodies, acknowledge*. Students read and answer the questions and compare answers with a partner before feedback.

Answers
1 China, Vietnam
2 Vietnam
3 India, Mexico
4 Denmark
5 Argentina, The Netherlands, Japan
6 Argentina
7 India, Japan
8 The Netherlands, Israel

> **Discussion box**
> **Weaker classes:** Students can choose one question to discuss.
> **Stronger classes:** In pairs or small groups, students go through the questions in the box and discuss them.
> Monitor and help as necessary, encouraging students to express themselves in English and to use any vocabulary they have learned from the text. Ask pairs or groups to feedback to the class and discuss any interesting points further.

9 Write

a) Ask students what they can remember from the text about Danny Wallace in Exercise 1. Students read the summary quickly to get a general impression of its quality. Discuss their opinions in open class. Without going into details, they should recognise that the text is far too long and rambling to be a good summary and that the general effect is very confusing. They may also notice that some information is inaccurate.

b) Students read the summary again and check the questions. Point out that they should decide not only if the summary is factually correct, but also if the writer has focused on key points and used his/her own words. Discuss the summary in more detail and help students to identify some of the problems, for example:

- It isn't clear that *Join Me* is an internet-based club with about 3,000 members all over the world.
- In paragraph 2, there is no mention of the acts of kindness that Danny does on Fridays – the writer has missed the main point. The statement that 'people sometimes hit you and run away' is inaccurate.
- In paragraph 3 the writer has copied long passages from the original text rather than selecting key points and using his/her own words. The sentence about 'stories about things they have done on the Tube or in the buses' is repeated (inaccurately) later. This paragraph contains a lot of unimportant information. At the same time, it doesn't mention the positive benefits that members of *Join Me* gain from their acts of kindness.

c) Tell students they are going to re-write the summary in Exercise 9a. Go through the guide with them to make sure they are aware of what needs to be included. If there is time, you may want to work through the first two steps of the guide with the class. Discuss the main ideas of the text together and write notes on the board. Then give students time to underline key points, and again give feedback before asking them to write their summary. Set a target length of about 150 words. Remind students to use their own words as far as possible and to use quotation marks when they quote directly from the text.

> **Language note**
> Quotation marks can be either double ("…") or single ('…'). Tell students that it doesn't matter which style they choose, but they should be consistent throughout their piece of writing.

OPTIONAL ACTIVITY
For further practice of summary writing, ask students to choose one of the longer reading texts from an earlier unit, and write a summary of it. Tell them they should write 150–200 words and use the guide in Exercise 9c to help them.

8 Peacemakers

Unit overview

TOPIC: Resolving conflicts and promoting peace

TEXTS
Reading: an article on the origins of the Nobel Peace Prize
Reading: a short biography of Wangari Maathai
Listening: an interview about a Nobel Peace Prize winner
Listening: song: *Peace, Love and Understanding*
Writing: a composition about an admirable person

SPEAKING AND FUNCTIONS
Discussing Nobel Peace Prize winners and candidates
Talking about how to resolve a conflict

LANGUAGE
Grammar: Past perfect passive; Past perfect continuous
Vocabulary: Conflicts and solutions
Pronunciation: Linking sounds

1 Read

If you set the background information as a homework research task, ask the students to tell the class what they found out.

BACKGROUND INFORMATION

The Nobel Peace Prize: is one of six Nobel prizes (the others are for Physics, Chemistry, Economics, Medicine and Literature) awarded every year in Scandinavia. The winner is decided by a group of five people who form the Norwegian Nobel Committee. The prize can be won by an individual or an organisation.

Martin Luther King Jr: (1929–1968) was a church minister and leader of the American civil rights movement which opposed racial discrimination against black Americans. King won the Nobel Peace Prize in 1964 before being assassinated in 1968. Martin Luther King Day (January 15th) was established in his honour. The *Jr* at the end of his name is short for *Junior*, as his father had the same name.

Nelson Mandela: (born in 1918) is a South African politician. He became leader of the African National Congress in 1961 and tried to end racial inequality (apartheid) in his country. He was put in prison for his political activities in 1963 and stayed there for 27 years. He became President of South Africa in 1994 and won the Nobel Peace Prize in 1993.

Aung San Suu Kyi: (born in 1945) is a supporter of democracy who won the Nobel Peace Prize in 1991. For more information about her, see the text on page 57 of the Student's Book.

Kofi Annan: (born in 1938) is from Ghana in Africa and from 1997 to 2006 he was the Secretary-General of the United Nations. He and the UN itself were joint winners of the Nobel Peace Prize in 2001 for 'their work for a better organised and more peaceful world'. During his term of office he was deeply committed to strengthening the role of the UN in promoting international peace and security.

Lech Walesa: (born in 1943) was a Polish electrician who became a trade union and human rights activist in Poland. In the 1980s he led the Solidarity trade union which opposed government repression, and after the fall of the Communist regime he became President of Poland from 1990 to 1995. He won the Nobel Peace Prize in 1983.

Mother Teresa: (1910–1997) was an Albanian-born Catholic nun who founded the Missionaries of Charity in India. Her work for the poor in Calcutta led to her winning the Nobel Peace Prize in 1979.

The First World War: is also called *World War I* and *the Great War*. It lasted from August 1914 to November 1918. The Allied Powers (led by Britain, France, Russia until 1917, and the United States after 1917) defeated the Central Powers (led by the German Empire, the Austro-Hungarian Empire and the Ottoman Empire).

Warm up

Books closed. Ask students to imagine that they have to give some prizes for special achievements: the class prize for music, the class prize for acting and the class prize for peace. Give students a short while to decide who they would give the prizes to and discuss interesting answers in open class. Ask students if they know of any real prizes in these three fields.

a) Ask students to look at the photos and elicit anything they know about the people. (The photos, top to bottom, show Alfred Nobel, Mother Teresa, Nelson Mandela, Kofi Annan and Lech Walesa.)

b) Pre-teach *fortune, dynamite, explosive* and *obituary*. Students read the questions and then read the text quickly to find the answers. Encourage them to look for the answers and not to spend time on new words.

Answers
1 By making explosives, including dynamite.
2 He saw his own obituary and he didn't want to be remembered only as the man who had invented a destructive weapon.

c) 🔊 Read through the text with the class, pausing where necessary to check comprehension and help with difficult vocabulary: *landmines, seamines, blast, weapon of mass destruction, promote, abolish, grave.* Then read the additional sentences (1–5). Ask students to look back at the text and to add the sentences in the appropriate spaces (A–E). Play the recording for students to check their answers. During feedback ask them to explain why they chose a certain sentence to fill each gap.

Answers
A 5   B 1   C 4   D 2   E 3

d) Students read the text again and number the events 1–8 in the order in which they occurred.
Stronger students: Let students try to order the sentences from memory before looking back at the text to check their answers.

Answers
Order of events: 7, 1, 3, 6, 8, 4, 2, 5

OPTIONAL ACTIVITY
Write the following sentences on the board. Ask students to decide if they are true or false and then to look back at the text and check their answers. Ask them to correct the false sentences.
1 *Alfred Nobel was the first winner of the Nobel Peace Prize.* (False. He created the prize.)
2 *Alfred was the first member of his family to develop explosives.* (False. His family had been developing explosives for many years when he joined the company.)
3 *Dynamite was safer than nitro-glycerine.* (True.)
4 *Alfred Nobel was not a rich man.* (False. He had a great fortune.)
5 *Alfred Nobel is still alive.* (False. He is in his grave.)

---

2 Grammar
Past perfect passive

a) Books closed. Ask students how many past tenses they can think of. Elicit *past simple, past continuous* and *past perfect*. Write the following sentences on the board and ask students which tenses are underlined.

Dan Brown <u>wrote</u> The Da Vinci Code. **(past simple)**
She <u>was cooking</u> dinner when I got home.
(past continuous)
When I opened the door, I realised somebody <u>had stolen</u> my computer. **(past perfect)**

Write the word *passive* on the board and ask students to change the three sentences into the passive by changing the underlined verbs:

The Da Vinci Code was written by Dan Brown.
Dinner was being cooked when I got home.
When I opened the door, I realised my computer had been stolen.

Books open. Ask students to complete the sentences from the text in Exercise 1.

Answers
1 had been   2 had been

b) Ask students to read through the rule and choose the correct options. Check the answers. Refer back to Exercise 2a to show students examples of the use of this tense.

Answers
to be, past participle

BACKGROUND INFORMATION
The League of Nations: was an international organisation founded after the Paris Peace Conference of 1919. The League's main goals were to stop war through collective security, to settle disputes between countries through negotiation and to improve global welfare.

---

c) Tell students they are going to read a text about the First World War. Ask them to give a bit of basic information about this war. Pre-teach difficult vocabulary: *peace treaty, railway carriage, vast amounts, opposing armies.* Students read the text and circle the correct verb forms. Ask them to compare answers with a partner before feedback.

Answers
1 was signed   2 were sent   3 had been killed
4 had been spent   5 had been destroyed
6 was taken   7 had been discussed   8 was fought

d) Students complete the sentences with the correct form of the verbs.

Answers
1 had been destroyed   2 had been sold
3 was killed   4 was held   5 hadn't been repaired
6 had been painted

Grammar notebook
Remind students to note down the rules for the past perfect passive and to write a few examples of their own.

3 Listen
If you set the background information as a homework research task, ask the students to tell the class what they found out.

BACKGROUND INFORMATION

Professor Wangari Muta Maathai: (born in 1940) is a Kenyan environmental and political activist. In 2004 she was awarded the Nobel Peace Prize for her contribution to sustainable development, democracy and peace – the first African woman to receive the award.

Bishop Desmond Tutu: (born in 1931) was the first black person in South Africa to lead the Anglican church. He became famous in the 1980s when he spoke out strongly against apartheid in support of 'a democratic and just society without racial divisions'. He was awarded the Nobel Peace Prize in 1984.

Nairobi: is the capital of Kenya. Nairobi has the highest urban population in East Africa, with an estimated population of between 3 and 4 million.

a) 🔊 Tell students they are going to hear an interview about a Nobel Peace Prize winner. Write her name on the board: *Professor Wangari Maathai*. Ask them to read through the questions and then play the recording, several times if necessary. Students listen and answer the questions.

TAPESCRIPT

Interviewer Following the news that Professor Wangari Maathai has just been awarded the Nobel Peace Prize, we have Martin Davies on the line, foreign correspondent based in Kenya, and a personal friend of Professor Maathai. Hello, Martin. So how is everyone taking the news there in Nairobi?

Martin Hello – well, we're all celebrating like crazy, as you can hear. Professor Maathai is just delighted.

Interviewer A few hours have passed since she got the message. How do you think she feels?

Martin I think, to be honest, she still can't quite believe it's true. She seems quite overwhelmed to have won this prize.

Interviewer And just why is it so important for her, and indeed for all environmentalists in Africa?

Martin Well, I think people are happy that Wangari's work has been recognised, that it has made such an impact on the Nobel Committee, the fact that the committee understands that it is often the fight over natural resources which causes conflict, and that working on these environmental issues is a way of resolving conflicts peacefully.

Interviewer And, in your view, what impact will this have on the role of African women in trying to build peace and a sustainable future in Africa?

Martin Well, I'm sure that many people who are involved in the environmental effort will be very, very encouraged by this prize. They will realise that what they're doing is extremely important, and I'm sure that that's true not only here in Africa, but also throughout the world.

Interviewer There's often a male structure in power in many African countries. Not just in Africa, of course, but if we look at Africa … do you think this prize can influence people, men especially, to understand the role of women more clearly?

Martin I'm quite sure that, now Professor Maathai has been awarded this prize, a lot of prejudices against women will be removed. I think I can say without exaggeration that everybody in this country, and I'm sure many people in Africa generally, are extremely happy, and they associate themselves with the prize – both men and women. And I'm sure that, at a time like this, men appreciate the role that women can play. I know that many men in this country are very proud. And they associate themselves with what the women have been doing.

Interviewer Well, there are still many problems in Africa, much work still to be done. In your view, what do you think will be the most pressing issues in the next few years?

Martin Well, the issue of the environment in Africa. It's a very important issue, among others, of course.

Interviewer Professor Maathai has taken huge personal risks in her fight for justice, human rights and the environment. What is it that makes her so brave? Do you think these are risks that we should expect more people to take?

Martin Well, I think that people react in their own way to the challenges that face them in their countries and in their regions, and quite often people have different ideas about how to approach those challenges. But everywhere in the world you will find a few very special people, people who stand up and face those challenges, taking many risks for what they believe in. People like Martin Luther King, who was honoured by the same Nobel Peace Prize, people like Mandela, Nelson Mandela, people like Bishop Desmond Tutu when he was fighting apartheid in South Africa. These are people with special qualities. They have also been recognised for their work by the Nobel Peace Committee, of course, but when they received their prizes, they had been working for many years for the things they believed in without any recognition for their work, just because they had faith in their own convictions and they were prepared to take the risks involved to make the world a better place to live in, to find solutions to the problems around them. These are very special kinds of people.

Interviewer Thank you very much, Martin, for your thoughts and insights. We'll let you go back to the celebrations.

Martin It's been a pleasure. Thank you.

Answers
1 He's in Nairobi, Kenya.
2 The news that Professor Wangari Maathai has won the Nobel Peace Prize.
3 Natural resources.
4 Because they associate themselves with what women like Wangari Maathai have been doing.
5 The environment.

b) 🔊 Read through the sentences with the class and check understanding. Play the recording again and ask students to number the events in the order in which they hear them. Check the answers. You may want to play the recording again, pausing as necessary for clarification.

Answers
1 Wangari Maathai feels overwhelmed that her work has been recognised by the Nobel Committee.
2 Professor Maathai's work will encourage people who work for the environment.
3 The prize will help to overcome prejudices against women.
4 Martin Davies praises people who take risks for what they believe in.
5 He mentions examples of people who fought for what they believed in.

> **Discussion box**
> **Weaker classes:** Students can choose one question to discuss.
> **Stronger classes:** In pairs or small groups, students go through both questions in the box and discuss them.
> Monitor and help as necessary, encouraging students to express themselves in English and to use any vocabulary they have learned from the text. Ask pairs or groups to feedback to the class and discuss any interesting points further. Students may like to vote on the person who should win the Nobel Peace Prize.

4 Grammar
Past perfect continuous

a) Look at the example sentence with the class and focus on the verb *had been working*. Tell students that this tense is called the past perfect continuous. Draw attention to the form (*had + been + -ing*).
Ask: *Did they work before or after they received their prizes?* (Before.) *Did their work happen at a particular time or was it an extended action?* (An extended action.) Students read through the rule and circle the correct option.

Answers
continuous, before

b) Ask students to read quickly through the text in Exercise 1a to find another example of the past perfect continuous. Ask them which happened first – Alfred joining the company or the development of explosives (*the development of explosives*). Draw attention to the time expression *for many years* and point out that the action of developing explosives continued for an extended period of time.

Answer
When Alfred joined the Nobel family company, it had been developing explosives for many years.

c) To clarify the difference between the past perfect and the past perfect continuous, write the following sentences on the board:
I recognised the hotel. I had stayed there in 2004. When I arrived, I met Isobel. She had been staying at the hotel for a few days.
Point out that both forms of the past perfect refer to an event that happened earlier than another event in the past. Ask students if they can say why the second example is different from the first. Elicit the point that we use the past perfect continuous to express continuous or repeated activities up to a point in the past. Students read through the sentences and decide which is the correct verb form. They could work on this in pairs. During feedback, you may find it useful to draw a timeline on the board to show when different actions took place.

Answers
1 was going   2 hadn't eaten   3 had been travelling
4 had received   5 had been looking

d) Students complete the sentences using the correct tense. Ask them to compare answers with a partner before feedback.

Answers
1 had been sleeping   2 had been crying
3 was shopping   4 had been waiting
5 was crossing   6 had been thinking

Grammar notebook
Remind students to note down the rule for the past perfect continuous and to write a few examples of their own.

5 Vocabulary
Conflicts and solutions

Warm up

To introduce the topic, ask students if they have ever had a serious argument with one of their friends or a member of their family. Ask them to discuss with a partner. What was the argument about? Did they make friends again? Did they go to somebody else for advice? Listen to a few examples in open class.

a) Read through the two sentences with students and ask them to fill the gaps. Make sure they understand that we *resolve* a problem or *find* an answer/solution to a problem.

Answers
resolve, find

b Tell students that they are going to read a page from a website which helps people resolve conflicts. Ask students to read the webpage and then to match the underlined expressions with the definitions. Students compare answers with a partner before feedback.

Answers
1 b   2 g   3 c   4 d   5 f   6 e   7 a   8 h

c 🔊 Ask students to complete the sentences using the underlined expressions. Point out that they will need to change the form of some of the verbs. Play the recording for students to check their answers.

TAPESCRIPT/ANSWERS
1 He's a bit upset because he's fallen out with his best friend.
2 Can you help me with my Maths homework? I keep getting stuck.
3 Let's reach a compromise. I'll do the washing up if you cook me dinner. OK?
4 I get angry at home because my parents always take my brother's side.
5 The presidents of the two countries are meeting to try and resolve the conflict that started last month.
6 Annie can help you with any problems you've got. She's really good at sorting them out.
7 Haven't you and your brother made up yet? I'm tired of seeing the two of you fighting all the time!
8 There are many countries in the world that always stay neutral when a war starts.

Vocabulary notebook
Encourage students to start a new section *Conflicts and solutions* in their notebook and add these words. They may find it useful to note down translations of the words too.

--- OPTIONAL ACTIVITY ---
For further practice of the vocabulary in this exercise, photocopy and hand out the following lists or write them on the board. Ask students to match 1–6 with a–f.

Answers:
1 d   2 f   3 a   4 b   5 c   6 e

1 She's very good at creating problems
2 The only way to resolve this conflict
3 I'm trying to find a solution to this problem
4 Jane and Fred fell out again last week, and
5 Why do you always have to take someone's side?
6 They failed to end the argument because

a but I keep getting stuck.
b they only made up yesterday.
c Why can't you stay neutral?
d but not so good at sorting them out.
e they couldn't reach a compromise.
f is to find out who started it.

6 Pronunciation
Linking sounds

a 🔊 Students turn to page 120 and read through the sentences. Play the recording and ask students to note how the underlined sounds are pronounced. Draw attention to the way a consonant sound at the end of a word links up with a vowel sound at the beginning of the next word: /meɪkʌp/, /sɔːtaʊt/, /faɪndə/, /getə/.

b 🔊 Play the recording again, pausing after each sentence for students to repeat.

7 Speak

Read the text with the class. In groups, students discuss ways of resolving the conflict. Ask different groups to present their solutions to the class and encourage others to comment and ask questions. Encourage the class to try to come to agreement about the best way of resolving the problem.

--- OPTIONAL ACTIVITY ---
If you have a strong class, you could ask pairs to write a dialogue between Monica and Jake, first arguing and then resolving their conflict. Invite different pairs to act out their dialogue for the class.

8 Listen and speak

If you set the background information as a homework research task, ask the students to tell the class what they found out.

BACKGROUND INFORMATION

Elvis Costello: (born in 1954) is a popular British musician, singer and songwriter. His real name is Declan MacManus. He became famous as part of the 'New Wave' of pop music in the 1970s. His hits include *Oliver's Army*, *Watching the Detectives* and *A Good Year for the Roses*. In recent years, Costello's albums have shown country, jazz and classical influences.

Nick Lowe: (born in 1949) is a singer, songwriter and producer. He has been recording since the 1960s. His hits include *So It Goes*, *I Love the Sound of Breaking Glass* and *Cruel to be Kind*.

Bob Geldof: (born in 1951) is an Irish singer, songwriter, actor and political activist. He sang with the Boomtown Rats in the 1970s and had two number one hits (*Rat Trap* and *I Don't Like Mondays*) before becoming even more famous as the organiser of the Live Aid and Live 8 concerts (see Background information for Unit 11, Exercise 9).

a 🔊 Ask students to look at the picture and the title of the song. Ask them to guess what the singer feels about peace, love and understanding. Play the song with books closed while students check their answers.

Unit 8

TAPESCRIPT
See the song on page 56 of the Student's Book.

(b) 🔊 Play the recording again. Students listen, read the lyrics and correct the underlined words. Let students compare answers in pairs before checking the answers. Play the recording again if necessary, pausing at the answers.

Answers
1 world   2 pain   3 know   4 times   5 cry

(c) Ask students what the singer means by the word *funny*. Discuss with the class why he asks the question.

Answer
b It's strange.

Did you know ...?

Read through the information in the box with the class. Ask students if they know any of the artists mentioned and invite them to give any interesting information they may know about them. Ask if they have seen any big concerts live or on TV.

9 Write

The planning for this exercise can be done in class and the writing can be set as homework.

(a) Ask students to read the text quickly and identify the topic of each paragraph.

Answers
Para 1 d   Para 2 b   Para 3 c   Para 4 a

(b) Students read the last paragraph of the text again and discuss the writer's admiration for Aung San Suu Kyi.

Possible answers
The writer admires her because she has acted with great courage for the good of her people, although this was dangerous for her personally. She held on to her ideals and tried to achieve them through peaceful means. The writer describes what is special about Aung San Suu Kyi and shows how her behaviour and beliefs fit with the values that he/she believes in.

(c) Students think of somebody that they admire. Read through the notes with the class and tell students to plan their composition using the same paragraph structure as in the sample text. Encourage them to think about why they admire the person they have chosen and to express this in the final paragraph. This task could be extended into a class presentation, with students putting their writing on the walls, passing them round for cross-reading or giving oral presentations based on their texts.

✱ Module 2 Check your progress

1 Grammar

(a) 3 What makes him seem friendly is that he's always singing.
4 It's important to keep calm.
5 What I find really annoying is that Paul always interrupts when I speak.
6 It's fun to speak a foreign language.
7 I've forgotten what she told me she wanted for her birthday.
8 It's normal to forget people's names sometimes.

(b) The word *would* should be crossed out in 1, 4 and 6.

(c) 2 would   3 may   4 May   5 can't   6 must   7 might

(d) 1 seeing   2 to phone   3 to have   4 apologising   5 to invite   6 playing   7 buying

(e) 2 had ... gone   3 had left   4 had been written   5 had been sold   6 had seen

(f) 1 had been working   2 had spent   3 had been waiting   4 had eaten   5 had been sitting down

2 Vocabulary

(a) 1 in   2 on   3 in   4 in   5 by   6 in

(b) 1 find   2 wrong   3 error   4 lengths   5 struggled   6 heartedly   7 properly

(c) 1 f   2 e   3 a   4 d   5 b   6 c

(d) *Across:*
1 sympathetic   3 witty   4 careless   5 smug   6 bubbly

Down:
2 intellectual   4 charming   5 shallow

How did you do?
Students work out their scores. Check how they have done and follow up any problem areas with revision work.

Module 3
Making a difference

YOU WILL LEARN ABOUT ...

Ask students to look at the pictures on the page. Ask them to read through the topics in the box and check that they understand each item. You can ask them the following questions, in L1 if appropriate:

1 *What can you see in the supermarket basket?*
2 *Who is the woman and what's her job?*
3 *Who's the singer on the left?*
4 *What's causing the damage in this photo?*
5 *What sport does this team play?*
6 *How could these birds help to produce energy for cars?*

In pairs or small groups, students discuss which topic area they think each picture matches. Check the answers.

Answers
1 Fair Trade
2 How famous people are helping the United Nations
3 Two concerts that tried to make a difference to our world
4 Threats to our environment
5 An unusual event to raise money for charity
6 Ways of reducing the amount of energy we use

YOU WILL LEARN HOW TO ...

Use grammar

Students read through the grammar points and the examples. Go through the first item with them as an example. In pairs, students now match the grammar items in their book. Check the answers.

Answers
Mixed conditionals: If you had brought the map, we wouldn't be lost now.
Future perfect: He'll have forgotten by tomorrow.
Future continuous: I'll be sunbathing on a beach this time next week.
Future time markers: You have until tomorrow to give me your answer.
Reduced relative clauses: *Imagine* is the song most played on British radio.
Question tags: He'll love it, won't he?
Phrasal verbs: Half the world gets by on less than $1 a day.
Revision of conditionals: If she had told you, you would have been angry.

Use vocabulary

Write the headings on the board. Go through the items in the Student's Book and check understanding. Now ask students if they can think of one more item for the *Ways of saving energy* heading. Elicit some responses and add them to the list on the board. Students now do the same for the other headings. Some possibilities are:

Ways of saving energy: ride bicycles, use solar power

Global issues: famine, drought, war

Expressing opinions: I think, in my opinion, from my point of view

Imprecise numbers: around, up to

Unit 9   61

9 Get involved

Unit overview

TOPIC: Taking social action

TEXTS
Reading and listening: a weblog about a sponsored climb up Mount Everest
Listening: a radio phone-in programme about giving the vote to 16-year-olds
Reading: an extract from *Lord of the Flies* by William Golding
Writing: a formal letter to raise money for charity

SPEAKING AND FUNCTIONS
Discussing raising money for charity
Discussing young people's right to vote
Talking about the rights and responsibilities of young people

LANGUAGE
Grammar: Conditionals review: zero, first, second and third conditionals; Mixed conditionals
Vocabulary: Ways of getting involved
Pronunciation: Contractions in third conditionals

1 Read and listen

If you set the background information as a homework research task, ask the students to tell the class what they found out.

BACKGROUND INFORMATION

Mount Everest: is a mountain on the border between Nepal and China. At 8,848 metres, it is the highest mountain on Earth. It is thought to be rising at a rate of around 4 mm per year.

Rugby: is normally played by teams of 15 players. It developed in the 19th century in England from the rules used to play football. The main differences from football are that in rugby the ball is oval instead of round and that the players are allowed to pick the ball up, run with it and throw it from player to player. They are not allowed to throw it forwards, only to the side or behind. Points are scored by carrying the ball over your opponents' goal line or by kicking a goal. Rugby is very popular in a number of countries including England, Wales, France and New Zealand.

Show Racism the Red Card: is an organisation that campaigns against racism in football. It is named after the referee's red card, which is shown to a player when he has committed a foul and must leave the pitch.

a Ask students to look at the photos and to suggest ideas in answer to the questions. Don't comment on their answers at this stage.

b Students read through the weblog quickly to check their answers for Exercise 1a. Remind them not to worry about every new word, but to make a note of any words they think might be important. Check the answers. Ask students what they know about the game of rugby and then ask how this activity can help a charity. Introduce the word *sponsor* and make sure students understand how sponsored events raise money.

Answers
They're on Mount Everest.
They're playing rugby.
They're doing it for charity.

c 🔊 Read through sentences 1–6 with the class. Then play the recording while students read and listen to the text. Pause where appropriate to check comprehension and help with difficult vocabulary. Students look back at the text to find the day on which each event happened. Warn them that they will have to read especially carefully to work out the answers for questions 2, 4 and 6. Ask them to compare answers with a partner before feedback.

Answers
1 Day 5 2 Day 2 3 Day 4 4 Day 10 5 Day 5
6 Day 8

OPTIONAL ACTIVITIES

Stronger classes: For further comprehension work, write the following sentences on the board and ask students to decide if they are true or false. If they are false, encourage students to explain why in their own words.

1 *Mike began supporting 'Show Racism the Red Card' when he heard about the rugby match.* (False. He began supporting them when his friend showed him a petition.)
2 *The players felt great when they reached Namche Bazaar.* (False. Most of them had headaches.)
3 *Mike had some free time on day 5.* (True.)
4 *Namche Bazaar is in a beautiful forest.* (False. They had walked through the forest before they got there.)
5 *The rugby game was played in a friendly way.* (False. It got competitive and two players were sent off.)
6 *One of his team got hurt.* (False. Mike thinks someone would have got hurt if they'd played any longer.)

The text includes some interesting idioms and phrases which you might like to present to students. Write the following on the board and ask students to work with a

---

62 Module 3

partner to work out translations in their own language.
to cut a long story short
make your way
get short of breath
do things the hard way
Ask students to think of sentences to show the meanings of these expressions.

> **Discussion box**
> **Weaker classes:** Students can choose one question to discuss.
> **Stronger classes:** In pairs or small groups, students go through the questions in the box and discuss them.
> Monitor and help as necessary, encouraging students to express themselves in English and to use any vocabulary they have learned from the text. Ask pairs or groups to feedback to the class and discuss any interesting points further.

2 Grammar
Conditionals review

Students covered conditionals in SB1, Unit 15, SB2, Unit 14 and SB3, Unit 14.

a Books closed. Write *four types of conditionals* on the board and elicit as much information as possible from students: the names of the conditionals, an example of each and explanations of when they are used. Students then open their books, look at the four examples and complete the table themselves. Write the table on the board and ask students to help you fill it in. Draw attention to example A and remind students that the two clauses can be reversed, with the *if* clause coming first or second.

Answers

	Example sentence	If clause	Main clause
Zero conditional	C	present simple	present simple
First conditional	B	present simple	will + infinitive
Second conditional	D	past simple	would + infinitive
Third conditional	A	past perfect	would have + past participle

b Read through the descriptions with the class. Students decide which conditional each sentence describes. Check the answers. Refer back to the examples in Exercise 2a and use these for further explanation if necessary.

Answers
1 third   2 zero   3 second   4 first

> **Language note**
> It is common to use imperatives in conditional sentences, for example: *If he phones, tell him I'm out. If the baby cries, give her some milk.*

c Students decide which conditionals are used in the sentences. During feedback, ask them to explain why a certain conditional is used in each case, referring back to the explanations in Exercise 2b.

Answers
1 second   2 zero   3 zero   4 third   5 first
6 first   7 third

> **Language note**
> Students may make the mistake of thinking they should use *will* in the *if* clause, as it has a future meaning, e.g. **If it will rain, I will take my coat.* You could point out some other sentence types where we use the present simple to refer to the future, for example:
> *When I see him, I'll call you.*
> *As soon as the concert finishes, we'll come home.*
> *I'll stay here until the bus arrives.*

OPTIONAL ACTIVITY
Write these sentence openings on the board:
If I hadn't eaten three hamburgers,
If I forget my mother's birthday,
If an alien walked into the classroom,
If I miss the bus,
If I had known you were coming,
Ask students to complete the sentences with suitable endings and compare answers with a partner. Monitor to ensure that students are using the correct forms. Listen to some of their ideas in open class.

Grammar notebook
Remind students to note down the rules for conditionals and to write a few examples of their own.

3 Vocabulary
Ways of getting involved

a Write the words *petition, demonstration, leaflets, donation, sponsored* and *volunteer* on the board and elicit the meanings. Refer students to the leaflet and ask them to try to complete the sentences using the words in the box. If they find this difficult, tell them to look back at the text in Exercise 1a for help. Stronger students should complete the exercise first and then look back at the text to check. After going through the answers with the class, say the full expressions and ask students to repeat them.

Answers
1 sign   2 Go on   3 Hand out   4 Make   5 get
6 Do

Unit 9

b) In pairs, students discuss the questions. Encourage them to use the new vocabulary as they speak. Ask a few students to tell the class about their partner's answers.

> **OPTIONAL ACTIVITY**
> If students are interested in charity, you might like to put them into small groups and ask them to create a poster for a fund-raising activity for a charity of their choice. Monitor to help with vocabulary. Display their work on the walls and let students circulate to read the posters.

Vocabulary notebook
Tell students to add these words to their notebook under the heading *Charities*. Also ask them to add any interesting words from the text in Exercise 1a.

4 Listen

a) Books closed. Write the following words on the board: *to vote, an election, the government, to run a country*. Make sure the meanings are clear and ask students what the connection is between the words (*politics*). Ask students if they know any other words connected to politics.

b) 🔊 Books open. Tell students they are going to hear three people talking on a radio show discussing whether 16-year-olds should have the right to vote. Before they listen, ask students if they have any opinions on the subject. Play the recording. Students listen and tick the correct boxes. During feedback, ask students what they heard on the recording to make them choose their answers.

TAPESCRIPT

Presenter They can leave school and get married. They can join the army and die for their country. If they earn money, they have to pay tax. So why can't they decide who runs the country? We're talking, of course, about 16-year-olds and what we want to know is: is it time that they got the vote? Our first caller is on line 3: Trevor from Rochester. Trevor, the airways are all yours.

Trevor Well, the first point I'd like to make is that if I'd decided to get married at 16, my decision would only have affected my wife and I. However, if I'd been given the vote at 16, my choice could have affected many more people. The problem is that many young people are not mature enough to take on such a big responsibility. I know I certainly wasn't.

Presenter So I take it that you're not in favour of the idea?

Trevor Not really, no. I think the main problem is that many young people are too easy to influence. And I should know because I teach them. If young people had the vote, politicians would try unfair tactics to get those votes. They might even try and buy them.

Presenter So you'd prefer to make them wait a while until they're more mature.

Trevor I think so. I think it makes sense.

Presenter Well, thank you for your opinion, Trevor. Line 1. Jenny from Sheffield. Jenny, tell us what you think.

Jenny Well I'd just like to say that I couldn't disagree more with your first caller. Young people are more than capable of making the right decisions about who runs this country. And if you give us the chance, we'll show you. I mean, he's completely missing the point. The real reason that 16-year-olds aren't given a vote is exactly because they think too much about things and they care about things like going to war, education and health. If young people had a vote, this government wouldn't have won the last election, that's for sure.

Presenter I take it you're not a great fan of the current government, then?

Jenny Absolutely not. They've done nothing for us young people at all.

Presenter How about this for an interesting idea, Jenny? What if there was a test for 16-year-olds who want to vote? The test would show whether you had an understanding of the issues you were voting on. If you wanted to vote, you'd have to pass the test.

Jenny But the problem is, who would write the test? Maybe the 'right' answers would be a way of making sure only people who'd vote for the government would get the vote.

Presenter So that's 'no' to the idea of the test then.

Jenny Absolutely. I think 16-year-olds are just as capable of making good decisions as older people. Most of this country votes the way the newspapers tell them to anyway. At least we get the chance to really discuss the issues at school.

Presenter Thank you, Jenny. A future Prime Minister maybe. OK, on line 2 we have Laurence from Ipswich.

Laurence Well, I hope Jenny is right about young people discussing politics at school. In my time we were too busy learning about Maths and English to talk about real issues. It's a shame. If I'd learned more about politics at school, I think today I'd understand how to vote better.

Presenter You sound like you're a little bit confused by today's political climate.

Laurence I suppose I am a little. I mean, it's getting very difficult to know who's on whose side. It seems to be all about personal power and very little to do with the health of our country.

Presenter But can we change all this by giving the vote to 16-year-olds?

Laurence I don't think it could make things much worse, although I must admit that I'm not entirely sure that most 16-year-olds care enough. Perhaps those who pay taxes should have the right to vote, regardless of their age. After all, it's your money the politicians are spending.

Presenter Well, on that interesting note, we'll take a break. I'll be back in a moment to take more of your calls. Should 16-year-olds have the vote? We want to know what you think. Call us now.

Answers
Trevor: older than 16
Jenny: 16 or younger
Laurence: older than 16

(c) 🔊 Read through the sentences with students and check any difficult vocabulary: *corrupt, immature, trust, personal power*. Play the recording again. Students listen and choose the correct endings to the sentences. Check the answers.

Answers
1 b   2 b   3 a

(d) 🔊 Ask students to read through the sentences, and play the recording again. Students decide which speaker said each of the sentences. You may like to ask stronger students to answer the questions from memory first, then play the recording again for them to check their answers.

Answers
1 Laurence   2 Jenny   3 Jenny   4 Jenny
5 Trevor   6 Laurence   7 Trevor

> **Discussion box**
> **Weaker classes:** Students can choose one question to discuss.
> **Stronger classes:** In pairs or small groups, students go through the questions in the box and discuss them.
> Monitor and help as necessary, encouraging students to express themselves in English and to use any vocabulary they have learned from the text. Ask pairs or groups to feedback to the class and discuss any interesting points further. As this issue may be of particular interest to students, you might like to arrange a debate. Divide the class into two halves (one half in favour of giving 16-year-olds the vote and the other half against). You might also ask one student to be neutral and leader of the debate. Students present their arguments. At the end, you can make a decision about which side won the debate and give reasons.

5 Pronunciation
Contractions in third conditionals

(a) 🔊 Students turn to page 121 and read through the sentences. Play the recording and ask students to listen carefully to the underlined words. Draw their attention to the way the words are contracted and linked together. Give special attention to the unstressed /ə/ sound in the contracted form of *have*, and the sound link with the word before: /wʊdəv/, /kʊdəv/. Ask students how *wouldn't have* and *couldn't have* are pronounced and elicit the correct pronunciation: /wʊdntəv/, /kʊdntəv/.

(b) 🔊 Play the recording again, pausing after each sentence for students to repeat.

6 Grammar
Mixed conditionals

(a) **Weaker classes:** Write the following sentences on the board:
If I had found a holiday job, I would have earned some money.
If I had found a holiday job, I .... now.
Point out that the first example is a normal example of the third conditional – we are imagining a situation in the past which did not happen. Focus on the second example and ask students if they can suggest an ending. Point out that although the *if* clause is the same, we are talking about <u>now</u> in the main clause. Elicit or supply a suitable ending (e.g. ... *I would have plenty of money now / I wouldn't be so poor now*) and write it on the board. Point out to students that this sentence does not follow the normal pattern for conditional sentences – it is a mixture of third and second conditionals. Follow the procedure for stronger classes.

Stronger classes: Students read the example sentences and answer the questions. Ask them to decide whether we are talking about the past or the present in the first and second clause of each sentence (*1: present in the first clause, past in the second; 2: past in the first clause, present in the second*). Explain that these are mixed conditionals, which are variations on the structures that students have learned.

Answers
1 No.   2 Yes.   3 No.   4 No.

(b) Read through the rules with the class and ask students to complete them. Check the answers.

Answers
- second, third
- third, second

(c) Students match the *if* clauses with the main clauses. Do the first sentence as an example if necessary. Students compare answers with a partner. Check the answers and point out that there is no difference in meaning if the clauses are reversed.

Answers
1 e   2 a   3 f   4 b   5 c   6 d

(d) Students combine the two sentences to make mixed conditionals. You could set them to work on this in pairs, and you may want to go through the exercise quickly with the whole class before they begin. Check the answers in open class.

Unit 9   65

Answers
2 If I really understood maths, I wouldn't have failed the test.
3 If I hadn't spent all my money on CDs, I would have some money today.
4 If I spoke Spanish, I would have understood what they said.
5 If I could swim, I would have been able to save the young girl.

Grammar notebook
Remind students to note down the rules for mixed conditionals and to write a few examples of their own.

7 Speak

a) Read through the list of actions with the class to check understanding. In pairs, students discuss and guess the legal age when young people can do each of these things in the UK. Tell them they are not expected to know the information – just to give the ages that they think are likely. Ask different pairs for their ideas, and then give them the actual answers.

Answers
buy a pet 12
work part-time 13
be legally responsible for a crime they commit 10
drive 17
buy a lottery ticket 16
have a tattoo 18
become a member of parliament 21
leave school 16
give blood 18
borrow money from a bank 18

b) Students work together to discuss the age when young people can do these things in their own country. There will probably be some disagreement on this. If possible, research the answers yourself prior to the class and give the information after students have had time to exchange ideas. Alternatively, you could ask students to find the answers themselves as a homework activity and to report back in the next lesson.

c) Read through the examples with the class. Ask concept check questions to ensure that students are clear about the meanings. Working individually, students think about consequences of changing the age limits and make similar sentences. Monitor to check progress and ensure that students are using the forms correctly.

d) In small groups, students compare their ideas. Get feedback from some individuals and write some of the most interesting ideas on the board. With weaker classes, let students read their answers. Stronger classes might try to remember their sentences without referring to their notes.

Literature in mind

8 Read

If you set the background information as a homework research task, ask the students to tell the class what they found out.

BACKGROUND INFORMATION

William Golding: (1911–1993) was a British writer who worked as an English and philosophy teacher in his early life and served in the navy during World War II. He wrote a number of books but is best known for his first novel, *Lord of the Flies*. He was awarded the Nobel Prize for Literature in 1983.

Lord of the Flies: was written shortly after the war and was published in 1954. It tells the story of a group of young boys who are stranded on a desert island without any adults after a plane crash. The society that they create on the island degenerates from an orderly, democratic and moral community into a more and more chaotic one, based on fear, superstition and violence. The clash of these values is focused in the conflict between Ralph, the boys' first leader, and Jack, who later takes power. The novel has become an English classic and is often set for study in school courses. It was filmed in 1963 and 1990.

In the extract, *the choir* refers to a group of boys dominated by Jack, who was a leading choir singer (chorister) at his English school. The conch was found by Ralph and he blew a sound on it to bring the boys together for their first meeting. It becomes a symbol of democratic order in the novel – at their meetings, whoever holds the shell is entitled to speak. Later in the story when rational order disintegrates, the conch is shattered.

a) Books closed. Write the following words on the board: *plane crash, children, survivors, leader, vote, domination*. Tell students that these words appear in the summary of a novel and ask them to work in pairs to discuss what the story might be about. Ask some pairs to give feedback. Students open their books and read the summary of the story. Were they right? Look at the photo and discuss whether or not students would be interested in reading the book, and why or why not.

b) Check the meaning of *candidates* and *election*. Students read the text quickly to find the answers to the question.

Answers
The candidates are Jack and Ralph. Ralph wins.

c) Pre-teach *chief, choir, chorister* and *head boy*. You may also want to pre-teach *conch* and provide a very brief background explanation. Read through the text with the class, pausing where necessary to check comprehension and help with some of the other difficult vocabulary. Students answer the questions and compare answers with a partner before feedback.

Answers
1. The conch is a shell.
2. Because he is the leading choir singer and head boy (at his school).
3. His stillness, his size, his attractive appearance and the conch.
4. The choir.
5. Everybody except the choir.
6. Students' own answers.

OPTIONAL ACTIVITY

Write the following definitions on the board and ask students to find words or phrases in the text to match them.
1. to complain to somebody – verb (**protest**)
2. doing what somebody else tells you – noun (**obedience**)
3. doing something when you don't really want to – adverb (**grudgingly**)
4. small brown marks on the face or body – noun (**freckles**)
5. when you go red because you are embarrassed – noun (**blush**)

Discussion box
Weaker classes: Students can discuss question 3 only.
Stronger classes: In pairs or small groups, students go through the questions in the box and discuss them.
Monitor and help as necessary, encouraging students to express themselves in English and to use any vocabulary they have learned from the text. Ask pairs or groups to feedback to the class and discuss. At the end, you could tell them a little about how the story actually develops in the book.

9 Write

The planning for this exercise can be done in class and the writing can be set as homework.

a) Look at the text and tell students it is a letter asking for donations to a charity. Read through the questions with students. Students read the letter and find answers to the questions.

Answers
1. James MacDonald.
2. A charity called *Have a Heart*.
3. A half-marathon.
4. Sponsorship of individuals by members of the public and institutional sponsorship by companies or organisations.
5. It's to a business.

b) As an example of a formal letter, this is a good opportunity to draw students' attention to the layout of the letter. Ask students to read the letter again and answer questions 1–4.

Answers
1. In the top right corner.
2. Dear Sir/Madam,
3. No, he doesn't.
4. Yours faithfully,

c) Ask students to plan how to raise money for a charity of their choice. If they have done the optional activity in Exercise 3, they might like to refer back to their poster. Students work in small groups to decide on the charity and how they hope to raise money. Encourage them to make notes.

d) Tell students they are going to write a letter to a company asking for their support. Ask them to organise their letter in paragraphs, using their notes from their group discussion. In a subsequent lesson, encourage students to read each other's letters and decide which charity would be most successful.

OPTIONAL ACTIVITY

If you would like to give your students practice in writing summaries, you could ask them to write a summary of each of the four paragraphs in James MacDonald's letter. If students find this difficult, give them an example for the first paragraph and show them how to pick out the main points to put in the summary.

10 SOS Earth

Unit overview

TOPIC: Global issues and threats to our environment

TEXTS
Reading and listening: a newspaper article about the dangers faced by the Earth
Listening: a radio programme about alternative energy supplies
Reading and listening: a conversation about pollution from a factory
Writing: a magazine article about life in the future

SPEAKING AND FUNCTIONS
Discussing global problems
Discussing ways of reducing the consumption of energy
Talking about activities at different times in the future

LANGUAGE
Grammar: Future continuous; Future perfect; Future time expressions
Vocabulary: Global issues; Conserving energy
Pronunciation: Contracted forms of *will have*

1 Read and listen

BACKGROUND INFORMATION

The World Wide Fund for Nature: is now generally known just by its initials, WWF. It was originally set up as an animal conservation group, but has broadened its activities to many other environmental areas. It lobbies governments, advises businesses and engages in education programmes. The organisation has about 5 million supporters worldwide.

a Draw a picture of the Earth on the board and brainstorm to elicit examples of problems facing the planet. Write these on the board, grouping different ideas together in topic areas. Look at the photos on page 68. Ask students to describe what they can see in the photos and what problems they represent. Students read the text quickly to see which of their ideas it mentions. Remind them not to worry about the meaning of every word, but simply to identify the topics that are covered. Check the answers and add any new problems to the list on the board.

b 🔊 Check that students understand the true/false statements, checking new vocabulary: *natural resources, cod, blame*. Play the recording while students read. You could pause as necessary to check comprehension and clarify any difficulties. Students decide if the statements are true or false and correct the false ones. They can compare answers with a partner before feedback in open class.

TAPESCRIPT
See the reading text on page 68 of the Student's Book.

Answers
1 F (The WWF is using this dramatic image to draw attention to the serious problems that the Earth faces.)
2 F (The report was based on scientific data.)
3 F (In the last 30 years we have used more than a third of the Earth's natural resources.)
4 F (Cod numbers have fallen by about 75% since 1970.)
5 F (There is less than 7% of the original forest left in South East Brazil.)
6 T
7 F (America uses around six times more of the Earth's resources than Ethiopia.)
8 T

Discussion box
Weaker classes: Students can choose one question to discuss.
Stronger classes: In pairs or small groups, students go through the questions in the box and discuss them.
Monitor and help as necessary, encouraging students to express themselves in English and to use any vocabulary they have learned from the text. Ask pairs or groups to feedback to the class and discuss any interesting points further.

2 Grammar
Future continuous

a Weaker classes: Books closed. Ask students what they are doing now and elicit an example sentence, e.g. *I'm sitting in the classroom now*. Ask about a time in the past (e.g. *at 8 o'clock this morning*), eliciting a sentence in the past continuous. Remind students that we use continuous tenses to refer to an activity in progress at a particular point in time. Now write the following sentence:
At 12 o'clock tonight I .... sleep......... .
Ask students to try to complete the sentence (*will be sleeping*) — give them the answer if they are unable to guess. Tell them we call this tense the future continuous. Students then follow the procedure for stronger classes.

Stronger classes: Ask students to look at the examples, and establish that they refer to the future. Read through the rule with the class, using the time

68 Module 3

line to show that the action (living) will already be in progress at a given time (50 years from now) and will continue after that time. Point out the similarities between the future continuous and other continuous tenses. Ask students to complete the rule.

Answers
will, *be*, present participle / -ing form of the verb

Future perfect

b) Weaker classes: Write the following sentence on the board:
By 2050 we will have used up our planet's resources.
Ask students if the action will take place before, in or after 2050 (*before*). Ask them if we know exactly when (*no, we don't — we only know it will be some time before 2050*). Students then follow the procedure for stronger classes.

Stronger classes: Ask students to look at the examples. Read through the rule and ask them to complete it. Emphasise that the future perfect action is something that will be completed before a given time in the future. Compare this with the future continuous, where the action will still be going on.

Answers
will, *have*, past participle

c) Read through the sentences with the class and check for any difficulties with vocabulary. Students complete the sentences using the future continuous or future perfect. Ask them to compare answers with a partner before feedback in open class.

Answers
1 have used up   2 have died out   3 be living
4 be looking   5 have cut down   6 be discussing

d) Read through the schedule with the class. Make sure that students are aware of the order and duration of events. Ask them to complete the sentences with the correct tense. Check their answers in open class.

Answers
2 By 2013 politicians will have decided on an undersea policy.
3 In 2020 engineers will be building homes under the sea.
4 By 2041 engineers will have finished the undersea project.
5 In 2045 people will be living under the sea.
6 By 2050 half the world's population will have moved to a home under the sea.

Grammar notebook
Remind students to note down the rules for the future continuous and future perfect and to write a few examples of their own.

3 Pronunciation
Contracted forms of *will have*

a) 🔊 Students turn to page 121 and read through the sentences. Play the recording and ask students to listen carefully to the underlined words. Draw special attention to the reduced form of *have* (/əv/).

b) 🔊 Play the recording again, pausing after each sentence for students to repeat.

4 Vocabulary
Global issues

a) Students complete the sentences using the words in the box. Tell them to guess unknown words and to use dictionaries to check if they have time. Check the answers. Then say the words and ask students to repeat them.

Weaker classes: Check the answers in open class at this stage.

Answers
1 species   2 resources   3 waste   4 atmosphere
5 temperatures   6 starvation

Students match the underlined phrasal verbs with meanings a–f. Remind them that phrasal verbs cannot be translated literally into other languages and that the two or three words together have a different meaning from when they are used separately.

Answers
1 b   2 e   3 d   4 f   5 c   6 a

b) Students work with a partner and discuss the sentences. Encourage them to agree on one sentence which they both find the most worrying and then to order the other sentences in order of importance.

c) Put students into small groups and ask them to compare lists. Ask a representative from each group to give feedback, and encourage further class discussion on interesting points.

--- OPTIONAL ACTIVITY ---
If students are interested in this area, divide the class into six groups. Ask them to choose one of the six sentences and to prepare a presentation describing the problem and offering possible solutions. Ensure that each of the six areas is covered by at least one group. After preparation, students give their presentation and invite questions and comment. You could ask the class to vote on which was the best presentation.

Vocabulary notebook
Encourage students to start two new sections in their notebook, *Global Issues* and *Phrasal verbs*, and to add the words from this exercise together with examples. They may find it useful to note down translations of the words too.

5 Listen

If you set the background information as a homework research task, ask the students to tell the class what they found out.

> **BACKGROUND INFORMATION**
>
> **Energy conservation:** In recent years, Britain has become more interested in energy conservation and 'green' living. People have become more aware of the fact that fuels are not limitless and there has been an increase in sales of energy-saving light bulbs, solar panels, etc. The government favours companies with ecologically sound policies and production methods. Many energy companies give free advice on saving energy. There has also been a big increase in recycling of paper, cardboard, glass and plastics.

a Look at the photos and the diagram on page 70. Ask students to discuss the questions in pairs. Also ask them to try to guess how the objects work. Discuss answers in open class, but do not comment at this stage.

b Tell students that they are going to listen to a radio programme about the environment. Students listen and number the photos and diagram in the order they are mentioned. Check the answer to the question in Exercise 5a.

TAPESCRIPT
Presenter And now with a look at some really cool environmental innovations, it's over to Toni MacKay with *The Science Spot*.
Toni Thank you, Jim. Now, as we all know, one of the biggest problems facing environmentalists today is the increasing demand for energy. The energy crisis is so great that some experts predict we've only got until 2010 to find a source of energy to replace oil. It comes as no surprise, then, that a lot of effort is being made to drastically reduce the amounts of natural resources we use to produce energy. We'll be seeing a lot of changes in the next decade to the types of fuel we use and the way we use it.

And one of the largest consumers of fuel are you car users – car manufacturers are working hard to come up with environmentally friendly alternatives to petrol-guzzling cars. In Brazil they've been developing cars with flexible engines. Flexible because they can run on more than one fuel source. These so-called 'Flex' engines can happily run on petrol or alcohol. The alcohol is made from sugar cane, a resource that there's no shortage of in Brazil. These engines not only reduce the amount of petrol used for getting from A to B, but are cheaper to run too.

Let's turn to chickens now. The jump from Flex engines to chickens isn't as strange as you might think. Now, like every other animal or bird, chickens produce – well, what shall we call it? – well, call it poo or manure or waste, it doesn't matter. What does matter is that some scientists in the USA have discovered that if you take chicken poo, turn it into a liquid, heat it and then mix it with diesel fuel, you can use it to run engines. The engines run just fine. They don't really know why, but it works. Who knows, in five years' time all our cars might be chicken-powered.

So, we're talking about fuels – but there are some changes happening too in places where we go to get fuel. Petrol stations aren't known as the cleanest of places and they're not normally high on the list of environmentally friendly locations – but a new garage at Hornchurch, just outside London, is trying to change all that. It's been built with solar panels and wind turbines to produce all the energy it needs – and rainwater is collected too, for things like flushing toilets. They've also built special places around the station for birds and fish! I wouldn't be surprised if we see a few more petrol stations like this by the end of the year.

OK, let's move on to other types of buildings, like homes and office blocks. Of course they use a lot of energy too – lighting, heating and air conditioning, lifts and so on. There's a new breed of building, like the Swiss Re building in London, otherwise known as 'the Gherkin', which was opened in 2003. Now, it's not everyone's favourite building by any means – you either love it or hate it. But the fact is that a building like this one uses something like half the energy of older, more conventional buildings, thanks to natural lighting and ventilation. Over the next few years, we'll be seeing more examples of environmentally friendly buildings, for sure.

Answers
Order: 1 car with Flex engine, 2 chickens,
3 petrol station, 4 Swiss Re building
They are all to do with saving energy or producing new forms of energy.

c Read through the sentences with the class and check any difficult vocabulary: *flexible, petrol, alcohol, diesel, poo, liquid, solar panels, conventional*. Play the recording twice and ask students to choose the correct answers. Let them compare answers in pairs before checking in open class. If necessary, play the recording again with pauses during feedback.

Answers
1 b   2 b   3 c   4 a   5 b

6 Vocabulary
Conserving energy

a Ask students if they know of any ways of recycling or saving energy. Do they do anything at home? Are there any facilities in their town? Pre-teach *waste paper, electrical appliances* and *long-life light bulbs*. Then ask students to use the verbs in the box to complete the sentences in the poster. If they aren't sure of some of the verbs, ask them to guess and check in a dictionary if they have time.

Answers
1 Recycle   2 Cut down   3 Take   4 Switch
5 Wash   6 Use   7 Unplug   8 Swap

b Ask students to think of other ways of using the four verbs. This exercise can be done as pairwork or as a brainstorm in open class.

Possible answers
1 a computer, a TV, a radio
2 plastic bags, bottles, metal objects
3 a computer, a TV, a CD player
4 the amount of petrol you use, the number of trips you make by car

c Tell students that energy saving and recycling are part of caring for the environment, or being 'green'. Read through the questions with students. Divide the class into small groups and ask them to discuss the questions. Monitor and help with vocabulary as required. Listen to some of their ideas in open class.

--- OPTIONAL ACTIVITY ---
As the basis for discussion, read out the following: *'Only after the last tree has been cut down, only after the last river has been poisoned, only after the last fish has been caught, only then will you find that money cannot be eaten.'* Tell students that this is a Cree Indian prophecy. Ask them to discuss the meaning with a partner, then write a one-sentence summary. Listen to some examples and ask students if they agree with the idea.

7 Grammar
Future time expressions

a Books closed. Write the following sentences on the board to introduce the target language:
1 _____ 2012, I will have passed my driving test. **(By)**
2 In four years' _____ I will have passed my driving test. **(time)**
3 Four years _____ now I will have passed my driving test. **(from)**
4 I'm going to stay at school _____ I'm 18 years old. **(until)**
5 I'm going to stay at school _____ two more years. **(for)**

If possible, elicit the missing words in the time expressions, clarifying the meanings as you go through them. Students may expect the answer for sentence 1 to be *in*. Recall the use of the future perfect and tell them that the sentence refers to an action completed <u>before</u> a time in the future (2012) – therefore the answer is *by*. Students open their books and complete sentences a–f with the phrases in the box.

Answers
b from now   c time   d for   e until   f during

> **Language note**
> Remind students to use an apostrophe in expressions like *in five years' time* or *in 20 minutes' time*, and to place it in the right position. These are examples of the possessive apostrophe being used with a plural noun. Students may make errors like **in four years time* or **in 20 minute's time*.

b Read through the rules with students and ask them to complete the sentences. Elicit some other example sentences using the time expressions.

Answers
during, for, by, until

Look
Read through the explanation and examples in the Look box. Make it clear that the only expressions that refer specifically to the future in Exercise 7 are *three days / a week (etc.) from now* and *in five years' / two hours' (etc.) time*.

--- OPTIONAL ACTIVITIES ---
Write the following on the board. Ask students to complete the sentences with suitable words from Exercise 7a. Check the answers.
1 *I want your homework _____ Wednesday. No later than that!* **(by)**
2 *I'll be seeing him _____ two days' _____ .* **(in ... time)**
3 *We'll be staying there _____ two weeks.* **(for)**
4 *The film is showing at the Roxy _____ Friday. They're showing something else after that.* **(until)**
5 *You can go to the party, but I want you to be back home _____ midnight.* **(by)**
6 *We're going camping twice _____ the summer holidays.* **(during)**
7 *I'll be starting university three weeks _____ now.* **(from)**
8 *You've got _____ tomorrow to give me your answer.* **(until)**

For more personalised practice, ask students to write predictions about what they will be doing and what they will have done at different times in the future. Encourage them to use a variety of time expressions from Exercise 7. Put students in pairs and ask them to read their sentences to their partner. Then listen to some examples in open class. If students enjoy this exercise, extend it and ask pairs to make predictions about other members of the class.

Grammar notebook
Remind students to note down the future time expressions, together with examples of their own.

8 Speak

Divide the class into pairs and give each partner a letter, A or B. Student A looks at the three questions on page 71, while student B turns to page 122 and looks at the three questions there. They will first need to select the correct time expressions in their questions. They then take it in turns to ask their questions and make a note of the answers. Circulate and check that they are using the language correctly. Ask some students to report back to the class on their partner's plans and predictions.

Answers
Student A: 1 by   2 in   3 during
Student B: 1 until   2 during   3 from

The factory

9 Read and listen

a) Pre-teach *smells* and *banners*. Ask students to read the questions and predict the answers but do not comment at this stage. Play the recording while students listen, read and check their predictions. Check the answers in open class.

TAPESCRIPT
See the dialogue on page 72 of the Student's Book.

Answers
It smells bad and it's polluting the river. They're going to start a petition / organise a demonstration.

b) Students read the text again and find the answers to the questions.

Weaker classes: Before students look at the questions, you may want to play the recording again, pausing as necessary to clarify any problems. Then read through the questions with the class and check that the meaning is clear.

Answers
1 By showing that she is concerned about the environment and prepared to take action.
2 Starting a petition, organising a demonstration with banners.
3 Because some of their friends have people in their families who work there.
4 Because the factory owners have agreed to repair any damage and put an end to pollution.

10 Everyday English

a) Students look back to the text in Exercise 9 and find out who said the expressions. Then ask them to study the context and decide what the expressions mean. Get them to repeat the full sentences from the text, giving attention to the intonation.

Answers
1 Matt   2 Matt   3 Matt   4 Joanne, Ash   5 Ash
a 2   b 4   c 5   d 1   e 3

b) Students complete the sentences. Check the answers and then ask students to practise dialogues 2–5 with a partner.

Answers
1 stuff like that   2 Come off it!   3 Since when?
4 So what?   5 Point taken.

OPTIONAL ACTIVITIES
See Unit 2, Exercise 11 Everyday English, Optional activities.

11 Write

The planning for this exercise can be done in class and the writing can be set for homework.

a) Ask students to look at the photos and describe what they see. Ask them to predict whether the text will be optimistic or pessimistic. Students read the article quickly and check their prediction.

Answer
The writer is optimistic.

b) Students read the article again and find which of the topics are covered. Ask them to say a little about the writer's opinions on these topics. Do they agree with them?

Answers
The writer covers:
- scientists' warnings concerning the Earth's future
- his/her own beliefs about what the future will be like
- peace vs. war
- people's life styles
- what people will eat / hunger in the world

c) Tell students they are going to write a magazine article entitled *Our life – 50 years from now*. Read through the writing guide with the class and encourage them to follow this procedure for their article. In a subsequent lesson, encourage students to read each other's articles and discuss their predictions in open class.

11 Stars step in

Unit overview

TOPIC: The involvement of famous people in social issues

TEXTS
Reading: an article on celebrity ambassadors for the United Nations
Listening: people's opinions about celebrities getting involved in politics
Reading: an account of Live Aid and Live 8
Writing: a composition on pop stars becoming political

SPEAKING AND FUNCTIONS
Discussing the promotion of causes by famous people
Expressing opinions on a range of social topics
Discussing quotations by famous people
Talking about charity concerts

LANGUAGE
Grammar: Reduced relative clauses; Question tags review
Vocabulary: Fame; Expressing your opinion
Pronunciation: Intonation in question tags

1 Read and listen

If you set the background information as a homework research task, ask the students to tell the class what they found out.

BACKGROUND INFORMATION

The United Nations (UN): is an international organisation that promotes cooperation and peace between countries. It was founded in 1945 after the end of World War II by the victorious world powers with the hope that it would act to prevent conflicts between nations by fostering an ideal of collective security. There are now 191 member countries and the UN plays a major role in peacekeeping. Goodwill ambassadors are famous people who promote the work of the UN around the world.

UNHCR: The office of the United Nations High Commissioner for Refugees was set up in 1950 to help refugees (people who have to leave their country for political reasons or because of war).

UNICEF: The United Nations Children's Fund aims to help and protect children in the areas of health and nutrition, education and protection against abuse, exploitation and discrimination.

Shakira Mebarak Ripoll: (born in 1977), better known simply as Shakira, is a Colombian Latin pop singer-songwriter. She released her first album in 1991 at the age of 13 and went on to massive success with her albums *Laundry Service* and *Oral Fixation*.

David Beckham: (born in 1975) is an English footballer who plays for LA Galaxy in America. He previously played for Real Madrid in Spain and Manchester United in England and was the captain of the English national team. He is married to former Spice Girls singer Victoria Beckham and they have three children. He advertises many well-known brands and regularly appears in tabloid newspapers.

Ronaldo (Ronaldo Luís Nazário de Lima): (born in 1976) is a Brazilian footballer who has contributed to two World Cup wins by the Brazilian national team (1994 and 2002). Ronaldo has also set a record of three FIFA World Player of the Year awards (1996, 1997 and 2002). He is regarded as one of the best players in the history of football.

Angelina Jolie: (born in 1975) is an American actress and former fashion model. She has received three Golden Globes as well as an Oscar for best supporting actress for her performance in the film *Girl, Interrupted*.

Mpule Kwelagobe of Botswana was crowned Miss Universe in 1999. She was the first black African to win the title.

Warm up

Write the name *United Nations* on the board and ask the class what they know about this organisation. Write notes on the board as students suggest ideas. Establish that the UN has a role in negotiations and peacekeeping between nations, but that it also does important humanitarian work. Introduce the terms *UNHCR* and *UNICEF* and elicit or provide some basic information about what these offices do.

a) Students look at the photos. Ask them to say what they know about the people and to guess what they have in common. Students read the text quickly to check their answers.

Answers
The top three photos show Angelina Jolie, Ronaldo and Mpule Kwelagobe. They all work with the United Nations and use their fame to help other people.

b) Read through the list of paragraph headings with the class. Ask students to match the headings with the paragraphs in the text.

Answers
A Para 3   B Para 2   C Para 1   D Para 4

Unit 11   73

c) 🔊 Read through the questions with the class. Students listen, read the text again and answer the questions. Ask them to compare answers in pairs before feedback. Play the recording again, pausing as necessary to check comprehension and clarify vocabulary.

Weaker classes: Let students read their answers aloud when they give feedback.

Stronger classes: Students should try to memorise their answers before giving feedback.

TAPESCRIPT
See the reading text on page 74 of the Student's Book.

Possible answers
1 They have appeared in public to promote issues like children's rights and the problems of homelessness and poverty.
2 She is famous for her humanitarian work for people left homeless through war.
3 The UN looks for people who are well known all over the world and will remain famous for a long time. They must also really care about helping other people.

> **Discussion box**
> **Weaker classes:** Students can choose one question to discuss.
> **Stronger classes:** In pairs or small groups, students go through the questions in the box and discuss them.
> Monitor and help as necessary, encouraging students to express themselves in English and to use any vocabulary they have learned from the text. Ask pairs or groups to feedback to the class and discuss any interesting points further. Students may like to vote on the most suitable person in their country to become a UN Goodwill Ambassador.

2 Grammar
Reduced relative clauses

a) Write the examples on the board. Ask students to work out where we can add *that is* and *who are*, and add these words to the sentences on the board. Point out that the clauses formed with the added words are normal relative clauses in the passive. Ask who the pronoun *who* refers to in the first example (*celebrities*) and what *that* refers to in the second (*the agency*). Ask students to identify the part of speech for *used* and *represented* (*past participle*). Explain that it is possible to leave out the relative pronoun and the verb *be* when the clause is in the passive. The meaning is carried by the past participle alone.

Answers
There are also celebrities <u>who are</u> used …
But perhaps the agency <u>that is</u> most represented …

b) Read through the rule with students and ask them to complete it.

Answers
passive, to be

> **Language notes**
> 1 Emphasise that we can reduce the relative clause like this only when it is in the passive. We can't say *There are a lot of stars represent UNICEF* – here the pronoun *who* must be used because the clause is active, not passive.
> 2 You may want to mention that when the clause is active, we can sometimes use the present participle instead of a full relative clause, e.g. *There are a lot of stars representing UNICEF.*

c) Tell students that they are going to read a text about another UNICEF Goodwill Ambassador. Look through the text with them, checking for difficulties with vocabulary. Students complete the text with the words in the box. When checking the answers, ask if the full relative clauses with *who* and *which* can be reduced, leaving out the pronoun and the verb *be* (*yes, they can*).

Answers
1 who is regarded   2 who was born   3 won
4 held   5 who was accompanied
6 which was given   7 attended   8 written

d) Draw students' attention to the words in italics in the sentences. Ask them to cross out those which are not needed. Emphasise that the extra words in sentences 1 and 2 are not incorrect – they just aren't necessary. Ask why *who* is needed in sentence 3 (*because the verb* plays *is active*).

Answers
The following words should be crossed out:
1 that was   2 that was

Grammar notebook
Remind students to note down the rules for reduced relative clauses and to write a few examples of their own.

3 Vocabulary
Fame

a) Ask students to read the sentences and try to choose the correct answer before looking back at the text for help. Encourage them to think of these expressions as single pieces of vocabulary even though they are made up of several words. Check the answers.

Answers
1 is famous for
2 made a name for themselves
3 made it big
4 household name
5 enjoyed a lot of success
6 sensation

b Students work in pairs to think of names of people that fit the descriptions. Ask different pairs for their ideas and invite others to say if they agree or disagree.

> **OPTIONAL ACTIVITY**
> For further practice of this vocabulary, play a guessing game. Ask students to write sentences about a famous person using some of the target language. They should not mention the person's name and should avoid saying *he* or *she* – tell them to use *X* instead. For example: *X made it big in the 1990s and is a household name all over the world. X is famous for acting in films like* Titanic *and* The Beach. (*Leonardo DiCaprio*) In small groups, students read out their sentences, while the others guess.

Vocabulary notebook
Encourage students to start a new section *Fame* in their notebook and add the expressions from Exercise 3. They may find it useful to note down translations of the words too.

4 Listen

Warm up

Ask students to think of famous people who are involved in politics, either in their country or in other countries. Write a few examples on the board.

a Write the names *Neil* and *Aisha* on the board. Tell students they are going to listen to these two people talking about famous people getting involved in politics. Play the recording while students answer the questions. Check the answers and, if necessary, play the recording again, pausing to check comprehension.

TAPESCRIPT
Neil Our politicians are often grey people – the public don't listen to them. And if the public don't listen, then we've got the problem of a public who don't take part in political life. If rock stars and film stars get the public to think about important issues, as far as I'm concerned, that can only be a good thing.
Aisha Our politicians know they're out of touch with the public, and so they're happy to be seen with the famous. They hope that some of the fame will rub off on them. And, as for the famous people – well, they don't usually understand the real issues. Perhaps they're well-motivated, but to my mind, they should keep their opinions to themselves.

Answers
1 Neil. Because it gets the public thinking about important issues.
2 Aisha. Because they don't understand the real issues.

b Explain to students that they are going to hear six more people answering the question *Should celebrities get involved in politics?* Play the recording twice. Students listen to the speakers' opinions and tick the correct box for each one. For the first listening, you could pause after each speaker to give students time to consider their answers.

TAPESCRIPT
Presenter Today we're out on the streets asking people 'Should celebrities get involved in politics?' Let's hear what ordinary people have to say about this.
Speaker 1 No, they shouldn't. I mean, I couldn't care less what these famous people think. The ones I hear on the radio or TV, they don't really know what they're talking about anyway, do they? So I don't pay any attention to them, I'm not influenced by them at all. To be honest, I think they should keep out of the way and leave politics to professionals, people who know what they're talking about, shouldn't they?
Speaker 2 It doesn't really matter either way. The way I see it, if there are people who are influenced by pop stars and so on, well, they aren't going to listen to politicians anyway, are they? And people who think seriously about politics won't be influenced by a rock star – they've formed their opinion already, haven't they? So it just doesn't matter.
Speaker 3 I'm against it. I'd have thought that politics is for politicians, just like music is for musicians and films are for actors. I mean, we wouldn't expect to see the prime minister getting involved in music, would we? If you ask me, these people should stick to what they know and keep out of politics altogether.
Speaker 4 I'm all for it, myself. It gets lots of people interested, doesn't it? Especially young people. I mean, it can't be a bad thing, can it, if people listen more because it's a famous person speaking, someone they look up to. They don't have to agree with the famous person, after all. But it's good because they listen and think.
Speaker 5 Well, I think it's a really good thing. There's a lot of people in this country who think it's boring to listen to these politicians on TV, and let's face it, they're right! You know, most of them look and sound really old and boring, yeah? So what's the problem if a famous person stands up and says 'Look, this is an important issue'? Then more people get involved. It's good, yeah. I'm all for it!
Speaker 6 Frankly, I really don't care. It's getting harder and harder to tell the difference between them, isn't it? The politicians and the celebrities, I mean. They're all the same. The politicians want to get elected again, and the pop stars want to have their face in the papers and sell more records. I guess that's cynical of me – well, it is, I know – but on the whole I just couldn't care less.

Answers
1 Same as Aisha   2 Neither   3 Same as Aisha
4 Same as Neil   5 Same as Neil   6 Neither

(c) 🔊 Read through the sentences with the class and then play the recording again. Students listen to identify the speakers, and then decide who the underlined pronouns refer to. Play the recording again for them to check their answers.

Answers
a   2; people who think seriously about politics
b   1; famous people
c   4; people
d   3; musicians and actors
e   6; politicians and celebrities
f   5; politicians

(d) Invite different students to state their opinions and to give reasons. Encourage class discussion.

5 Vocabulary
Expressing opinions

(a) Ask students to complete the phrases using the words in the box. Then say the phrases and ask students to repeat. Point out that they should place a stress on *I*, *me* or *my* for emphasis.

Answers
1 mind   2 thought   3 concerned   4 ask
5 opinion   6 see

(b) Read through the expressions with students and ask them to decide if they are used to agree, disagree or neither. Check the answers.

Answers
1 ✗   2 ✓   3 ∅   4 ✓   6 ✗   7 ∅

(c) Read the topics in the box and elicit some initial responses – positive or negative. In groups, students discuss their opinions more fully. Encourage them to use the expressions in Exercises 5a and 5b, and to give reasons for their opinions.

--- **OPTIONAL ACTIVITY** ---
If students enjoy this activity, you might like to expand it into an open class debate. Ask students to decide on one of the topics that interests them. Divide the class into two groups, one in favour of the topic and the other against. Give each group a set amount of time to organise their arguments, then ask them to debate the topic. Encourage as many people as possible to give their opinions.

Vocabulary notebook
Encourage students to start a new section *Expressing opinions* in their notebook and add the expressions from Exercise 5. They may find it useful to note down translations of the words too.

6 Grammar
Question tags review

Students covered question tags in SB2, Unit 5.

(a) Write some simple sentences on the board:
You've got a dog.
She can speak French.
They didn't finish their homework.

Ask students to turn the sentences into questions using question tags. Elicit the correct tags (*haven't you? can't she? did they?*) and write them on the board. Remind students that question tags are formed with a positive or negative auxiliary or modal. Show how the tense and subject of the tag depend on the first part of the sentence. Ask students why we use question tags. Establish that we use them when we want to check information or when we are inviting someone to agree with us.

Students now open their books, read the sentences and choose the correct question tags.

Answers
1 doesn't it   2 can it   3 haven't they   4 do they
5 are they   6 isn't it   7 shouldn't they
8 would we

(b) Read the rule with the class and ask students to complete the sentence. Refer them back to Exercise 6a for examples of the different types of question tags.

Answers
negative; positive

> **Language notes**
> 1 Point out that in conversation we often don't expect answers to questions with tags – they may be simply a way of encouraging someone to follow and give assent to what we are saying.
> 2 Question tags usually follow the positive–negative or negative–positive patterns described in the rule. However, in some circumstances we may use a positive tag after a positive statement or a negative tag after a negative one, e.g. *An octopus has got three hearts, has it? You aren't going to the party, aren't you?* We use this form when expressing surprise or disbelief at something somebody has said. The tag suggests: 'I find that hard to believe – is it really true?'

(c) Ask students to read through the sentences and look for modal verbs before completing them with the appropriate question tags. You may want to look at sentence 5 with the class as an example, showing that we use the modal *would* in the tag (not the auxiliary *have*). Ask students to compare answers with a partner before feedback.

Answers
1 wasn't 2 did 3 was 4 didn't 5 wouldn't
6 shouldn't 7 won't 8 do

Grammar notebook
Remind students to note down the rules for question tags and to write a few examples of their own.

7 Pronunciation
Intonation in question tags

a) 🔊 Write these two sentences on the board:
It's cold, isn't it?
A mosquito is an insect, isn't it?

Point out the difference between these two sentences. In the first, the speaker knows it's cold and is just expecting the other person to agree – he/she doesn't need to know the answer to the question. In questions like this, the intonation falls at the end. In the second sentence, the person isn't sure of the information and really wants an answer. In this case, the intonation rises.

Students turn to page 121 and read the sentences. Point out that in all these sentences the intonation could go either up or down at the end, depending on whether or not the speaker really wants to know the answer. Play the recording. Students mark the sentences with arrows to show the intonation they hear.

Answers
1 ↓ 2 ↓ 3 ↑ 4 ↑ 5 ↑ 6 ↓ 7 ↑

b) 🔊 Ask the question and play the recording again, pausing after each sentence. Ask students to repeat and to answer the question for each sentence.

Answers
Looking for information: 2, 3, 5, 7
Making conversation: 1, 4, 6

c) With the whole class, say the sentences with rising and falling intonation and ask students to repeat. In pairs, students practise saying the sentences in the two different ways. Their partner tells them which type of question they have used.

8 Speak

> **BACKGROUND INFORMATION**
>
> **Kofi Annan:** see Background information for Unit 8, Exercise 1.
>
> **Bono:** (born as Paul David Hewson in 1960) comes from Dublin, Ireland, and is the lead singer of the Irish rock band U2. He is also an outspoken political commentator who campaigns for debt relief for the Third World. He was nominated for the Nobel Peace Prize in 2003 and 2006.
>
> **Bob Geldof:** see Background information for Unit 8, Exercise 8.
>
> **Tracey Ullman:** (born in 1959) is a British singer, actress and comedian. After success on British TV in the 1980s, she was given her own US show, *The Tracey Ullman Show*, which won four Emmy awards.

a) Read through the quotations and check difficult vocabulary: *prosperous, spare me, perceive*. Invite some students to say which quotation they like best and why, but don't go into great detail here.

b) In small groups, students discuss their opinions. Encourage them to use some of the expressions from Exercise 5 to help them express their opinions.

c) Students discuss the question in their groups. Ask different groups to report back to the class and invite others to comment.

— **OPTIONAL ACTIVITY** —
When you are monitoring students speaking, note down some sentences that are incorrect and some that are particularly good. Collect a range of sentences that include structures practised in recent units. At the end of a speaking activity, write ten of the sentences on the board. Make sure there is a mixture of right and wrong sentences. In pairs, students decide which ones are right and correct those which are wrong. Go through the answers with the class. Point out good examples of structures or vocabulary used correctly.

Culture in mind
9 Read

If you set the background information as a homework research task, ask the students to tell the class what they found out.

> **BACKGROUND INFORMATION**
>
> **Bob Geldof:** see Background information for Unit 8, Exercise 8.
>
> **Midge Ure:** (born as James Ure in 1953) is a Scottish rock guitarist, singer and songwriter who had particular success in the 1970s and 1980s. He had huge hits with the songs *Vienna* (as singer of the group Ultravox) and *If I Was* as a solo artist. He co-wrote the Band Aid single with Bob Geldof in 1984 and helped organise the Live Aid and Live 8 concerts.

a) Write *Live Aid* and *Live 8* on the board and ask students what they know about them. Elicit as much information as possible. Look at the photos on page 78. Explain that these are all musicians who

Unit 11   77

performed in Live 8 and ask students to name them if they can. Focus on the title of the text and ask them what they think it means. Students read the text quickly to check their answer. Ask them to decide whether or not music can make a difference, based on the information in the text.

Answer
Students' own answer

(b) Read through the text with the class, pausing where necessary to check comprehension and help with difficult vocabulary: *gigs, victims, spectators, relief, simultaneously, coincide, foreign debt, aid, accessed.* Students read statements 1–7 and decide which of the concerts they refer to. Ask them to compare answers with a partner before feedback.

Answers
1 Live Aid   2 both   3 Live Aid   4 both
5 Live 8   6 Live 8   7 Live 8

OPTIONAL ACTIVITY
Write these sentences on the board and ask students to decide if they are true or false. If the answer is not in the text they should write *Don't know*.
1 *The Live Aid concert ended famine in Ethiopia.* (Don't know.)
2 *There were only four concerts on 13th July 1985.* (False. There were others.)
3 *They recorded a single after Live Aid.* (False. The shows were a follow-up to a single.)
4 *All the artists on the single were British or American.* (False. They were mainly British and American.)
5 *Live 8 was organised to persuade world leaders to change their policies.* (True.)
6 *You can still show your support for Live 8 on the internet.* (True.)

Discussion box
Weaker classes: Students can choose one question to discuss.
Stronger classes: In pairs or small groups, students go through the questions in the box and discuss them.
Monitor and help as necessary, encouraging students to express themselves in English and to use any vocabulary they have learned from the text. Ask pairs or groups to feedback to the class and discuss any interesting points further.

10 Write

The planning for this exercise can be done in class and the writing can be set as homework.

(a) Tell students that they are going to read a composition about politicians becoming media stars. Students read the text and make a note of the different arguments for and against politicians becoming media stars. Draw attention to the organisation of the composition and the content of each paragraph. Let students discuss their findings with a partner before feedback.

Answers
For: Entertainment is part of our daily lives, so politicians need to adapt to this and appear on TV chat shows. The more we see politicians, the more we get to know them. Good politicians can get more support if they appear a lot on TV.
Against: Politics shouldn't be about fun. Politicians shouldn't be distracted from important work by seeking celebrity status. Politicians spoil enjoyable TV shows. Politics should be about truth and reality, not entertainment.

(b) Ask students to read the composition again and complete it with the words in the box. Check their answers.

Answers
1 past   2 days   3 course   4 addition   5 hand
6 same   7 but   8 things

(c) Read through expressions a–h and check that students understand them all. Students look again at expressions 1–8 in the text and match them with a–h. Check the answers, and point out the usefulness of all these expressions in signalling to the reader how ideas are linked together.

Answers
a On the other hand
b All things considered
c In the past
d Of course
e these days
f In addition
g In the same way
h Last but not least

(d) In pairs, students discuss the writer's opinions and conclusion. Ask students to decide which of the opinions they agree or disagree with. Ask for feedback from a few pairs and discuss any interesting points in open class.

(e) Tell students they are going to write their own composition entitled *Should pop stars become political?* Read through the writing guide with them and encourage them to follow this procedure for their composition. Give them as much time as possible for the planning and organisation stages in class. Monitor and check their progress. In a subsequent lesson, ask students to read each other's compositions and give each other feedback.

12 The global village

Unit overview

TOPIC: Awareness of global issues

TEXTS
Reading and listening: an article about Fair Trade
Reading and listening: a webpage about the world's population and the distribution of wealth
Listening: Song: *Saltwater*
Writing: a report on a class survey

SPEAKING AND FUNCTIONS
Discussing Fair Trade products
Discussing the world's population and the distribution of wealth
Talking about imported culture and products

LANGUAGE
Grammar: Phrasal verbs review
Vocabulary: Meanings of phrasal verbs
Pronunciation: Shifting stress

1 Read and listen

Warm up

Books closed. Write the following foodstuffs on the board: *chocolate, tea, coffee, wine, bananas, rice.* Ask students which countries these things come from. Ask students whether they think it is cheap to buy food from developing countries abroad. If so, why? Do they think people should be paid the same amount for producing these things, regardless of where they live? Use this discussion to pre-teach the key words *developing countries, consumers* and *wages*.

a) Write the words *Fair Trade* on the board and elicit or explain the meaning of each word. Then tell students that *Fair Trade* is the name of an organisation and ask them to guess what it might do.

b) Tell students they are going to read an article about Fair Trade. Students read the text quickly to check their predictions in Exercise 1a. Encourage them not to worry about every difficult word, but to concentrate on the task. When you check the answer, make sure students understand that the products are labelled *Fair Trade* in the shops so that customers know which ones they are.

Possible answer
Fair Trade is a movement that aims to make sure that food producers in developing countries get a fair price for their products. When Fair Trade products are exported and sold abroad, there is an agreement that a fair percentage of the selling price will go to the producer.

c) 🔊 Check that students understand the true/false statements. Play the recording while students read and listen. Pause as necessary to check comprehension and clarify difficult new vocabulary. Students decide if the statements are true or false – you could also ask them to correct the false ones. They can compare answers with a partner before feedback.

TAPESCRIPT
See the reading text on page 80 of the Student's Book.

Answers
1 T 2 T 3 T 4 F (Only 8% are providing this option.) 5 F (80% buy them to help the poor.)
6 F (They think it's important that producers get a fair wage.) 7 T 8 T

Discussion box
Weaker classes: Students could discuss question 2 only.
Stronger classes: In pairs or small groups, students go through the questions in the box and discuss them.
Monitor and help as necessary, encouraging students to express themselves in English and to use any vocabulary they have learned from the text. Ask pairs or groups to feedback to the class and discuss any interesting points further.

2 Grammar

Phrasal verbs review

Students covered the grammar of phrasal verbs in SB3, Unit 16.

a) Remind the class that phrasal verbs have two or more parts and give a few familiar examples. Ask students to look at the text in Exercise 1 again and underline all the phrasal verbs they can find. Ask them to look at the verbs in their context and to match nine of them with definitions 1–9. Check the answers.

Answers
1 give back 2 put up with 3 get by
4 taken off 5 looked into 6 find out
7 make up for 8 get away with 9 bring round

Read through the rule with the class, looking carefully at the examples. Point out that there is no rule to help us decide whether a phrasal verb is separable or not. It is up to students to make a note of whether a phrasal verb is separable or inseparable every time they learn a new one. If they aren't sure about this, a good dictionary will tell them if a verb is separable or not.

b Students decide whether the verbs are separable or not. Tell them to look back at the text for help and to use dictionaries where necessary. Check the answers.

Answers
1 give back – B   2 put up with – C   3 get by – A
4 take off – A   5 look into – A   6 find out – B
7 make up for – C   8 get away with – C
9 bring round – B

> **Language note**
> The verb *take off* is inseparable if it means 'to rise' (e.g. *sales took off, the plane took off*). However, it is separable when it means 'to remove clothes' (e.g. *I took off my jacket / I took my jacket off*). Other meanings of *take off* are covered in Exercise 3.

c Students put the words in order to make sentences. Go through the example and point out the alternative answer. Ask students whether *give back* is separable or inseparable (*separable*). Check the answers and elicit the two possibilities for sentence 4.

Answers
2 I won't put up with it.
3 I've got enough money to get by.
4 I looked the word up in my dictionary. / I looked up the word in my dictionary.
5 It didn't make up for what you said.
6 She didn't bring me round to the idea.
7 The police are looking into the robbery.
8 We never found out what happened.

Grammar notebook
Remind students to note down the rules for phrasal verbs and to write a few examples of their own.

3 Vocabulary
Meanings of phrasal verbs

a Remind students that some phrasal verbs (e.g. *take off*) can have more than one meaning and that, depending on the meaning, the verb may be separable or inseparable. Read through the sentences with the class. Elicit the meaning of *take off* in each sentence and ask whether the verb is separable or inseparable.

Possible answers
1 started going well (inseparable)
2 imitating (someone) to make fun of them (separable)
3 leaving the ground (inseparable)
4 ran away (inseparable)
5 remove (separable)

b Weaker classes: Go through the two meanings of each of the phrasal verbs in the box, giving examples. Then follow the procedure for stronger classes.

Stronger classes: Students work in pairs to complete the sentences. Encourage them to work out the verb for each pair of sentences and to use a dictionary to check. Point out that they will need to use different forms of the verb to fit the sentences.

Answers
1 a bring ... round   b bring ... round
2 a went up   b gone up
3 a send ... off   b sent off
4 a take back   b takes ... back
5 comes across   b came across
6 making ... up   b make up

Vocabulary notebook
Encourage students to add the new verbs to the section *Phrasal verbs* in their notebook. For all verbs in this list, encourage them to make a note of which are separable and which are inseparable and to write an example sentence for each. If the verbs have different meanings, they should write an example for each meaning. They may find it useful to note down translations of the verbs too.

4 Read and listen
Warm up

Ask students to guess how many people live in the world and how many live in Asia, Africa and Europe. What percentage of people do they think have an internet connection / own a car / have a bank account / have electricity in their houses? Invite students to offer their guesses, but don't comment on them at this stage.

a Tell students they are going to look at some statistical information from a website. Read through the first paragraph of the text with them and make sure they understand the concept of viewing the world as a 'village' of 100 people. In groups, students read the text, discussing and guessing the missing information together. Ask them to fill in their answers in pencil.

b 🔊 Play the recording while students listen, read and complete the gaps with the correct information. Students compare answers with a partner. Then play the recording again, pausing if necessary for clarification. Check the answers in open class and invite students to comment on the information.

TAPESCRIPT
Welcome to our Global Village – the village Earth. In our village there are 100 people: 51 female and 49 male. 61 people are Asian. 12 people are European. 14 people are Americans, from North and South America. And there are 13 Africans.
13 people don't have enough to eat, or are actually dying from hunger.
More than 40 people in the village live without basic sanitation, and 16 people live without water that can be drunk.
Roughly 14 adults in the village are illiterate. Only seven are educated at secondary level. Eight people have a computer, and four have an internet

connection. Eight people have a car each, and 10 per cent of the houses are powered by electricity. Some people keep their food in a refrigerator, and their clothes in a wardrobe; they have a roof over their head and they have a bed to sleep in – and they represent about 75 per cent of the entire population of the village.

Six people in our village own 59 per cent of the entire wealth of all the people in our community. 47 people have two dollars a day or less to live on. 25 people struggle to live on a dollar a day or less. Perhaps if you have a bank account, you're one of the 30 wealthiest people in the village.

Of all the money that the village spends every year, about 5.5 per cent is spent on weapons and war, roughly 3.4 per cent is spent on schools and university, and something like 2.6 per cent is spent on keeping people healthy.

Next year, there will be 105 people in the village. Work with passion,
Love without needing to be loved,
Appreciate what you have,
And do your best for a better world.

Answers
1 men   2 Asia   3 Europe   4 America   5 Africa
6 eat   7 education   8 connected   9 wardrobe
10 population   11 a dollar   12 wealthiest   13 war
14 education   15 healthy   16 have   17 better

> **Discussion box**
> **Weaker classes:** Students could discuss question 1 only.
> **Stronger classes:** In pairs or small groups, students go through both questions in the box and discuss them.
> Monitor and help as necessary, encouraging students to express themselves in English and to use any vocabulary they have learned from the text. Ask pairs or groups to feedback to the class and discuss any interesting points further.

─ OPTIONAL ACTIVITY ─
Do some work on estimating numbers. Ask students to look through the text and underline six examples of approximate numbers (*More than 40 people, Roughly 14 adults, about 75 per cent, two dollars or less, about 5.5 per cent, something like 2.6 per cent*). Then ask students to look again at the text and decide if the following sentences are true or false. Ask them to correct the false sentences.
1 *Roughly* half the population haven't got enough food. **(False. 13% of people don't have enough to eat.)**
2 *Something like* 90% of houses haven't got enough electricity. **(True.)**
3 *Somewhere in the region of* 12% of people own a car. **(False. 8% own a car.)**
4 *Approximately* a third of the village have a bank account. **(True.)**

5 *A quarter or so* of the people in the world haven't got a bed to sleep in. **(True.)**
6 *More or less* half the people live on $2 or less a day. **(True.)**
7 *More than* 95% haven't got a computer. **(False. 92% haven't got a computer.)**
8 *Fewer than* 15% can't read. **(True.)**

5 Pronunciation
Shifting stress

a) 🔊 Students turn to page 121 and read the first sentence. Explain that the other two sentences use exactly the same words, but the stress will be different each time. Play the recording and ask students to underline the word that has the greatest stress in each sentence. Check the answers, then play the recording again and ask students to repeat.

Answers
1 half   2 second   3 English

b) Ask students to match each sentence with one of the phrases. Ask them to say each sentence with the phrase added at the end, stressing the contrasted words, e.g. *Roughly half the population speak English as a second language, not French*.

Answers
1 sentence 3   2 sentence 1   3 sentence 2

c) Students read the sentence and the three options. Ask them to decide where the stress should go for each option. In pairs, students practise saying the sentence, varying the stress. One student can say the first part of the sentence, and the other should complete it with the right phrase. Listen to some examples in open class.

6 Speak

a) Set a time limit of three minutes for this activity. Students write as many examples as they can for each category. Ask some pairs for examples and ask a few follow-up questions, for example: *Where is that programme from? Which is your favourite American show? Have any of these groups done a tour in our country? Do we produce (name of product) here?*

b) Read through the examples with the class. In pairs, students discuss the items listed in Exercise 6a, estimating the percentage that comes from abroad and supporting their estimates with reasons/examples. Students compare their answers in class discussion. You could refer them back to the language used for expressing opinions covered in Unit 9 and encourage them to use some of these expressions.

OPTIONAL ACTIVITY
You could ask students to do some research on the internet to find out any interesting information they can on this topic, e.g. the percentage of locally made programmes on TV or the percentage of certain foodstuffs which are imported. Ask them to report their findings in English in the next lesson.

7 Listen and speak

If you set the background information as a homework research task, ask the students to tell the class what they found out.

BACKGROUND INFORMATION

The New Seekers: were originally formed after the successful Australian folk-pop group The Seekers broke up in 1969. They have made many changes in their line-up over the years, but the group is still performing in the UK and Europe. *I'd Like to Teach the World to Sing* was their most famous song, selling almost a million copies in the UK alone.

The commercial that featured the original version of the song was one of the most successful ever made, and is believed to have helped Coca-Cola regain its position at the top of the soft drink market in the USA in the 1970s.

a) Look at the song title and elicit some suggestions about the possible subject of the song.

b) Play the recording. Students listen and check their predictions in Exercise 7a. Then ask them to read through the lyrics and guess the order of the lines. Play the recording again. Students number the lines in the correct order (1–17).

TAPESCRIPT/ANSWERS
I'd like to build the world a home
And furnish it with love
Grow apple trees and honey bees
And snow-white turtle doves

I'd like to teach the world to sing
(Sing like me)
In perfect harmony
(In perfect harmony)
I'd like to hold it in my arms
And keep it company

I'd like to see the world for once
All standing hand in hand
And hear them echo through the hills
Oh, peace throughout the land
(That's the song I hear)

I'd like to teach the world to sing
In perfect harmony

c) Students match the words with the definitions. Check that they understand the meaning of *sing in harmony*.

Answers
1 c   2 a   3 d   4 b

d) Students discuss the questions in pairs. Listen to their ideas in open class.

Did you know …?

Read the information in the box with the class. Ask students if they know any other good songs that have been used for TV or radio ads.

8 Write

The planning for this exercise can be done in class and the writing can be set as homework.

a) Tell students that they are going to read a report of a student survey. Ask them to read the report quickly and answer the questions.

Possible answers
It was about the popularity of local TV programmes, music and other products compared with those from abroad.
The student wasn't surprised by the results.

b) Students read again and match the headings with the paragraphs. Check the answers and ask some questions about the topics, e.g. *Who was surveyed? Did most people prefer foreign TV programmes / food / clothes? Why wasn't the writer surprised?*

Answers
A Para 2   B Para 4   C Para 1   D Para 3

c) Students read the report again and find the words and expressions. Ask them to them compare answers with a partner before feedback.

Answers
1 was aimed at finding out, investigated
2 More than 70 per cent, about 15 per cent, approximately half, something like 60 per cent
3 a) outcome   b) in line with   c) backed up

d) Students check the use of reported and direct speech in the report. Point out that general responses are usually summarised in reported speech, but direct speech can be used effectively to give typical or unusual examples.

Answer
Both.

e) Ask students to suggest questions which might have been used in the survey. Point out that it is important that most questions have either a *yes/no* answer or present a choice between several options. This makes it possible to compare answers and draw some conclusions. Elicit suitable questions and write them on the board.

Possible answers
Do you think TV shows from your own country are better than the ones from abroad?
Do you prefer listening to music from your own country or abroad?
How often do you eat food from abroad?
Would you like to eat more local food?
What percentage of the products you use come
a) from this country?   b) from abroad?
How many of your clothes were made in other countries? ☐ All of them? ☐ More than half of them? ☐ About half of them? ☐ Less than half of them? ☐ None of them?

f Tell students they are going to carry out a class survey on internet use. Read through the steps in open class. Students work together in groups to write a list of about five questions. Each person should make a copy of the questions and leave space on their survey sheet to record interesting comments or examples from individuals. Monitor and help with any difficult vocabulary. Tell students to record their own answers first.

Students now stand up and move around the room, surveying other students. Tell them to announce their group before they start asking their questions. If the person has already been interviewed by a member of their group, they should move on and find someone else. After a short time, students regroup and work out the percentages. Make sure every student makes notes of their group's findings, as the basis for their report.

Students write their report, following the steps in the writing guide. Remind them of the paragraph organisation of the model text (see Exercise 8b) and ask them to use the same structure in their report. In a subsequent lesson, you could ask a student from each group to present their findings to the class.

Module 3 Check your progress

1 Grammar

a 2 would get / would have got 3 'll give up
4 would have bought 5 would go / would have gone 6 hadn't barked

b 2 be doing 3 be flying 4 have finished
5 have discovered 6 be thinking 7 have fallen

c 2 during 3 for 4 from now 5 until 6 by

d The italicised words should be crossed out in sentences 3 and 4.

e 2 can't you 3 did she 4 wouldn't you
5 aren't they 6 will you 7 don't you

f 2 Take off your shoes when you come in. /
   Take your shoes off when you come in.
3 I didn't come across your glasses in the kitchen.
4 I looked up the address in the phone book. /
   I looked the address up in the phone book.
5 Don't worry, you can make up for it later.
6 She eventually brought me round to the idea.
7 Teachers are looking into the possibility of building a new theatre.

2 Vocabulary

a 1 out 2 up 3 of 4 up 5 up

b Across:
1 donation 3 petition 6 sponsored
Down:
1 demonstration 2 raise 4 voluntary
5 leaflets

c 1 for 2 name 3 big 4 household 5 enjoyed

d 2 I'm all for it.
3 I couldn't care less.
4 It doesn't really matter.
5 It can't be a bad thing.
6 I'm completely against it.
7 It's not a good idea.

How did you do?
Students work out their scores. Check how they have done and follow up any problem areas with revision work.

Unit 12 83

Module 4
Around the world

YOU WILL LEARN ABOUT ...

Ask students to look at the pictures on the page. Ask them to read through the topics in the box and check that they understand each item. You can ask them the following questions:

1 *Why do people come to this place?*
2 *Who is this actor?*
3 *Where does this man come from?*
4 *What sound is this person making?*
5 *Where is this place?*
6 *What countries can you see on this map?*

In pairs or small groups, students discuss which topic area they think each picture matches. Check the answers.

Answers
1 Choosing the music we hear in different places
2 Using films to make people feel better
3 Musical instruments around the world
4 A very different kind of language
5 A dangerous trip in the Grand Canyon
6 Different accents and dialects in English

YOU WILL LEARN HOW TO ...

Use grammar
Students read through the grammar points and the examples. Go through the first item with them as an example. In pairs, students now match the grammar items in their book. Check the answers.

Answers
Passive report structures: He is believed to be in Brazil.
Participle clauses: Smiling, the man walked towards me.
Clauses of purpose: They phoned the police in order to get help.
Result clauses: We had such a good time that we decided to go back next year.
Verbs + *wh* clauses: I have no idea where they are right now.
Indirect questions: Could you tell me where this instrument comes from?

Use vocabulary
Write the headings on the board. Go through the items in the Student's Book and check understanding. Now ask students if they can think of one more item for the *Noises people make* heading. Elicit some responses and add them to the list on the board. Students now do the same for the other headings. Some possibilities are:

Understanding language: work out the meaning, catch what someone says
Geographical features: hill, mountain, river
Reacting to films: cheer, fall asleep, cover your eyes
Music: song, rhythm, chorus

13 Language

Unit overview

TOPIC: Different ways of speaking

TEXTS
Reading and listening: an article about a very unusual language
Listening: a discussion about regional accents
Listening and speaking: people speaking English in different accents
Reading: an extract from *The World According to Garp* by John Irving
Writing: a narrative about a misunderstanding concerning language

SPEAKING AND FUNCTIONS
Talking about languages that are dying out
Discussing regional accents
Talking about understanding language
Responding to and telling a funny story

LANGUAGE
Grammar: Passive report structures
Vocabulary: Understanding language
Pronunciation: Words ending in *-ough*

1 Read and listen

If you set the background information as a homework research task, ask the students to tell the class what they found out.

BACKGROUND INFORMATION

Silbo: The intonation patterns of the whistled language Silbo follow the same patterns as the Spanish dialect that is spoken on La Gomera. Users of Silbo also use repetition and context to convey their message. Whistled languages survive today in Papua New Guinea, Mexico, Vietnam, Guyana, China, Nepal, Senegal and a few mountainous pockets in southern Europe. There are thought to be as many as 70 whistled languages still in use, although only 12 have been described and studied scientifically.

The Canary Islands: (population 2 million) are a group of seven islands of volcanic origin in the Atlantic Ocean. They are located off the north-western coast of Africa and belong to Spain. The name is thought to originate in the Latin term *Insularia Canaria* (Island of the Dogs), named by the Romans when they discovered a large number of wild dogs on the islands.

UNESCO: (United Nations Educational, Scientific and Cultural Organisation) is an agency of the United Nations established in 1945. Its purpose is to contribute to peace and security by promoting international collaboration through education, science and culture.

a Ask the question and brainstorm ideas with the class, writing notes on the board. Use this warm-up to pre-teach *whistle*. Ask students why people whistle (*because they're happy, for music, to catch someone's attention, etc.*). Ask if anyone in the class can whistle well.

b Ask students to say what they can see in the photos and what they know about the Canary Islands. Students read the article quickly and find the answers to questions 1–3.

Answers
1 On La Gomera, one of the Canary Islands.
2 Whistling.
3 Children have to study it up to the age of 14.

Did you know …?

Read the information with students. Ask them why they think there are so many languages in the world and why so many are disappearing.

c 🔊 Check that students understand the questions. Make it clear that *die out* means the same as *become extinct*. For question 5, explain the meaning of *canary* (= bird). You may want to give a brief explanation of *UNESCO* and to pre-teach the word *heritage*. Play the recording while students read. You could pause as necessary to check understanding and clarify any difficulties. Students answer the questions and compare answers with a partner before feedback in open class.

TAPESCRIPT
See the reading text on page 90 of the Student's Book.

Answers
1 It's one of the Canary Islands, off West Africa.
2 It is thought to have arrived with early African settlers 2,500 years ago.
3 They used it as a way of communicating over long distances.
4 3,000 students study *Silbo* but only a few can communicate fully in it. People like Cabello use it to communicate with their families and friends.
5 No, probably not.
6 Because people from La Gomera emigrated there in the past.

Unit 13

7 He's leading an effort to get UNESCO to declare *Silbo* a 'cultural heritage'.
8 It is not used for romance, because everyone on the island would be able to hear what was being said.

> **Discussion box**
> **Weaker classes:** Students can choose one question to discuss.
> **Stronger classes:** In pairs or small groups, students go through the questions in the box and discuss them.
> Monitor and help as necessary, encouraging students to express themselves in English and to use any vocabulary they have learned from the text. Ask pairs or groups to feedback to the class and discuss any interesting points further.

2 Grammar
Passive report structures

a Read through the sentences with the class. Students look back at the text to find and underline sentences with the same meaning.

Answers
1 Only a few people are believed to be able to communicate fully in the whistling language.
2 There is thought to be no connection between the islands' name and the birdsong-like way of communicating.
3 This unusual way of communicating is said to have arrived with early African settlers.
4 People throughout La Gomera are known to have used *Silbo* in the past as a way of communicating.

b In pairs, students complete the four sentences with the verbs from the text.

Answers
1 are believed to be
2 is thought to be
3 is said to have arrived
4 are known to have used

c Ask students to describe the difference in verb form between the sentences in Exercise 2a and those in the text. Point out that the word *Experts* does not appear in the passive structure – the source of the belief or knowledge is not identified. However, the implication is that the belief is generally shared.

Answer
The verbs in the text are passive, while sentences 1–4 are active.

d Students discuss which sentences refer to the present and which to the past. Point out that the passive verbs are followed by *to* + infinitive when referring to the present and *to* + *have* + past participle when referring to the past.

Answer
Sentences 1 and 2 refer to beliefs or knowledge about the present. Sentences 3 and 4 refer to beliefs or knowledge about the past.

> **Language notes**
> 1 Note that continuous forms of the infinitive can also be used with this structure, e.g. *Temperatures around the world are known* **to be rising**. *Humans are believed* **to have been living** *in this valley for thousands of years.*
> 2 The passive form of the verbs is also often used with the dummy *it* and followed by *that* + a clause, e.g. *It is thought that the name Canary Islands has a Latin origin.*

e Look at the example and ask students to rewrite the other sentences in a similar way. They could work on this in pairs. Before they start, you may want to go through a couple more of the sentences as examples with the class.

Answers
2 Chinese is said to be a difficult language to learn.
3 Some languages are known to disappear every year.
4 Whistling languages are believed to exist in other countries.
5 The words for *finger* and *toe* are said to be the same in some languages.
6 French and Latin are known to have influenced the English language.
7 Many European languages are believed to have originated in India.
8 Hundreds of languages are said to have died out in the past.

Grammar notebook
Remind students to note down the rules for passive report structures and to write a few examples of their own.

─ **OPTIONAL ACTIVITY** ─
Brainstorm the names of some famous people and write them on the board. In pairs, students write a mixture of true and false sentences about these people, using passive reporting structures, e.g. *Brad Pitt is said to have 16 cats. Mariah Carey is known to have bought a house in Spain.* Monitor to make sure that students are using the structures in the correct way, and encourage them to use their imagination. Then put pairs together to form small groups and ask them to tell each other their sentences. They should try to convince the other pair that their information is likely to be true, adding extra detail if possible. The others say whether or not they believe the information they hear. Ask a few different students to say one of their sentences to the class and invite the others to comment.

Module 4

3 Pronunciation
Words ending in *-ough*

a 🔊 Students turn to page 121 and read through the words. Play the recording, pausing after each one for students to repeat. Draw attention to the different vowel sounds and the /f/ ending in 1, 2 and 5.

b 🔊 Play the recording, pausing after each sentence for students to repeat.

4 Listen

If you set the background information as a homework research task, ask the students to tell the class what they found out.

BACKGROUND INFORMATION

Birmingham: is a city in the West Midlands area of England. It has a population of 992,400. Birmingham is famous for industry and manufacturing. It is the birthplace of heavy metal music and bands like Black Sabbath, Led Zeppelin and Judas Priest.

Liverpool: (population 444,500) in north-western England became the largest British port after London in the 18th and 19th centuries. It is well known as the home of The Beatles and Liverpool Football Club. The word *Scouse* is believed to come from a German sailor's dish called *Labskaus*.

Newcastle: (population 269,500) is in the north-east of England, once famous for its shipbuilding industry. Geordie dialect words have origins in Norse and Old English and the Geordie accent is one of the strongest in Britain – many people find it difficult to understand a strong Geordie accent.

Manchester: (population 437,000) is not far from Liverpool. It is a centre of the arts, the media, higher education and big business. The city is world-famous for its sport, being home to Manchester United and Manchester City football clubs.

Glasgow: (population 629,500) is the largest Scottish city and the commercial, business and industrial centre of Scotland. Standard Scottish sounds very different from standard English, and in addition there are local dialects spoken in different parts of the country, including Glaswegian, or 'the Glasgow patter'.

Estuary English: is a term first used in 1984 to describe an accent used in London and south-eastern England. This style of speech is spreading across southern England and many other local accents are slowly disappearing.

Lead in

Ask students if they think there is a strong local accent in their part of their country. Does their accent sound different from those of TV news presenters or political leaders? Do they know of any local words and expressions that are used only in their own area/region or only by certain groups of people? Discuss these questions with the class and elicit examples if possible.

a 🔊 Look at the map of the UK, say the names of the cities and ask students to repeat them. Tell them they are going to listen to the beginning of a TV programme about local accents. Play the recording. Students listen and draw lines to match the accents with the cities.

TAPESCRIPT
Hello, and welcome to the show. The first thing we're going to talk about this week is accents. Regional accents are still very much a part of British life. From Estuary English in parts of London to Brummie in Birmingham, people around the country pronounce words in different ways. Just ask people to say a word like *bath*, and in most places in the south you'll hear it said with a long 'a' – *bath*, like *car* – while in the north, it's generally pronounced with a short 'a', *bath* like *cat*.

Sometimes, of course, people use quite different words altogether. Up in Newcastle, where people speak with a Geordie accent, you'll hear people talk about a *canny ganzy* instead of a *nice pullover*, while in places around Manchester and Liverpool, *shorts* become *keks*. And talking of Liverpool, who hasn't heard the Scouse accent that The Beatles made famous around the world in the 1960s? In Scouse, some vowel sounds that you'll hear down south hardly exist, so that *fairy* and *furry* are pronounced almost identically.

Accents are a really important part of people's lives and their personal identities, and many people are very proud of the way they speak. That's certainly true of people in Manchester who speak Mancunian English, and in Glasgow where they speak Glaswegian. But accents can cause some problems too. We asked Jenny Cooper, our favourite Brummie, to talk to some teenagers about their accents. This is what they had to say …

Answers
Brummie: Birmingham
Scouse: Liverpool
Geordie: Newcastle
Mancunian: Manchester
Estuary English: London
Glaswegian: Glasgow

Unit 13 87

Language note
Students may have heard the word *cockney* and think this refers to the dialect or accent used throughout London. In reality, *cockney* is a term for a working class person in the East End of London and the cockney accent is quite different from Estuary English spoken by many Londoners. Students may be interested to hear about cockney rhyming slang, in which words are replaced by rhyming words. Examples include *Can I have a butcher's?* (butcher's hook = look) and *I haven't got any bread* (bread and honey = money).

b 🔊 Make sure students are clear about the difference between *accent* and *dialect*. Play the recording again while students listen and find examples. Students discuss their answers with a partner before feedback. Play the recording again, pausing for clarification if necessary. Check the answers.

Answers
1 *Bath* is pronounced /bɑːθ/ in the south and /bæθ/ in the north. *Fairy* and *furry* sound the same in Liverpool.
2 They say *a canny ganzy* in Newcastle to mean *a nice pullover* and they say *keks* in Liverpool to mean *shorts*.

Look
Draw students' attention to the adjectives commonly used to describe accents. Go through them with the class and elicit the meanings. Note that *a heavy accent* and *a strong accent* mean the same.

c 🔊 Draw attention to the names of the four speakers. Explain that these people will be using different UK accents on the recording – it may not be easy to understand them because of variations in their pronunciation. Play the recording. Students read, listen and write the name of the city for each speaker. During feedback, ask where the presenter comes from (*Birmingham*).

Presenter Hi there! Well, as Andy said, this week's topic is regional accents. I've got a slight accent myself of course – everyone has. Mine's from Birmingham. And what's interesting is that maybe 30 years ago I wouldn't have got the job on this show because of my accent! So, attitudes have changed. But how much? We've invited a few people in to talk to us about their accents and what they feel about them. First of all, here's Marie from Dundee in Scotland.
Marie Hi.
Presenter Marie, tell us how you feel about your accent.
Marie Well, I'm really proud of it! It's absolutely part of who I am. I'm Scottish and I'm happy about that. And of course I don't notice it, I mean everyone where I live speaks like me of course, so, you know, it's just me.
Presenter Have you ever had any problems?
Marie You mean people not understanding me?
Presenter Yeah, that kind of thing.
Marie Not really. Except a few years ago when I was in London and once or twice people didn't get what I said. But these days everyone's got a different accent and I think people in Britain accept that. You hear all kinds of different accents now on TV, like you said, so I don't think accents matter any more in Britain, really.
Presenter OK, thank you, Marie. Now, let's bring in Patrick, he's from Dublin. Patrick, do you feel the same way as Marie?
Patrick Oh yeah, a hundred per cent. I mean, as far as being proud is concerned. Well, I'm not sure if 'proud' is the right word, but certainly my accent is part of me and I never want to change it. Erm, I have had a little problem, though, nothing much.
Presenter Oh?
Patrick Yeah, I grew up in Ireland, but about three years ago our family moved to London and so I started in a new school and one or two of the other kids, I mean not many, they gave me a bit of a hard time at first, but it didn't last. You know, they just laughed a bit when I spoke – they said I was incomprehensible! It didn't last too long, though.
Presenter Didn't hurt you?
Patrick Sorry, I didn't catch that.
Presenter I mean, you didn't get upset at all, they didn't hurt you?
Patrick Oh, no! No, it was no big deal really.
Presenter OK, thank you. Now, next we've got Tina – she's from London, and Tina, you've got a slightly different story, right?
Tina A little, yeah. Erm, well, as you can tell I'm from the East End of London, that's where I'm from, and erm, I left school actually about two years ago when I was 16 and I wanted to get a job and I'm pretty sure that at least one job I didn't get because of my accent.
Presenter Oh, and why's that?
Tina Well, I don't know for sure – but I wanted to work as a shop assistant in a West End store, and it was quite a posh place, you know, selling really expensive clothes in an expensive part of London, and I wrote and they invited me for an interview, and as soon as I said hello I could see, you know, they didn't like the way I spoke, and the interview lasted about five minutes and they wrote a week later saying 'No thanks'.
Presenter Did they say why?
Tina Yeah, they said I didn't have experience. Well, of course I didn't have experience, I was only 16 and I'd just left school. So why did they interview me? I just think they were lying.
Presenter So are you going to change how you speak?
Tina No way, no!
Presenter Good for you. And now from Liverpool we've got John. What's your view about all this, John?
John Well, I think what everyone's said is very interesting. Erm, I think in Liverpool when I leave

school, if I want to get a job I won't have any problems because almost everyone's got the same accent. Err, maybe I'd have a problem if I went somewhere else, London or somewhere, I don't know.

Presenter Is your accent important to you?

John Not especially. I mean, it's OK, I'm not ashamed of my accent. But it could change. You know, if I went and lived somewhere else, it'd probably change a bit. You have to fit in, don't you? I mean, if I went to live in Australia or something, I might lose my accent. I mean, after a few years I'm sure I'd be speaking differently, maybe a kind of mixture of Liverpool and Australia!

Presenter Well, that would be different! OK. Now, can I ask you all …

Answers
Marie: Dundee (Scotland)   Patrick: Dublin
Tina: London   John: Liverpool

(d) 🔊 Read through the sentences with the class. Ask students if they can remember any of the answers without listening again. Play the recording again. Students listen, complete the sentences and compare answers with a partner. Play the recording once again to check, pausing at the answers.

Answers
1 Patrick   2 John   3 Tina   4 Tina   5 Presenter
6 Marie   7 John   8 Marie

> **Discussion box**
> **Weaker classes:** Students can choose one question to discuss.
> **Stronger classes:** In pairs or small groups, students go through the questions in the box and discuss them.
> Monitor and help as necessary, encouraging students to express themselves in English and to use any vocabulary they have learned from the text. Ask pairs or groups to feedback to the class and discuss any interesting points further.

5 Vocabulary
Understanding language

(a) 🔊 Tell students that all the expressions in this exercise are to do with understanding / not understanding what somebody has said to us. Ask them to read the sentences and choose the correct words to complete them. If they aren't sure of some answers, ask them to guess and to check new words in a dictionary if they have time. You could tell them to cover the table in Exercise 5b while they complete the sentences. Play the recording for students to check their answers.

Answers
1 word   2 totally   3 catch   4 make   5 got
6 out   7 gist   8 lost

(b) Check that students understand the words in the table. Ask them to complete the table using the expressions from Exercise 5a. Check the answers.

Answers
the gist; couldn't make out, didn't catch, a word; lost

(c) In pairs, students complete the dialogues. Point out that there are several different possible answers for each sentence. Ask students to practise saying the dialogues in pairs.

Suggested answers
1 understood
2 can't make out / catch
3 understood/got a lot of what
4 get / catch / pick out a few words
5 understood/got/caught the gist
6 lost me / was totally incomprehensible

(d) Look at the picture and ask what is happening. Give students time to make a short dialogue using appropriate expressions from the exercise. You could ask them to work on this in pairs and then choose a few pairs to read out their dialogue as expressively as possible.

Vocabulary notebook
Encourage students to start a new section *Understanding language* in their notebook and add these expressions. They may find it useful to note down translations too.

6 Listen and speak

(a) 🔊 Focus on the four flags and the names of the countries. Ask students if they can think of something that the countries have in common. Establish that they are all English-speaking, and ask students if they can say why this is so (*because they all used to belong to the British Empire*). Explain that in this listening they will hear four people speaking about their countries in their national accents. Play the recording. Students decide which country speakers are from and write the numbers 1–4.

TAPESCRIPT
Speaker 1 Hi, I'm Meg. I don't know if you know much about my country – you've probably never been there, I guess, it's a long way from most other places! I'll tell you what I really like about living there – I live down in Sydney, down in the south – and that's the climate. I mean, we just have really, really nice weather almost all year round and it means you can get outside a lot and go to the beach and just do lots of things without being stuck inside, know what I mean? I mean, there are other good things about Australia too, of course there are, but that's what I like best, the weather. I just love the fact that you can have barbecues all year round.

Unit 13   89

Speaker 2   I hope you can understand everything I'm saying OK, because English isn't my first language. My first language is Hindi – it's the language of Delhi, the city where I live – but I speak English quite a lot too. We used to speak English a lot when I was at school and it's a language we use quite a lot here in India because it's such a big country and there are so many different languages here – Urdu, Tamil, Gujarati, Punjabi and so on. There are so many languages it's impossible for anyone to understand anyone else, so some newspapers and things are in English but it isn't the first language here in India by any means. If you look at the films, for example, they're never in English, they're always in one of the Indian languages.

Speaker 3   I live in Vancouver, BC. It's a pretty cosmopolitan place, Vancouver – there are people there from all parts of the world so you see all kinds of different faces and hear all kinds of different languages too. Mostly that's because of immigration, of course. There are lots of immigrants here from Vietnam and Hong Kong and places like that. A lot of people think that because Vancouver's in Canada, the second language must be French, but it isn't – the second language here is Chinese. That's because there are so many people here from Hong Kong. Everything here is written in English and French because that's the law in Canada, but you'll only hear French spoken over on the east coast, in Quebec and Montreal.

Speaker 4   I live in the land of sun and great music! But that's not all – here in Jamaica we love cricket too. You can see people playing cricket all over the place – on the beaches, in the streets, in yards – they don't need a special place, anywhere is good enough, especially for the small boys who want to play when they're not in school. And of course in Kingston there's a stadium, it's called Sabina Park, where they play the Test matches – that's the international matches if you don't know much about cricket – and me, I just love going there to watch and to listen to the people playing the steel drums and shouting and things, it's just the best atmosphere in the world, man!

Answers
1 Australia   2 India   3 Canada   4 Jamaica

b) 🔊 Play the recording again. You could pause after each speaker to give students time to make a brief note of the topic. Emphasise that they should listen for the main points, without including details. If necessary, play the recording a third time.

Possible answers
1   The weather/climate is very good in Sydney.
2   In India there are lots of languages. English is spoken by most people, but not as a first language.
3   In Vancouver it's very cosmopolitan. Chinese (not French) is the second language.
4   In Jamaica they love playing and watching cricket.

c) Give students time to compare answers with a partner or in a small group before pooling information in open class. Students discuss the four speakers' accents. Encourage them to use expressions from Exercise 5b to help them describe how much they understood.

Literature in mind

7 Read

If you set the background information as a homework research task, ask the students to tell the class what they found out.

> **BACKGROUND INFORMATION**
>
> **John Irving:** (born in 1942) is an American novelist and screenwriter. Since achieving great critical and popular acclaim after the international success of *The World According to Garp* in 1978, he has written eight best-selling novels, including *The Fourth Hand* and *A Prayer for Owen Meany*. Many of his novels have been made into films, including *The World According to Garp* (1982, starring Robin Williams and Glenn Close) and *The Cider House Rules* (1999, starring Tobey Maguire and Michael Caine).
>
> **New Hampshire:** is a US state in the New England region of the USA. It is bordered by Massachusetts, Vermont, Maine and Quebec, Canada.

a) Ask students to think back to when they were small. Were there any words they misunderstood? Perhaps they have smaller brothers or sisters – do/did they misunderstand words? Give some examples of your own if possible. Ask students to discuss in pairs. Then invite them to tell the class about any particularly good or funny examples.

b) Pre-teach *undertow* or ask students to find it in a dictionary.

c) Focus on the book cover and use the illustration to pre-teach *toad*. Then read through the introduction with the class. Explain that Duncan is Garp's elder son and Walt is the younger. Students read the text and answer the questions. There is quite a lot of new vocabulary in this text, but encourage students to work without help from you or a dictionary at this stage. Ask them to underline any words and phrases they don't understand. Give them time to compare answers with a partner and to discuss the possible meanings of the new words together. After feedback, you may want to read through the text with the students, pausing to check their comprehension and their grasp of vocabulary.

Answers
1 There was a dangerous undertow.   2 The Under Toad.   3 Four years.   4 When they were anxious or had a sense of danger.

OPTIONAL ACTIVITIES

Write these definitions on the board and ask students to find the words in the text:
1 moved back (**retreated**)
2 pull (**drag**)
3 look closely (**peer**)
4 rest on top of the water (**float**)
5 being very afraid of (**dreading**)

Alternatively, you could split the text into two halves at the sentence *What are you doing, Walt?*. Divide the students into two groups, A and B. Group A students look up difficult words from the first part of the text and B students do the same with the second half. Then put students in A/B pairs to answer each other's questions about the vocabulary. This is an opportunity for students to practise using dictionaries.

Discussion box
Weaker classes: Students can choose one question to discuss.
Stronger classes: In pairs or small groups, students go through the questions in the box and discuss them.
Monitor and help as necessary, encouraging students to express themselves in English and to use any vocabulary they have learned from the text. Ask pairs or groups to feedback to the class and discuss any interesting points further.

8 Write

The planning for this exercise can be done in class and the writing can be set as homework.

(a) Ask students to look at the pictures and describe what they see. Can they guess what the story is going to be about? Students read the text to find out which pictures are not part of the story. Tell them not to worry about the gaps in the text, but just to follow the basic events of the story. Check the answers.

Answers
2 and 5 do not form part of the story

(b) Students read the text again to find the two expressions and their meaning in standard English.

Answers
keks (= shorts), Black Beauty (cola and ice cream)

(c) Check that students understand the words in the box. Point out that they are adverbs or adverbial phrases and that they are used to describe how actions take place. Students complete the text. During feedback, point out that adverbs / adverbial phrases are especially useful in a narrative, as they help to make the actions more lively and dramatic.

Answers
1 suddenly   2 immediately / unfortunately
3 desperately / in a panic   4 Unfortunately
5 In a panic / Desperately   6 easily / immediately
7 Fortunately   8 exactly

(d) Tell students that they are going to write a story with the title *A misunderstanding*. Ask students to take some time to think of an incident (real or fictional), then to make notes of the main events of the story and to plan three or four paragraphs. Encourage them to use adverbs / adverbial phrases.

14 The wonders of the world

Unit overview

TOPIC: Wonderful places in the world

TEXTS
Reading: three short texts about extraordinary places
Listening: a story about a dangerous trip in the Grand Canyon
Listening and reading: a conversation about exam results and possible travels
Writing: a composition describing a place

SPEAKING AND FUNCTIONS
Discussing natural and man-made wonders of the world
Retelling a story
Describing an interesting trip

LANGUAGE
Grammar: Participle clauses; *didn't need to / needn't have*
Vocabulary: Geographical features; Travel verbs
Pronunciation: /ɪ/ *sit* and /iː/ *see*

1 Read and listen

If you set the background information as a homework research task, ask the students to tell the class what they found out.

BACKGROUND INFORMATION

The Great Barrier Reef: is the world's largest coral reef, located off the coast of Queensland in north-east Australia. It is over 2,000 kilometres long and can be seen from space. Like all coral reefs, it shelters a huge variety of fish and other marine life.

The polyps that create coral reefs are tiny creatures with a sac-like body, a hard internal skeleton and a mouth fringed by small tentacles for feeding. They form colonies, attaching themselves to the branching, rock-like skeletons left behind by previous polyps. They need warm, clear, shallow water to survive. Reefs around the world are in great danger because of pollution, physical damage and rising sea temperatures.

The Northern Lights: are also known as the *aurora borealis* which is Latin for 'northern dawn'. These remarkable displays of light occur most often from September to October and from March to April in the northern parts of the Nordic countries, Alaska, Canada and Russia. There is an equivalent in Antarctic skies during the southern hemisphere winter, called the *aurora australis*.

Victoria Falls: is one of the world's most spectacular waterfalls. The falls are situated on the Zambezi River, on the border between Zambia and Zimbabwe, and are roughly 1.7 km wide and 128 m high. The falling water generates spray and mist that can rise to heights of over 1.6 km, and is visible from up to 40 km away.

Warm up

Books closed. Write the title of the unit on the board: *The wonders of the world*. Ask students what they understand by the title and which things they would call the wonders of the world. Are there any natural wonders in their country? Elicit ideas and write examples on the board.

a Books open. Students look at the photos and match them with the names. Ask students to say what they know about each of these places.

Answers
a Victoria Falls b Northern Lights
c Great Barrier Reef

b Tell students they are going to read three different texts about the places in the photos. Ask them to read quickly to decide what types of text they are. Tell them to ignore unknown words and the gaps in the third paragraph at this stage. During feedback, ask them how they decided on their answers.

Answers
1 Northern Lights text   2 Barrier Reef text
3 Victoria Falls text

c Look at the questions and check understanding of *horizon* in question 3. Ask students to read the texts again themselves, using a dictionary for new words if they can't guess the meaning. Alternatively, read the texts with the class, checking comprehension and helping with difficult vocabulary. Students answer the questions and compare answers with a partner before feedback.

Answers
1 It is the longest of the world's natural wonders, 2,000 km in total. It's made up of the skeletons of marine polyps. Pollution and man-made damage are the biggest threat to the reef.
2 chug, screech, roar
3 1 commonly known   2 considered to be
   3 above the horizon   4 a must

92 Module 4

d) 🔊 Students listen to the recording to check their answers to question c in Exercise 1.

TAPESCRIPT
See the reading text on page 96 of the Student's Book.

OPTIONAL ACTIVITY

Write the following sentences on the board. Students decide if they are true or false or if the answer is not in the text. During feedback, ask students to give evidence supporting the true statements and to correct the false ones.
1 *The writer is excited about visiting the Great Barrier Reef.* **(True)**
2 *The reef is endangered.* **(True)**
3 *Before the men began to hear the waterfall, everything was silent.* **(False. There was the chug of the boat and the screech of parrots.)**
4 *The boat went over the waterfall.* **(Don't know)**
5 *Many people died after watching the Northern Lights.* **(False. Some people thought they were bringers of death.)**
6 *The Northern Lights appear suddenly in the sky.* **(False. They start as a dim glow, then grow until they fill the sky.)**

---

2 Grammar
Participle clauses

a) **Weaker classes:** Write the following sentences on the board:
1 *While I was sitting on my bed, I called Lisa.*
2 *When I had called her, I went downstairs.*

Ask students how many actions there are in each sentence (*two*) and if they happened at the same time or one after the other (*1 at the same time, 2 one after the other*). Now write the same sentences with participle clauses:
1 <u>Sitting</u> on my bed, I called Lisa.
2 <u>Having called</u> her, I went downstairs.

Point out that the meaning is the same, but here we are using an *-ing* verb form to replace the subject and the full verb. Follow the procedure for stronger classes.

Stronger classes: Ask students to look at the two examples and to identify the subject in the underlined part of each sentence. Check the answers. Make it clear that there are two clauses in each sentence, and that both have the same subject.

Answers
A the aurora borealis   B I

b) Ask students to work with a partner to match the sentences with the meanings. Make sure they recognise that in sentence 2 the first action happened before the second. Then read through the rule with the class and elicit the words to complete them. Refer back to the example sentences in Exercise 2a to clarify the rule.

Answers
1 b   2 a
Rule: present, past

Look
Read through the examples in the Look box to emphasise that the subject must be the same in both clauses.

> **Language note**
> Students may make the mistake of using participle clauses when the subject is different, making sentences like: **Riding my bicycle, a dog ran into the road* or **Having switched on the computer, it suddenly stopped working.* You may like to give students some incorrect examples like these and show how they don't make sense.

c) Look at the example with the class. Point out that we use the present participle *Swimming* here because this action was happening at the same time as the action *I saw*. You might want to go through the whole exercise with the class before students write their answers.

Answers
2 Having seen the show, we walked slowly back to our hotel.
3 Having discovered the falls, David Livingstone named them after the Queen of England.
4 Looking up at the sky, the visitors see wonderful lights.
5 Falling 100m into the Batoka Gorge, the water makes an incredible noise.
6 Having flashed for hours, the lights disappear.
7 Listening to the sounds of nature, the men felt very alone.

OPTIONAL ACTIVITY

Write on the board the following sentence openings, referring to the Great Barrier Reef trip:
Having always wanted to see the Great Barrier Reef, …
Arriving at my hotel in Cairns, …
Having booked a snorkelling tour, …
Diving into the sea, …
Ask students to think of some possible endings for the sentences, using their own ideas.

Grammar notebook
Remind students to note down the rules for participle clauses and to write a few examples of their own.

3 Vocabulary
Geographical features

a) 🔊 Students match the words with the pictures and compare answers with a partner. Play the recording for them to check their answers. Then play the recording again and ask them to repeat the words.

Unit 14   93

TAPESCRIPT/ANSWERS

a	4	a canyon	f	2	a bay
b	5	a waterfall	g	7	a cliff
c	1	a coral reef	h	6	a mountain range
d	10	a desert	i	9	a glacier
e	3	a lake	j	8	a plain

b) In pairs, students think of as many examples of the features as possible in three minutes. Ask them to go right through the list first, writing one item for each feature if possible. They can then go back and add more if they have time. Ask different students to give their answers. Ask a few questions about where the places are and what they are like.

4 Speak

BACKGROUND INFORMATION

Seven wonders of the world: The original list of the seven wonders of the world was written in the second century and included works located around the Mediterranean. Only one still exists – the Great Pyramid of Giza. The following is an example list of the top seven wonders existing today (compiled by Hillman Wonders): the Great Pyramid of Giza, the Great Wall of China, the Taj Mahal, the Serengeti migration, the Galapagos Islands, the Grand Canyon, Machu Picchu.

In pairs, students make lists of natural and man-made wonders. In open class, ask some pairs for their ideas and write them on the board. Try to create a list of seven wonders (natural and man-made) which the whole class agrees on.

5 Listen

If you set the background information as a homework research task, ask the students to tell the class what they found out.

BACKGROUND INFORMATION

The Grand Canyon: is a very dramatic steep-sided gorge, carved by the Colorado River in northern Arizona, USA. The canyon is about 446 km long, ranges in width from 0.5 to 29 km and reaches a depth of more than 1,600 m.

a) Students look at the photos. Read out the questions and discuss ideas with the class.

b) 🔊 Tell students that they are going to hear the first part of a story about some young people who went hiking in the Grand Canyon. Read through the sentences. Explain the meaning of *rim* and *lodge*, and check pronunciation of the place names. Play the recording twice. Students listen and put the sentences in order. You may want to play the recording again, making pauses to check understanding.

TAPESCRIPT

Annabel Christine, I hear you went on holiday to the Grand Canyon.
Christine That's right.
Annabel So what was it like?
Christine Really, really beautiful. The first day we walked along the rim of the canyon looking down. It's a breathtaking view. You can see the Colorado River from up there, and you really feel so small. You can't help thinking about the millions of years it must have taken the river to cut into those massive rocks and create a canyon like that.
Annabel Wow! It sounds like you had a really beautiful holiday.
Christine Yeah, we did, but I don't want to think about what happened on the second day.
Annabel Really? What happened?
Christine Well, there were eight of us. And we wanted to go down into the canyon. The people in the lodge recommended going down a path called the Bright Angel Trail.
Annabel Uh huh.
Christine They told us to be careful and they gave us all lots of kinds of advice.
Annabel Like what?
Christine Well, they told us that we needed to set off really early in the morning, and plan our hike carefully, you know.
Annabel You mean to take a map with you and things like that?
Christine Well, they didn't need to tell us to take a map, we're not that stupid! They said that we needed to make sure that we didn't go too far in one day. The Bright Angel Trail goes right down to the Colorado River, but they said there was no way you could do this and go back up to the lodge in one day. You need to take two days or just go to what's called the Indian Garden Campground and then come back up to the rim.
Annabel So what did you decide to do?
Christine Well, we didn't want to go for two days, so we decided just to go to the Indian Garden Campground.
Annabel All right. Seems to make sense.
Christine Yeah, but unfortunately … Well, we set off early the next day, as we were told, you know, at 6.30 or so, and we got down the trail really fast. It was pleasantly cool, and it didn't seem so difficult. It only took two hours to get to the Indian Garden Campground.
Annabel So what was the problem?
Christine Well, we thought, 'Let's go a bit further', you know, so we went on to the next point on the trail which is called the Plateau Point. From there you get a brilliant view over the gorge. It's just fantastic.

Annabel Uh huh.
Christine Well, that's when the problems started, because some of us ...

Answer
3, 4, 1, 5, 6, 2

c) Students match the two parts of the warnings.

Answers
1 c 2 a 3 d 4 b

d) 🔊 Ask students to predict what happened in the next part of the story. Write the names *Ken* and *Chuck* on the board, and pre-teach *suspension bridge*, *dizzy*, *sunstroke* and *mule*. Play the recording several times while students listen and make notes. Then give them time to think about how to reconstruct the story from their notes. In pairs, students take turns to retell the story. For feedback, retell the story in open class, with different students contributing one sentence each.

TAPESCRIPT

Christine Well, that's when the problems started, because some of us wanted to go back up to the rim, but the others, especially Ken and Chuck, wanted to go further down to the bridge.
Annabel The Bright Angel Suspension Bridge?
Christine Yeah, that's right.
Annabel So did you split up?
Christine No, we didn't. We stayed together and headed down to the bridge. But by now it was about 11 in the morning, and quite hot, you know. Down there you're basically in a desert.
Annabel Did you have enough water?
Christine Well, we thought we did. But by the time we got to the suspension bridge it was 12.30 and baking hot. We'd drunk most of the water. This was when I started to worry. But I had no idea what really lay ahead of us. You know, it's the opposite of climbing a mountain ...
Annabel The opposite of climbing a mountain? What do you mean?
Christine Well, up to then we'd only gone down into the Canyon, and it hadn't really been a problem, apart from the heat, you know, but then we had to go back up – and we'd never expected it to be so difficult.
Annabel Uh huh.
Christine Well, when you climb a mountain, you go up first, and if you can't get to the top you just turn, and you go back down, and that's easier than going up, right? But here we were faced with the opposite.
Annabel Right! I'd never thought of that!
Christine Well, anyway, things got really heavy. We went back up to the Indian Garden Campground, and refilled our water supply there. We were thinking that it took us about two hours to get down there in the morning, so it probably wouldn't take us more than three hours to get back up, you know.
Annabel And that was impossible?
Christine Absolutely. The first thing was the heat. It was just so hot. I'd never felt anything like it in my life. And then the trail! It's just so steep. It was awful. And then half way up, Chuck suddenly felt dizzy. He just couldn't go on any more. He must have had sunstroke, or something. So we poured all our water over his head to cool him down.
Annabel So you had no water left!
Christine That's right. I was really getting worried.
Annabel What did you do? Could you get any help?
Christine Well, good question. We had our mobile phones with us, of course, but in fact we needn't have taken them because they didn't work in the canyon, and so all we could do was shout and shout, but we needn't have bothered. Nobody could hear us, of course. It just made us all feel more exhausted.
Annabel Oh dear. So what did you do?
Christine Well, we were desperate. We couldn't stay overnight on the trail, right? There was no way we could have got back up without any water left, and it was almost getting dark. So we really were in a difficult situation.
Annabel Sounds like it.
Christine Anyway, to cut a long story short, some of the park rangers had seen us from below. And when we were just about to give up hope, suddenly we saw them slowly coming up towards us on two mules.
Annabel Wow. You must have been relieved!
Christine Yeah, imagine. The rangers were a bit angry with us, though. They warned us to be more careful next time.
Annabel I guess they needn't have told you?
Christine That's right, but I can understand why they were so angry. I only read afterwards that every year 250 people have to be rescued from the canyon!
Annabel Wow! I didn't know that! Anyway, what about Chuck? Was he all right in the end?
Christine Yeah, they put him on a mule, and they gave us all water, and we slowly went back up. We only got back to the lodge at midnight, you know. Chuck was still exhausted the next day, and he and Ken were really sorry, but ...

6 Grammar
didn't need to / needn't have

a) Read through the example sentences and elicit answers to the concept questions.

Answers
1 No. 2 Yes.

b) Read through the rule with the class. Students complete the sentences. To clarify, you might like to write the following on the board:
I didn't take my phone because I <u>didn't need to take</u> it.
I took my phone, but I <u>needn't have taken</u> it.

Talk through the sentences with students and check that they understand the difference in meaning.

In the second example, draw attention to the structure: *needn't* + *have* + past participle. Emphasise that *needn't* is not followed by *to*.

Answers
didn't do something; did something

> **Language notes**
> 1 Note that when *need* or *don't need* is followed by another verb, we always use *to*, e.g. *We didn't need to use our map.* We can't say **We didn't need have used our map*. The structure with *have* + past participle is used only with *needn't*, which is a special case.
> 2 You may like to take this opportunity to remind students that when we use modal verbs to talk about the past, they are also followed by *have* + past participle, e.g. *I think I might have made a mistake. They're not here – they must have gone home. You shouldn't have bought that car.*

(c) Students complete the sentences with the correct phrases. Ask them to check their answers in pairs before feedback.

Answers
2 needn't have taken
3 needn't have bought
4 didn't need to phone
5 needn't have phoned
6 didn't need to buy

(d) Ask students to complete the sentences with the correct form of the verb in brackets. Do the first two sentences as examples with the class. Students write their answers and compare answers with a partner before feedback in open class.

Answers
1 needn't have worried
2 didn't need to get up
3 needn't have taken
4 needn't have bought
5 didn't need to use
6 didn't need to wait

Grammar notebook
Remind students to note down the rules for these structures and to write a few examples of their own.

7 Vocabulary
Travel verbs

(a) Look at the pictures and ask students to describe what they can see. Elicit verbs that might be used in connection with the pictures and write these on the board. Students complete the verbs in the three sentences from the listening text.

Answers
1 on   2 off   3 back

(b) Read through the table of travel verbs with students. Individually or in pairs, they complete the table using the words in the box.

Answers
1 holiday   2 home   3 taxi   4 bicycle   5 flight
6 car

(c) Students complete the sentences, referring back to the table as necessary. You could ask stronger students to complete the sentences without looking at the table and then to check their answers at the end.

Answers
1 drove   2 went, set, got   3 went, took, got
4 got, rode   5 going, go   6 got/went, go
7 going away   8 gets, rides   9 're leaving / setting off

> **OPTIONAL ACTIVITY**
> In pairs or small groups, students work through the table of verbs, making sentences based on their own experience, e.g. *I went for a walk last Saturday. I've never been on a cruise.* Encourage students to ask their partners for further information and to expand on their sentences. Listen to some examples in open class.

Vocabulary notebook
Encourage students to start a new section *Travel verbs* in their notebook and add these words. They may find it useful to note down translations of the words too.

8 Pronunciation
/ɪ/ *sit* and /iː/ *see*

(a) 🔊 Say the words *sit* and *seat*, exaggerating the difference between the two vowel sounds. Students turn to page 121 and read quickly through the words. Play the recording twice. Students tick the words they hear and then listen again to check. Play the recording again and ask students to repeat.

TAPESCRIPT/ANSWERS
1 bit   2 sit   3 feet   4 green   5 heat   6 neat
7 ship   8 win

> **OPTIONAL ACTIVITY**
> For further practice of the difference between these sounds, put students in pairs and ask them to say the words to each other. Their partner has to guess which of the words they are saying.

(b) 🔊 Ask students to read through the sentences. Play the recording, pausing after each sentence for students to repeat, first all together and then individually.

9 Speak

a) Weaker classes: To help students with ideas, make a very basic sentence about a trip you have made, e.g. *Two years ago I went on holiday to Prague.* Elicit a list of questions that students could ask you about the trip and write them on the board in note form, e.g. *When / set off? How / get there?* Invite students to ask you about your trip, and give answers. Then ask them to report back some of the things you told them. Follow the procedure for stronger classes.

Stronger classes: Students think of an interesting trip they have made. Encourage them to remember particular facts and interesting details. In pairs, students take it in turns to ask questions about their partner's trip, making notes of the answers. Tell them to follow up information with further questions and to ask for explanations if they need them.

b) Students take it in turns to tell the story of their partner's trip. Their partner listens and makes any necessary corrections. Monitor and give help with vocabulary if needed.

c) Regroup the students into new pairs. Students retell the story of their previous partner's trip to their new partner. As feedback, ask different students to report a few interesting things that they have heard from either of their partners.

10 Round the world

Listen and read

a) 🔊 Look at the photo and ask students what they think is happening. Establish that the sheets of paper contain exam results. Read out the questions and ask students to predict the answers but do not comment at this stage. Play the recording while students listen, read and check their predictions. Check the answers.

Answers
They got their final exam results. Ash did best.

TAPESCRIPT
See the dialogue on page 100 of the Student's Book.

b) Students read the text again and find the answers to the questions.

Weaker classes: Before students look at the questions, you may want to play the recording again, pausing as necessary to clarify any problems. Then read through the questions with the class and check that the meaning is clear.

Answers
1 He thinks they might be studying for exams again because they might not pass.
2 Joanne: Brazil for the sun and beaches
  Caroline: somewhere in Asia to see the other side of the world
  Ash: India, because it must be a fascinating place and he would love to visit cities like Delhi and Mumbai
  Matt: Australia for the surfing
3 He thinks they speak Spanish in Portugal, he says *Bombay*, not *Mumbai*, and he thinks Perth is the capital of Australia.
4 Joanne: pleased
  Caroline: quite pleased
  Matt: very disappointed
  Ash: happy and surprised

11 Everyday English

a) Students look back to the text in Exercise 10 and find out who said the expressions. Then ask them to study the context and decide what the expressions mean. Get them to repeat the full sentences from the text, giving attention to the intonation.

Answers
1 Joanne 2 Caroline 3 Joanne 4 Matt
1 c 2 d 3 b 4 a

b) Students complete the sentences. Check the answers and then ask students to practise the dialogues with a partner.

Answers
1 Get out of here!
2 a bit of a nightmare
3 How does that grab you?
4 Take it easy

OPTIONAL ACTIVITIES

Tell students that if we want to be less exact when describing something we can:
- add *-ish* to ages and some adjectives, especially colours (e.g. *fiftyish, greenish, coldish*)
- add *or so* when talking about numbers (e.g. *thirty or so, four weeks or so*)
- use expressions like *kind of* or *sort of* with adjectives (e.g. *kind of weird, sort of interesting*)

Ask students to find examples in Exercise 10 (*kind of nervous, a few days or so, OKish*).

Write the following sentences on the board and ask students to make the underlined adjectives less exact. The answers given here are suggestions – others are possible.

1 *The man was fifty and his hair was grey.* (fiftyish, greyish)
2 *He's been doing the job for three weeks, but he's still slow.* (three weeks or so, sort of slow)
3 *I was nervous during the interview, so I think I said some stupid things.* (kind of nervous, sort of stupid)
4 *The weather yesterday was warm – the temperature was twenty degrees.* (warmish, twenty or so)

Unit 14

12 Write

The planning for this exercise can be done in class and the writing can be set as homework.

a Tell students that they are going to read a composition describing somebody's favourite place. Ask them to read the text quickly and identify the place.

Answer
The writer's bedroom.

b Students read the composition again and answer the questions. They could work on this in pairs.

Possible answers
1 The unusual colour (he/she seems to be an imaginative person with a strong personality); the objects in the room (he/she seems to be untidy and he/she enjoys watching the world on his/her own).
2 The questions make you feel that the writer is talking to you personally. They make you want to continue reading to find the answers.

c Read through the instructions with students. Point out that grouping ideas in longer sentences often produces a richer description than writing a series of short sentences. Ask students to look at each group of ideas and to combine them to make a sentence. They could think about this on their own for a few minutes, then work with a partner to decide on the best way to combine the ideas. When they have reached a decision, ask students to look back at the text and compare their answers. Ask students if they think they have created descriptions that are as good as or better than the original and listen to some ideas in open class.

Answers
Students' own answers

d Ask students to think of three objects that have some importance to them. Tell them to brainstorm ideas about each object and to make brief notes. They then combine their ideas into one or two sentences. Encourage students to show their sentences to a partner.

e Tell students they are going to write a composition about their favourite place or object. Encourage them to:
- brainstorm ideas and take notes.
- experiment with different ways of putting together their ideas to make interesting sentences.
- ask questions in the text to make the reader want to read on.
- use interesting adjectives.

In a subsequent lesson, ask students to read each other's compositions. If you take in the work to mark, you could make a list of particularly interesting descriptive sentences from different compositions. Hand them out to the class and discuss why they work well.

--- OPTIONAL ACTIVITY ---
Stronger classes: Ask students to read the composition again quickly and then close their books. Write the following words on the board: *tiny, wild, Switzerland, juicy, pop stars, overlooks, joke.* Ask students to work in pairs and discuss how the words were used in the composition. Encourage them to try to reconstruct the passage of description where they appeared. Students look back at the text to compare their answers with the original.

15 Movie magic

Unit overview

TOPIC: Films and their effects on people

TEXTS
Reading and listening: an article about using films as therapy
Listening: a discussion about films by Steven Soderbergh
Reading: an article about the film industry in India
Writing: a film review

SPEAKING AND FUNCTIONS
Discussing the idea of film therapy
Discussing films and their suitability for different people
Talking about the film industry in different countries

LANGUAGE
Grammar: Clauses of purpose: *to / in order to / so as to*; Result clauses with *so/such (that)*
Vocabulary: Reacting to films
Pronunciation: Word stress in multi-syllabic words

1 Read and listen

If you set the background information as a homework research task, ask the students to tell the class what they found out.

BACKGROUND INFORMATION

On the Waterfront: (1954) is a classic film directed by Elia Kazan. A young dockworker Terry Malloy, played by Marlon Brando, discovers and makes a stand against the union corruption and violence in which his much-loved elder brother (Rod Steiger) is involved. The film received eight Oscars in 1955.

Falling Down: is a 1993 film directed by Joel Schumacher and starring Michael Douglas as an engineer whose car breaks down. He walks home through Los Angeles and is disgusted by the awful things he sees. He reacts with violence and tries to improve the dreadful city.

Warm up

Ask students how often they watch films. Ask them to name any films that are particularly important to them, or which they like watching again and again. Can they say why?

a) In pairs, students discuss the question. Ask some pairs for their ideas and invite the rest of the class to comment or add their own ideas.

b) Pre-teach *unlock emotions*. Students read the text quickly to decide on the best title. You could set a two-minute time limit, encouraging a quick reading to get the general idea of the text. Tell them to ignore the gaps in the text at this stage.

Answer
2 Films help unlock emotions

c) 🔊 Read through the phrases with students and help with difficult vocabulary: *implications, releasing, betrayal, deeply buried, clients, confront, immediate*. Students put the phrases into the correct places in the text. Play the recording while students read and listen to check their answers. Play the recording again, pausing as necessary for clarification.

TAPESCRIPT
See the reading text on page 102 of the Student's Book.

Answers
1 e 2 b 3 d 4 f 5 c 6 a
(corrections: 1 c, 5 e)

d) Ask students to read the questions and help with any difficulties. Students read the text again and answer the questions. Ask them to compare answers with a partner before feedback.

Answers
1 The Royal College of Psychiatrists.
2 *On the Waterfront*.
3 About 33%.
4 Because they are happier to relate to fictional characters than to real people.
5 It helped him to understand that he needed to release his anger more often rather than holding on to it.

Discussion box
Students discuss the questions. Monitor and help as necessary, encouraging them to express themselves in English and to use any vocabulary they have learned from the text. Ask pairs or groups to feedback to the class and discuss any interesting points further.

2 Grammar
Clauses of purpose: *to / in order to / so as to*

a) **Weaker classes:** Books closed. Write the following on the board:

Why do you come to school?
Because I want ...
Why do you go to the cinema?
Because I want ...

Unit 15   99

Elicit answers from students, e.g. *Because I want to learn English*, *Because I want to watch a film*. Tell students that it is possible to remove *Because I want* from the sentences without losing meaning. The word *to* on its own carries the idea of purpose. Ask further questions (*Why do you go to the bank / the clothes shop?* etc.) and encourage students to answer beginning with *To*. Then follow the procedure for stronger classes.

Stronger classes: Ask students to read the examples. Point out that *to* on its own means the same as *so as to* and *in order to* – they are all used to express purpose. Students complete the rule. Draw attention to example 3 and clarify the point about the use of *not*. Explain that when the purpose is negative, we must use *so as not to* or *in order not to*. We can't say **I came in quietly not to wake the baby.*

Answer
so as to, in order to; to

(b) Students match the questions with answers a–f. Check the answers. They then make sentences as in the example. Ask them to compare answers with a partner before feedback.

Answers
2 f She cried a lot in order to release her emotions.
3 a They went to the DVD store to get some films to watch.
4 b People go to libraries to borrow books.
5 c Studios make films so as to make money.
6 e Psychiatrists' clients lie on a couch so as to relax.

─ OPTIONAL ACTIVITY ──────────
Ask students to think of several things they did last weekend and why they did them. In pairs, students tell their partner about each action and their partner has to guess why they did it, using *to*, *so as (not) to* or *in order (not) to*.

Grammar notebook
Remind students to note down the rules for this structure and to write a few examples of their own.

3 Grammar
Result clauses with *so/such (that)*

(a) Books closed. Write on the board:
The book was really exciting. I read it in one day.
Tell students that we can make this into one sentence, using either *so* or *such*. Write up the two alternatives:
The book was so exciting that I read it in one day.
It was such an exciting book that I read it in one day.
Give students a few moments to consider the differences between the two sentences, but do not analyse at this stage. Students open books at page 103. Ask them to complete the sentences using the phrases in the box. They can find the sentences in the text to check their answers.

Answers
1 so frustrated   2 such an impact
3 such strong emotions   4 so easily

(b) Students complete the rule. Emphasise the point that *such* is followed by adjective + noun.

Answers
so, such

> **Language note**
> You may want to tell students that it is possible to use *so* and *such* without a *that* clause, e.g. *It was so boring! It was such a boring film!* This usage is very common in conversation.

(c) Students join the sentences using *so* or *such ... that*. As you check the answer to number 2, ask students to change the word order and make an alternative sentence with *so*. (*The film was so moving that I almost cried.*) Do the same with sentences 3 and 4. (*It was such a boring film that ... This actor is so bad that ...*)

Answers
2 It was such a moving film that I almost cried.
3 They were so bored by the film that they fell asleep.
4 He's such a bad actor that you feel like laughing when you watch him.
5 Cinema tickets are so expensive these days that more and more people hire DVDs.
6 Film therapy is so effective that many people overcome their problems.
7 Film therapy is such an effective approach that it's backed by the Royal College of Psychiatrists.
8 Spielberg makes such great films that he's known all over the world.

(d) Students think of their own sentences using the phrases in the box. Give them one or two examples of your own to get them started. In pairs, students compare sentences. Monitor and check that they are using the correct structures. Ask a few pairs to tell you some of their partner's sentences.

─ OPTIONAL ACTIVITY ──────────
Write the following on the board:
1 *hot – have a cold shower to cool down* (It was so hot that I had a cold shower to cool down.)
2 *expensive – borrow £500 to buy it* (It was so expensive that I had to borrow £500 to buy it.)
3 *silly film – walk out* (It was such a silly film that we walked out.)
4 *heavy box – not carry it* (It was such a heavy box that they couldn't carry it.)
5 *worried – not sleep* (I was so worried that I couldn't sleep.)
Ask students to work together and make sentences using *so* or *such*. Do the first one with them as an example. The answers given above are suggestions – other answers using different subjects and tenses are possible.

Grammar notebook
Remind students to note down the rules for this structure and to write a few examples of their own.

4 Pronunciation
Word stress in multi-syllabic words

a 🔊 Students turn to page 121 and read through the words. Play the recording. Students listen and underline the syllable with the main stress in each word.

Answers
1 <u>the</u>rapy   2 thera<u>peu</u>tic   3 <u>med</u>icine
4 me<u>dic</u>inal   5 <u>com</u>edy   6 co<u>me</u>dian
7 i<u>den</u>tify   8 identifi<u>ca</u>tion

b 🔊 Play the recording again, pausing after each word for students to repeat.

5 Speak

If you set the background information as a homework research task, ask the students to tell the class what they found out.

BACKGROUND INFORMATION

Leonardo DiCaprio: was born in 1974 in Los Angeles. He has appeared in over 20 films including *Romeo and Juliet* (1996), *Titanic* (1997), *The Beach* (2000) and *Catch Me If You Can* (2002).

Steve Martin: (born in 1945 in Texas) is an American comedian, writer, producer and actor. He has starred in over 40 films including *The Jerk* (1979), *The Man With Two Brains* (1982), *Roxanne* (1987) and *The Pink Panther* (2006).

Sigourney Weaver: (born as Susan Weaver in 1949 in New York) is an actress famous for films such as *Alien* (1979) and its three sequels, *Ghostbusters* (1984) and *Copycat* (1995).

Bill Murray: (born in 1950 in Chicago) is an American comedian, actor, producer, director and poet. After a successful career as a TV comedian, Murray has gone on to make over 30 films including *Groundhog Day* (1993), *Space Jam* (1996) and *Broken Flowers* (2005).

The Aviator: is a 2004 film directed by Martin Scorsese. It tells the story of the romances and mental problems of Howard Hughes, the American aeroplane tycoon and film-maker. Hughes was known as the richest man in the world in the 1930s.

Cheaper by the Dozen: is a 2003 film starring Steve Martin and Bonnie Hunt as a couple with 12 children who move from the country to the city. The Steve Martin character is left alone to look after the children for two weeks.

Alien 4: (1997, also called *Alien: Resurrection*) is the fourth in the series of *Alien* science fiction films in which Sigourney Weaver fights horrible creatures. In this film, she is cloned and resurrected 200 years in the future.

Lost In Translation: is a 2003 film directed by Sofia Coppola and tells the story of the friendship between two lonely Americans (Bill Murray and Scarlett Johansson) in modern-day Japan. The film concentrates on the cultural differences between Japan and the USA.

Warm up
On the board, make a list of the words for film types in Exercise 5a. Ask students to give examples for each type of film.

a Look at the photos with the class and ask students if they recognise any of the actors. Focus on the film titles and ask if anyone has seen any of these films. If so, invite students to say a little about them. Students read the descriptions and decide which type of film they are. Check the answers in open class.

Answers
The Aviator – drama
Alien 4 – horror
Cheaper by the Dozen – comedy
Lost in Translation – romantic comedy

b Ask students how they feel when they go to the cinema. What type of films make them feel happy/sad/scared? Tell them that they are going to read about some people who want to try film therapy. Students read the descriptions of the people and work with a partner to decide which of the films would be most suitable as therapy for each person and why. Ask students to make brief notes about their decisions. Note that there are no 'correct' answers to this question – students will have different opinions. During feedback, try to come to a class decision about the best film for each person.

Answers
Students' own answers

c In small groups, students discuss which other films they have seen that they think might be suitable as therapy for the people. Listen to some ideas in open class.

6 Listen

If you set the background information as a homework research task, ask the students to tell the class what they found out.

BACKGROUND INFORMATION

Steven Soderbergh: (born in 1963) is an American film producer and director. His first film *Sex, Lies and Videotape* won the Palme D'Or at Cannes Film Festival when he was 26 years old.

Unit 15

He has since made many other films. He won the Oscar for Best Director for *Traffic* in 2000.

Julia Roberts: (born in 1967) is an American actress. Her most famous film is *Pretty Woman* (1990) in which she starred as a prostitute who finds love with Richard Gere. She has starred in over 30 films and has won many prizes including the Oscar for best actress in 2000 for *Erin Brockovich*. She is very popular with the general public and is often called 'America's Sweetheart'.

The Coen brothers: (Joel and Ethan Coen) started making films together in the early 1980s. They are known for their dark comedies, including *Raising Arizona* (1987), *Fargo* (1996) and *The Ladykillers* (2004).

a) 🔊 Ask students if they have seen any films by Steven Soderbergh. Write the titles *Bubbles, Ocean's Eleven, Ocean's Twelve, Erin Brockovich* and *Traffic* on the board. Also write the title *Fargo* and tell students that it is a film by the Coen brothers. If students have seen any of the films, ask them to say which ones they enjoyed and to give a very brief description of the plot. Tell them they are going to listen to two people discussing the films. Play the recording while students listen and tick the boxes.

TAPESCRIPT

Vince Here's that DVD you lent me, Cathy. Thanks.
Cathy Oh, yeah – *Bubbles*. Did you enjoy it?
Vince Yeah, it was really exciting. It had me on the edge of my seat the whole film. I thought it was really good.
Cathy Really? I thought it was a bit boring, a bit too long. I think he's made better films.
Vince Who?
Cathy Steven Soderbergh – the director.
Vince Oh? It's a Soderbergh film? I didn't realise. He's the guy who made *Ocean's Twelve*. Did you ever see that?
Cathy Yes, I did. What did you think of that?
Vince I thought it was excellent – really, really funny. There were times when I just fell about laughing.
Cathy Yes, it was pretty funny – but not as good as *Ocean's Eleven*. Now that was a funny film!
Vince Yeah, but you know – I preferred the other one!
Cathy Oh, well, let's agree to differ!
Vince OK! But what other films of his do you like?
Cathy Well, I really enjoyed *Erin Brockovich* – you know, the one with Julia Roberts.
Vince Oh right, yes – she's a lawyer who's investigating pollution or something.
Cathy Yes, that's right. A lot of people get really sick and she finds out that a big company is putting chemicals in the water, and she tries to prove it and the company tries to stop her.
Vince That's the one.
Cathy Yeah, I thought it was a really good, really interesting film – and a film that shows that Julia Roberts can actually act!
Vince Yes, I know what you mean! And it was pretty exciting too – I mean, not like *Traffic*, but quite exciting.
Cathy *Traffic*? You liked that?
Vince Yeah – didn't you?
Cathy Well, no, it was too long and too boring. I was really yawning by the end.
Vince How can you say that? I thought it was so exciting! All those drug dealers trying to get him. And it was sad, too – you know, the bit where Michael Douglas's daughter almost dies. I thought it was very moving – I cried my eyes out! But don't tell anyone!
Cathy Don't worry – your secret's safe with me!
Vince Hey, changing the subject a little bit – well, changing directors, anyway. My friend Graham lent me this brilliant DVD, a film called *Fargo*. It's by the Coen brothers. Do you know it?
Cathy I've heard of it, but I've never seen it.
Vince Well, it's a bit old now – but it's wonderful! One minute you're laughing, the next minute it's really scary and exciting. Shall I ask Graham to lend it to you?
Cathy OK, if it comes with your recommendation, I might like it – even though we don't agree on everything!

Answers
1 Vince 2 Vince 3 Cathy 4 Cathy 5 Vince
6 Vince

b) 🔊 Read the questions with students and check that they understand the meaning of *agree to differ*. Play the recording while students answer the questions. Check the answers. Then play the recording again, pausing for clarification if necessary.

Answers
1 Whether *Ocean's Twelve* or *Ocean's Eleven* is the better film.
2 Julia Roberts.
3 It's about a lawyer investigating a company which is polluting the water.
4 Michael Douglas's daughter.
5 Because one minute you're laughing, and the next minute it's scary and exciting.

7 Vocabulary
Reacting to films

a) Tell students they are going to read a questionnaire about four different types of film. Students read and complete the gaps with the words in the box. To check the answers, go through all three alternatives for each question in the questionnaire and elicit the meanings. Ask students what type of film each question is asking about (*1 comedy, 2 drama, 3 horror, 4 horror/thriller*).

Answers
1 funny 2 sad 3 scary 4 exciting

b Students do the quiz, then turn to page 122 to find out their score. Encourage them to discuss their answers in pairs or small groups. Then listen to some of their responses in open class.

c Students match the definitions with the expressions in the questionnaire.

Answers
1 yawning 2 fall about laughing
3 scream 4 cry your eyes out 5 chuckle
6 bite your lip 7 on the edge of your seat
8 jump out of your seat

d Students complete the sentences with six of the expressions from the questionnaire.

Answers
1 yawning 2 jumped out of my 3 my eyes
4 bit my 5 fell about 6 the edge of my

Vocabulary notebook
Encourage students to start a new section *Reacting to films* in their notebook and add these expressions. They may find it useful to note down translations too.

OPTIONAL ACTIVITY
Ask students to think of two films of different kinds that they have seen. Tell them to make notes about each one, focusing on:
- who starred in the film.
- what happened in it.
- what they especially liked about it.

Encourage them to use some of the expressions from Exercise 7 in their descriptions. You may like to give them an example of your own to show the type of description you are looking for. Monitor and help with vocabulary if necessary. When students have made notes and thought carefully how to describe the films, put them in small groups to explain their choices. Listen to some of the descriptions in open class.

Culture in mind

8 Read

If you set the background information as a homework research task, ask the students to tell the class what they found out.

BACKGROUND INFORMATION

Bollywood: is the informal name given to the popular Hindi language film industry of India, based in Mumbai. In terms of films made and tickets sold, the Indian film industry is the biggest in the world. However, it makes less money than Hollywood. (In 2002, Bollywood sold 3.6 billion tickets and had an income of $1.3 billion.

Hollywood films sold 2.6 billion tickets and made $51 billion.) Until recently, the films covered traditional themes and had low production values. Since the 1990s, however, more money has been spent on films and stories have focused on modern urban living. Bollywood films always include songs, but the star actors do not normally sing them – they mime to a recording by professional singers.

Hollywood: is a district in Los Angeles, California, USA. It is the centre of the American film and TV industry. Films have been made in Hollywood since the 1900s. It became the home of the major production studios Paramount, RKO, 20th Century Fox, MGM and Warner Brothers. Every year the Oscar ceremony is held in Hollywood. In recent years the control of the major studios has been reduced and a lot of independently made films have become very successful.

a Write *Hollywood* on the board and ask students what they know about it. Ask them to discuss in pairs and make notes. Listen to some of their ideas and write them on the board.

b Ask students if they have heard of Bollywood. Explain that it is the Indian equivalent of Hollywood. Students read the text quickly to find similarities and differences between the two film industries. They can compare answers with a partner before feedback in open class.

Possible answers
Similarities: they both produce very popular films, they both started off making silent films and began making 'talkies' in the 1930s.
Differences: more films are produced by Bollywood and the films are made much more quickly and cheaply than in Hollywood.

c Read through the text with the class, pausing where necessary to check comprehension and help with difficult vocabulary: *nickname, massive, henna, musical, box office success, piracy, profit*. Focus on the questions 1–5 and check that students understand the meaning of *plot*. Students answer the questions and compare answers with a partner before feedback.

Answers
1 It's a play on the word *Hollywood*, with the B coming from *Bombay*.
2 In the 1950s, because many Indians came to England and brought their culture with them.
3 England played India in a cricket tournament.
4 Boy meets girl, they fall in love and they struggle for family approval.
5 A lot of people copy their films, so the studios lose money. Also younger generations are getting bored with the predictable story-lines. Film-makers are trying to prevent piracy and to change the plots.

Discussion box
Weaker classes: Students can choose one question to discuss.
Stronger classes: In pairs or small groups, students go through the questions in the box and discuss them. Monitor and help as necessary, encouraging students to express themselves in English and to use any vocabulary they have learned from the text. Ask pairs or groups to feedback to the class and discuss any interesting points further.

OPTIONAL ACTIVITY
Write the following sentences on the board and tell students that they are all false. In pairs, students try to remember what the text said and make the sentences true. Encourage them to write their answers, then compare them with the original text.
1 *Bollywood films are made one at a time.*
2 *Bollywood films have always been very popular in Britain.*
3 *In the UK, only Indian families watch Bollywood films.*
4 *There are four main characters in Bollywood films – two people in love and two funny characters.*
5 *All Bollywood films make a profit.*

9 Write

If you set the background information as a homework research task, ask the students to tell the class what they found out.

BACKGROUND INFORMATION
School of Rock: (2003) is a comedy directed by Richard Linklater. The child actors in the film really play all the music and the star, Jack Black, is a musician as well as an actor – he records and tours in the pop group Tenacious D.

The planning for this exercise can be done in class and the writing can be set for homework.

a) Ask students to imagine that they can learn anything they want at school. Which subjects would they like to include in the school timetable? Listen to a few of their ideas. Then tell them they are going to read about a film in which students learn to play rock music at school. Students read the synopsis and answer the questions. Tell them not to worry about the words in bold at this stage.

Answers
Students' own answers

b) Ask students to read the text again and to answer the questions.

Possible answers
1 It is all factual information about the film.
2 The story is told in the present simple as this makes it more immediate.
3 There is a lot of information about the main events in the first part of the film.
4 He stops at an important point so that the reader wants to know what happens next.

Language notes
1 We use the present simple as the main tense to tell the story of films and books. In a sense, the action is not finished as it still exists in the film/book and is therefore permanent. We also often use the present simple when telling jokes.
2 On internet film sites, writers use the word *spoiler* for a synopsis which tells the ending of a film. Any such review should begin with the expression *spoiler warning*.

c) Draw students' attention to the pronouns in bold in the text, and remind them that pronouns refer back to someone/something previously mentioned. Students read the text again and identify who/what each pronoun refers to. Ask them why the pronouns are used (*to avoid unnecessary repetition of nouns*).

Answers
It stars Jack Black: the film
his dream of living: Dewey's
it's becoming almost impossible: his dream of living a rock 'n' roll lifestyle
his band: Dewey's
his on-stage clowning: Dewey's
they have a better chance: the other band members winning without **him**: Dewey
his services: Ned's
his flatmate: Dewey's
their teacher: the ten-year-olds'
He puts **them**: the kids
their weekly music lesson: the children's
There he sees: in the music room
his kids: Dewey's

d) Tell students they are going to write a synopsis which tells part of the story of a film they have seen recently. Tell them to plan what information they are going to include and to think about where they will end the story. Encourage them to:
• give a few basic facts about the film at the beginning.
• focus on the story.
• use the present simple for telling the story.
• use pronouns to avoid repetition and make sure it is clear who/what they refer to.
• end at a suitable point, without giving away the ending.

In a subsequent lesson, encourage students to read and discuss each other's synopses.

16 Music in the air

Unit overview

TOPIC: Music and its effect on people

TEXTS
Reading and listening: an article about choosing music for different purposes
Listening: a radio programme about musical instruments from around the world
Listening: a song about music
Writing: a mini-saga, a limerick or a haiku

SPEAKING AND FUNCTIONS
Discussing the influence of music in different situations
Making comparisons about music
Discussing musical preferences

LANGUAGE
Grammar: Indirect questions
Vocabulary: Making comparisons stronger; Listening to music
Pronunciation: *re*cord (noun) vs. re*cord* (verb) (etc.)

1 Read

If you set the background information as a homework research task, ask the students to tell the class what they found out.

BACKGROUND INFORMATION

Background music: In 1922 in the USA, the Muzak company began to sell background music to be played in shops and factories. Studies have shown that background music can affect people's state of mind without them realising it, and they can be influenced to work harder or to spend more money in shops. These days, a great deal of money is spent on researching which types of music will relax people or make them shop more.

Bluewater Shopping Centre: is a large out-of-town shopping mall just outside London. It has over 330 stores and 40 cafés, bars and restaurants.

Paul Oakenfold: is a record producer and DJ, especially well known for his remixes. Remixing uses computer programs to create new versions of previously recorded music – changing the rhythm or instrumentation, adding new musicians, combining effects from different recordings, etc.

The *1812 Overture*: is by Tchaikovsky and is famous for its use of cannons and bells in its climactic finale.

Frank Sinatra: (1915–1998) was an American singer and film actor who became enormously popular in the 1940s and remained one of the world's best-selling and most influential recording artists throughout the 1950s and 1960s.

***White Christmas*:** is a Christmas song written by Irving Berlin. It was first sung by Bing Crosby in the 1942 film *Holiday Inn*. It won the Oscar for best song the same year and went on to sell 30 million copies.

Tranmere Rovers: is a football club based near Liverpool in north-west England.

Baroque music: is a style of classical music from the 17th and 18th centuries. Some of the great Baroque composers are Bach, Handel and Vivaldi.

Warm up

Books closed. Ask students to discuss the following questions in small groups, and then to give feedback to the class.

What type of music do you most enjoy?
What type of music do you least enjoy?
Where do you most enjoy listening to music?

a) Students list places where they often hear music without choosing to. Ask different students for their examples and write them on the board. Ask what sort of music they hear in these places and whether they like it.

b) Tell students that they are going to read an article about music in public places. Students read the article quickly to see which of the places listed on the board are mentioned. Tell them not to worry about unknown vocabulary and to ignore the gaps for the time being. Discuss answers in open class.

c) 🔊 Explain that sentences a–e are extra sentences from the text. Ask students to read the text again and choose the correct sentence for each gap. They could work on this in pairs. Play the recording for students to check their answers. Ask them to explain why they chose each sentence, encouraging them to show how it links with other sentences in the text. Play the recording again, pausing as necessary to check comprehension and help with difficult vocabulary.

Answers
1 a   2 d   3 e   4 b   5 c

d) Students answer the questions and compare answers with a partner before open class feedback.

Answers
1 When it gets busy.
2 Because a lot of people came to tell them when they played *White Christmas* at Easter.

Unit 16   105

3 They have certain songs which they play at different stages of the game.
4 They have to turn music down so that it isn't too loud.
5 Because it helps them to relax.

— OPTIONAL ACTIVITY —
Write the following words on the board. Ask students to read the text and find words with a similar meaning.
1 *escape* (get away)
2 *not often* (rarely)
3 *choices* (selections)
4 *asking* (consulting)
5 *sure* (certain)
6 *to give you a truthful answer* (to be honest)

Discussion box
Weaker classes: Students can choose one question to discuss.
Stronger classes: In pairs or small groups, students go through the questions in the box and discuss them. Monitor and help as necessary, encouraging students to express themselves in English and to use any vocabulary they have learned from the text. Ask pairs or groups to feedback to the class and discuss any interesting points further.

2 Grammar
Indirect questions (1)

Students covered indirect questions in SB3, Unit 12.

(a) **Weaker classes:** Write the following question on the board:
Where is Timbuktu?
Elicit some suggested answers, and then write this sentence opening on the board:
I don't know …
Tell students that we don't say *I don't know where is Timbuktu*. If possible, elicit the correct form and write it on the board:
I don't know where Timbuktu is.
Point out that the question is now a statement (there is no question mark at the end) and draw attention to the difference in word order. Then follow the procedure for stronger classes.

Stronger classes: Read through the examples from the text. Then elicit the direct questions. Point out that in the examples, these questions are now embedded inside statements. We still use the question word, but the words following it are no longer in question form. As in any other statement, the subject comes before the verb, and we do not use the auxiliary *do*.

Answers
1 do they
2 the customers

(b) Read the rule with students and use the previous examples to show how indirect questions are formed.
Answers
invert, sometimes; don't invert, never

(c) Look at the example with the class. Ask students to join each pair of sentences in a similar way. They should start with the words in the second sentence. Students compare answers with a partner before feedback.
Answers
2 I don't know how much it costs.
3 It's easy to find out where people buy CDs.
4 We don't always know when people need to listen to music to relax.
5 I'm not sure how often they change the music they play in shops.
6 I wonder when music was first played in shops.

Grammar notebook
Remind students to note down the rules for indirect questions and to write a few examples of their own.

— OPTIONAL ACTIVITY —
Write the following sentence openings on the board:
1 *I don't know …*
2 *I'd like to find out …*
3 *I'm not sure …*
4 *Maybe you can tell me …*
5 *I wonder …*
Ask students to think of ways of completing them, using the question words *who, what, when, where* and *why*. They should use each question word only once. Ask different students to read out their sentences. Invite others to respond, either by giving the information if they know it or by saying *I don't know* if they don't.

3 Vocabulary
Making comparisons stronger
Warm up

Briefly revise comparisons using comparative adjectives and *(not) as … as*. Write *pop music – classical music* on the board and elicit some example sentences comparing the two.

(a) Explain that the words in the second column of the table can be added to comparisons to make them stronger. Students complete the sentences in the table, then look back at the text to check. Go through the answers. Then write on the board:

The tips are	much a lot far	better.
Classical music is	not nearly as nothing like as	enjoyable.

106 Module 4

Make it clear that the expressions in each group are interchangeable – the meaning is the same.

Answers
1 as   2 more   4 lot worse   5 nothing like
6 far

(b) Work through sentences with students and ask them to decide which make comparisons and which emphasise similarity.

Answers
1 All the sentences.   2 Sentence 1.

(c) Students add words to make the comparisons stronger. Ask them to use all the words/phrases from Exercise 3a in their answers. Students compare answers with a partner before feedback in open class. Explain that the words added to make comparisons stronger are often stressed for extra emphasis when we say them. Encourage students to do this when giving feedback.

Possible answers
1 Shopping centres would be much nicer without music.
2 MP3 players are a lot cheaper than they used to be.
3 Classical music is far more relaxing to listen to than dance music.
4 The piano is even harder to learn than the guitar.
5 CDs should be much less expensive than they are.
6 Films are just as enjoyable as music.
7 Learning English is nothing like as difficult as some people think.
8 Music isn't nearly as important as many people say it is.

(d) In pairs or small groups, students discuss the statements in Exercise 3c. Listen to some of their thoughts in open class and discuss any interesting points further.

── OPTIONAL ACTIVITY ──
Record a selection of types of music (about six different types, each about 20 seconds long) on a cassette. Write the following adjectives on the board: *catchy, noisy, exciting, boring, irritating, relaxing.* Play your cassette and ask students to give each music extract a score from 1 to 10 for each of the six adjectives. They then make sentences comparing the music, using the target language from Exercise 3, e.g. *I thought number 1 was much more relaxing than the others.* Monitor and check that they are using language correctly. Ask students to work in small groups and discuss their reactions to the songs. You may like to ask the class to vote on the best song.

Vocabulary notebook
Encourage students to start a new section *Making comparisons stronger* in their notebook and add these words in example sentences.

4 Speak

Give students a few minutes to think of sentences by themselves. You may like to give them some example sentences of your own to get them started. Tell them they do not have to write about music for sentences 4–6. Circulate and help with vocabulary as necessary. In pairs, students compare sentences. Ask some students to report back on their partner's answers.

5 Listen

Warm up

Books closed. Ask students to name all the musical instruments they know, and write the words on the board. You could group them under the headings *Strings, Wind, Keyboard* and *Percussion*. Ask different students to say which instruments they have tried to play. Encourage students to add any new words to their vocabulary notebook under the heading *Music*.

(a) Look at the photos of instruments. Ask students if they recognise any of them. If not, can they imagine what the instruments sound like?

(b) Students match the instruments with the countries, making guesses if they are not sure. Ask for their answers, but don't comment at this stage.

(c) Tell students they are going to listen to a radio programme in which a music expert talks about the instruments. Students listen and check their answers to Exercise 5b.

TAPESCRIPT
Presenter Well, our next guest is a lady who knows just about everything there is to know about music and musical instruments from all around the world. Please welcome Hope Staunton.
Guest Hi, Jeremy.
Presenter So, Hope, I believe you've just brought out a book about world music.
Guest That's right. I spent about a year and a half travelling round the world doing my research and the book's out next week.
Presenter Hard life, eh?
Guest That's right.
Presenter Can I ask you where you went?
Guest Oh, it would take me a long time to tell you! All over the place, basically. But I learned lots about musical instruments, some that perhaps you've heard of and maybe some that aren't so familiar.
Presenter And you've brought one or two along to the studio with you today.
Guest That's right – and also a couple of people who can play them for us.
Presenter Now, this first one, this one I recognise. This is a set of bagpipes.
Guest That's right. These are quite well known, of course, and these bagpipes are from Scotland.

Presenter But lots of countries in Europe play bagpipes, don't they?

Guest Yes, that's right. Bagpipes have been around for about two thousand years, in fact, and old ones have been found all over the place, erm, especially North Africa and Eastern Europe, but in the British Isles too, of course.

Presenter So can we hear a bit?

Guest Sure.

Presenter Gosh, that makes your blood go faster, doesn't it? Right, what's next?

Guest Well, let's stick to wind instruments just for the moment. Here are two more instruments that you play by blowing. This enormous thing here is an alphorn.

Presenter And can you tell us where it's from?

Guest Well, this is a Swiss Alphorn but there are versions of this instrument in Scandinavia, in Lithuania, and in Spain in the Pyrenees. They're all wooden but some are straight and some are curved. Erm, they used to be played across valleys as a kind of communication, but nowadays only at festivals and things.

Presenter It looks pretty hard to play!

Guest Well, you need good lungs, yes! It's about four metres long, so you have to blow hard.

Presenter So let's hear it.

Presenter Well, thank you for that. Now, this next instrument's not too dissimilar to the alphorn. And I've got a feeling it's from Australia.

Guest Spot on, Jeremy. It's a didgeridoo, a native Australian instrument. It's not quite as big as the alphorn, considerably smaller in fact, it's about one and a half metres long, although there are bigger ones. It used to be played in ceremonies like weddings and funerals. Now you can hear it in all kinds of modern music. Would you like to hear it?

Presenter Absolutely!

Presenter What a great sound. Now, the other instruments you have are not wind instruments, right?

Guest Right. This next one is from Trinidad, from the Caribbean islands, and it's pretty well known in Britain now.

Presenter A steel drum – I love these! You hear them a lot at events like the Notting Hill Carnival. Do we know when they were first developed?

Guest Yes, we do. They're really very recent – erm, the first ones were made in the twentieth century, in fact ...

Presenter Oh!

Guest ... and, yes, there are four different sizes of drum. They're played in orchestras or bands, erm, usually four people but sometimes up to a hundred players!

Presenter Wow – that must be loud.

Guest It is! But for now, let's listen to just one! Here we go.

Presenter Hey, I love that sound! But I like this one too. What's this?

Guest It's called a berimbau, and it's from Brazil. It's a stringed instrument, as you can see ...

Presenter But only one string.

Guest Yes, and then this brown box, called a gourd, changes the notes a bit. They use the berimbau a lot in all kinds of Brazilian music, but originally it came from Africa, it came to Brazil with the African slaves who were sent there, and it's still very, very popular and a great instrument to listen to. It's great for rhythm!

Presenter OK – let's hear it.

Presenter Very different – the more I hear it, the more I like it. And what's the last one?

Guest Well, this is called a bonang. It's used to play a kind of music called gamelan ...

Presenter Right.

Guest ... and gamelan comes from Indonesia, especially from Java and Bali, it's a very popular kind of music there.

Presenter Still played?

Guest Oh, yes, very much so, it's used as accompaniment to lots of things like theatre and so on, still played a lot. This is what the bonang sounds like.

Presenter That's lovely. So different from anything else we've heard.

Guest Yes, absolutely.

Presenter Well, thank you, Hope. I'm sure many of our listeners will be looking forward to learning more from your new book ...

Answers
1 e   2 f   3 a   4 c   5 d   6 b

d 🔊 Read through the sentences with students and check understanding. Then play the recording. Students listen and answer the questions. Play the recording again, pausing if necessary for clarification.

Answers
1 In North Africa and Eastern Europe.
2 They were used for communication across valleys. They're now played at festivals.
3 At weddings and funerals.
4 There are four different sizes.
5 Four.
6 It has one string. It came from Africa.
7 The bonang.

e 🔊 Students listen to the instruments and name them. Ask students to discuss which instrument they like most/least and encourage them to use language covered in Exercise 3. Listen to some of their answers in open class.

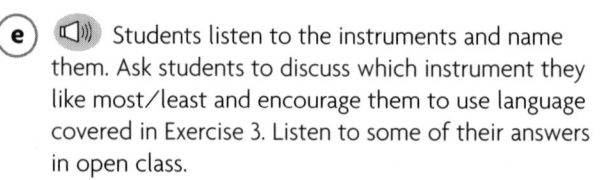

Answers
1 alphorn   2 berimbau   3 steel drum
4 bagpipes   5 bonang   6 didgeridoo

6 Vocabulary

Listening to music

a) Read through the sentences with the class. Students match the underlined words with the definitions. If they are unsure about some of the vocabulary, encourage them to guess the meaning from its context. During feedback, say the words and ask students to repeat them.

Answers
1 d 2 h 3 c 4 f, e 5 a, g 6 j 7 b 8 i

b) Students read the sentences in Exercise 6a again and decide if they are true for them. Ask them to change the sentences if they disagree.

Answers
Students' own answers

c) In pairs, students discuss their opinions. Monitor and help with vocabulary if necessary. Listen to some of their answers in open class.

Vocabulary notebook
Encourage students to add these words to the *Music* section in their notebook. They may find it useful to note down translations of the words too.

7 Pronunciation

re*cord* (noun) vs. *re*cord (verb) (etc.)

a) 🔊 Explain that certain words in English look identical, but are pronounced differently depending on what part of speech they are. Students turn to page 121 and read through the sentences. Play the recording. Ask students to underline the stressed syllable in each of the words in italics and to say if the word is a noun or a verb. Play the recording again, pausing after each sentence for students to repeat.

Answers
1 re*cord* (noun)   2 re*cord*ed (verb)
3 ex*tract*ed (verb)   4 *ex*tract (noun)

b) 🔊 Play the recording again. Students listen and repeat.

8 Grammar

Indirect questions (2)

a) Weaker classes: Write the following question on the board:

How much did you pay for those shoes?

Point out that it might seem a bit impolite to ask this question. However, we can add words at the beginning so that the question is less direct. Write the sentence openings *Can I ask you* and *Could you tell me* and help students to form the following:

Can I ask you how much you paid for those shoes?
Could you tell me how much you paid for those shoes?

Now follow the procedure for stronger classes.

Stronger classes: Look at the examples and ask students to choose the correct words.

Answers
1 you went   2 it's from   3 they were first developed

b) Students underline the *Wh-* question words in the examples in Exercise 8a. Point out that they now appear in the middle of the sentences.

c) Read through the rule with students and ask them to complete it. Point out the similarity to the previous indirect questions studied in Exercise 2: the subject comes before the verb and we don't use the auxiliary *do*. However, we must use a question mark at the end because the whole sentence is in the form of a question: *Can I ask you (something)?*

Answer
statement

d) Students read the interview and change the direct questions to indirect questions. Ask them to compare answers with a partner before feedback. Point out that the interview is a formal situation and the interviewer is using the indirect form in order to be polite.

Answers
2 Do you know when disco music started?
3 Do you know exactly how many disco CDs you've got?
4 Could you tell us where you keep them?
5 Have you got any idea how much money you've spent on them?
6 Can you remember which was the first disco record you bought?
7 Can you tell me which piece of disco music you like the most?
8 Can you tell me how often you listen to it?

e) Students work in pairs and ask each other the questions. They might like to insert their favourite type of music to replace *disco*. Encourage them to use vocabulary from Exercise 6 in their answers.

Grammar notebook
Remind students to note down the rules for indirect questions and to write a few examples of their own.

9 Speak

If you set the background information as a homework research task, ask the students to tell the class what they found out.

BACKGROUND INFORMATION

Hip-hop: is also referred to as *rap*. It is made up of rapping (speaking very quickly in rhyme) and mixing or DJing (mixing different types of music and sounds). There is usually quite a simple rhythm with a heavy drumbeat and a strong melodic background, over which the singer

Unit 16 109

speaks. Lyrics are often aggressive comments on politics and relationships. It is currently the most popular style of popular music in many parts of the world. Artists include Tupac Shakur (2Pac), Eminem and Fifty Cent.

Dance music: Any music used for dancing could be referred to as dance music, but in recent years, the term has been used to refer to electronic music used for dancing. It usually has a strong repetitive beat and is either instrumental or has very simple lyrics. There are many different styles of dance music including *techno, house, trance, electro* and *breakbeat*.

Disco music: refers to the dance music played in discotheques in the 1970s. It became very popular after the film *Saturday Night Fever* in 1977 and has come back into fashion in recent years. Popular disco artists include The Bee Gees, Michael Jackson, Village People and Kool and the Gang.

Check that students understand the meaning of the words in the box by asking for one or two examples. Students work in pairs or small groups and discuss the questions. Encourage them to speak in full sentences and to use comparisons. Monitor and help with vocabulary if necessary. In feedback discuss the questions further and find out what the most popular type of music is in the class.

--- OPTIONAL ACTIVITY ---
If students are interested in this area, ask them to prepare presentations on their favourite type of music. This could be given as a homework task and students could bring in pieces of music to illustrate their presentations.

10 Speak and listen

If you set the background information as a homework research task, ask the students to tell the class what they found out.

BACKGROUND INFORMATION
Sister Sledge: is an American musical group formed in 1972 and consisting of four singers, all of whom are sisters: Kim, Debbie, Joni and Kathy Sledge. Their biggest success came in 1979 with the popular disco anthems *We Are Family*, *He's the Greatest Dancer* and *Lost in Music*. They also achieved an international number one hit with *Frankie* in 1985.

The song *Lost in Music* has been in the charts three times in the UK, in 1979 (number 17), in 1984 (number 4) and in 1993 (number 14).

(a) Read through the phrases and ask students to match them with their definitions. They should be able to deduce the answers, even though some words will be new to them.

Answers
1 d   2 e   3 b   4 c   5 a

(b) Ask students to read the lyrics and help them with difficult vocabulary: *quit, tragedy, temptation, melody, vanity, sanity*. Ask them to think about the sorts of words that will be needed to fill the gaps. Then play the recording. Students complete the song lyrics. Check the answers and play the recording again, pausing if necessary.

TAPESCRIPT
See the song on page 112 of the Student's Book.

Answers
1 trap   2 alive   3 tragedy   4 fans   5 band   6 survive

Did you know ...?
Read through the information and find out if students know any other songs by Sister Sledge. Ask if they know any other musicians who became famous when they were children. What do they think it would be like to become famous at the age of 12?

11 Write

(a) Pre-teach *saga* and *humorous*, and make sure students know the meaning of *poem/poetry, rhythm* and *rhyme*. Ask them to read the descriptions (1–3) and match them with the texts. You may choose to read the texts aloud yourself, creating a sense of drama and tension until the last moment in text B and bringing out the regular rhythm and rhyming pattern of text C. As you check the answers, discuss the poems briefly. Ask students what is being described in the haiku and ask what they thought was happening in the mini-saga before they read the last sentence. Ask them to pick out the stressed words and the rhyming words in the limerick (note that *Crewe* is pronounced /kru:/).

Answers
1 B   2 C   3 A

(b) In pairs, students discuss which of the texts they like best and why. Listen to some pairs' opinions in open class.

(c) Read through the descriptions with the class. Students choose one of the types and start planning their own piece of writing. You could ask them to choose one of the types as a class exercise and set another as homework.

Mini-sagas: A good way to approach this is to use a well-known story (for example, a legend or fairy story). Elicit some ideas for a story like this. Point out

Module 4

to students that they will have to be very selective about the events they include, and that the effect of doing this is often funny.

Haiku: Haikus are short, but this does not make them easy to write. Look back at text A and ask students to check the number of syllables in each line. You could take one of the example topics and gather suggestions from the class to form a first line of five syllables on the board.

Limericks: It is important that students hear the rhythm, so practise by repeating the example, then simply the rhythm (da DUM da da DUM, etc.).

Point out that the first line of a limerick often gives the name of a person or place. You could write an example on the board (e.g. *There was a young lady called Jane* or *There once was a boy from Japan*) and get the class to help you form a second rhyming line (e.g. *Who went round the world in a train / Who lived in the back of a van*). Elicit other rhyming words that they could use for their last line (e.g. *rain, brain, Spain, insane / man, can, began*, etc.).

(d) If you set the writing as a homework task, ask students to read each other's work in a subsequent lesson. Invite some students to read out their work to the class.

Module 4 Check your progress

1 Grammar

(a) 2 are thought   3 are known   4 is thought
5 is said   6 are expected   7 are thought

(b) 3 Looking out of the window, she thought about her father.
4 Walking through the valley, she felt at one with nature.
5 Having climbed the mountain, they sat down to look at the view.
6 Having swum across the lake, he collapsed on the shore.
7 Seeing the *aurora borealis*, we gasped in amazement.
8 Having seen the waterfall ahead of them, they tried to change direction.

(c) 2 It wasn't raining, so we didn't need to take our raincoats.
3 I needn't have studied all weekend because the test on Monday was cancelled.
4 There was no test so I didn't need to study at the weekend.
5 We didn't need to cook any food because there was a restaurant.
6 I needn't have bought him any chocolate because he told me he is allergic to it.

(d) 2 I studied hard so as to get better marks than last time.
3 He wore his best clothes in order to impress her.
4 She put the money in her pocket in order not to lose it.
5 We kept very quiet so as not to disturb him.

(e) 2 such   3 so   4 such   5 so   6 such a

(f) 2 Do you know how many people there were at the party?
3 I have no idea what time the shops open.
4 Let's find out when the concert starts.
5 Can you tell me what they wanted to know?
6 I don't know who the teacher said was responsible.

2 Vocabulary

(a) 2 word   3 lost   4 catch   5 gist   6 pick

(b) 2 edge   3 fell   4 cried   5 bite   6 chuckled

(c) *Across:*
3 bay   4 lake   6 glacier   7 coral reef
Down:
1 range   2 plain   5 canyon

(d) 2 F   3 T   4 T   5 F   6 F

How did you do?
Students work out their scores. Check how they have done and follow up any problem areas with revision work.

Unit 16

Project 1
A class presentation: a unique mind

Divide the class into pairs.

1 Getting information

a) Ask pairs to brainstorm to make a list 'mankind's greatest minds'. You could give an example of your own from each category to get them started.

b) Encourage pairs to choose two people who they are interested in and want to know more about. Monitor to make sure that pairs have all chosen different people.

c) Students do some preliminary research, either at home or in the library, on the two people they have selected. They could take a 'timeline' approach and organise information chronologically.

d) Students compare notes on their two people and decide which of the two they will use for their presentation. Encourage them to work through the questions in the book and to make sure they have an answer for each question. If not, they should go back and do further research. Stress the importance of quotations, other people's opinions and anecdotes, as these points make presentations interesting.

2 Prepare the presentation

a) Look at the mind map on page 116. Show students that they should choose four or more main areas to focus on and build up the mind map using your own example.

b) In pairs, students decide which points each of them is going to focus on. Students may choose to do this in different ways, either one after the other, doing half each, or alternating several times during the presentation. If they have found pictures, maps, etc. that they can use in their presentation, one person can hold these up at relevant points while the other speaks. They may want to use the board to write key names or places.

c) Students rehearse the presentation in pairs and give each other suggestions if it needs improving.

3 The presentation

a) In pairs, students come to the front and give their presentations to the class. Encourage them to use their notes as little as possible and to keep their heads up and look around the classroom. Their classmates should write questions to ask later. If you have a large class, you may like to have students giving presentations over a series of lessons, rather than one after the other.

b) After the presentation, invite questions from the rest of the class. The speakers should answer as if they were the person in the presentation. Encourage them to guess the answers if they do not know them.

Project 2
A group presentation: design your own charity

Divide the class into groups of three or four.

1 Do your research

a) Look at the photos and ask students to describe what they can see. What are the charity workers doing and what are they aiming to achieve? Give students time to decide which type of charity they want to set up and whether they want to work locally or nationally.

b) In their groups, students discuss the aims of their charity. Encourage them to think carefully about what results they want to achieve.

c) Brainstorm the names of a few charities and elicit some examples of slogans. Students then decide on the name and slogan for their charity and design an eye-catching logo.

d) Students discuss the questions and work together to plan the activities of their charity. Encourage them to be as practical and specific in their planning as possible.

2 Prepare the presentation

a) Students work together to decide what information they are going to include on their poster and make a rough sketch of the design. Ask them to draw or find suitable pictures. Give each group a large piece of paper to make a final version of their poster. If possible, they should also create a leaflet which describes their charity in more detail. You could photocopy each group's leaflet, or students may be able to design it on a computer and print out copies themselves. The leaflets can then be handed out to other students before the group's presentation.

b) Ask students to plan what they are going to say. They should divide different parts of the presentation amongst themselves and make notes of what they are going to say. Remind them not to read from their notes, but just to use them to refer to where necessary. Give students time to practise their presentations and give each other feedback.

3 The presentation

a) Ask each group to come to the front, stick their poster to the board or the front wall and present their charity. Encourage them to speak clearly and project their voices. Stand at the back of the class yourself to make sure they are audible. Give time at the end of each presentation for other students to ask questions.

b) You may like to end with a discussion of whether they could use their ideas in any way in the school or in their community.

Project 3
A class survey: your ecological footprint

Divide the class into groups of four or five.

1 Choose the area you want to research

a) Look at the photos with the class and refer them back to the reading in Unit 10 Exercise 1. Remind them that the more a country pollutes the planet or consumes natural resources, the bigger its ecological footprint, so a big footprint is a bad thing. Explain that they are going to do a survey to find out about the class's ecological footprint. Write the list of topics on the board and discuss briefly how activities in each of these areas may harm the environment.

b) In their groups, students focus on the topics on the board and think about the sort of information they will want to gather in their survey. Read through the ideas on page 118 to get them started. Ask each group to elect one person to take notes.

2 Prepare and carry out the survey

a) Students transform their notes into questions for use in the survey. Read through the examples of different question types. Encourage students to choose mostly *Yes/No* or ranking questions, to get answers which can be compared and scored. Tell them to work out a scoring system for their survey. Make sure that all students in the group write down the completed survey questions.

b) Students in each group agree on who they are each going to interview, so that they cover the whole class. Students circulate, ask their questions and make a note of the answers.

3 Write up the results

a) Back in their groups, students add up the scores from their questionnaires and work out a total score.

b) Students work together in their group to write a report, summarising the information for each topic and drawing conclusions. Encourage them to create graphs as in the example to illustrate the information they have gathered.

4 Present your report

Ask students to decide who will present each part of the report, and give them time to rehearse. Then ask groups to present their report to the class. At the end of each presentation, invite other students to comment or ask questions. Finally, in open class, discuss whether the groups' results tallied and whether the class footprint is large or small. Invite students to suggest ways to make it smaller.

Project 4
An information booklet: a foreign country

1 The task

Read through the topics with the class, clarifying vocabulary as necessary. You may like to ask students to think of examples for each topic in their own country.

2 Do your research

a) In pairs, students choose a country that they would like to find out and write about. Encourage them to choose a lesser-known country rather than a very familiar one, and try to ensure that pairs are working on a range of different countries.

b) In their own time outside class, students research the information in step 1. You might like to give them a word limit, so they know how much information they need to find. In a subsequent lesson, students share their findings with their partner and decide what information they will use in their booklet.

3 Design your booklet

a) Ask students to find or produce suitable pictures and maps to go into their booklet.

b) Students work together to write an introductory paragraph which explains why they chose the country. Monitor and help with vocabulary as necessary.

c) Students plan their booklet. They should decide on the best order in which to present information, what headings and sub-headings are suitable for each section and where their maps and illustrations should go. Encourage them to include as many interesting facts as possible.

d) Students write up their notes into paragraphs. Monitor and note down any problems to discuss at the end of the activity.

e) Students write a contents page which reflects the headings they have used in the booklet.

4 Presentation

Ask each pair to prepare to present their country. Encourage them to take a few notes about each area so they do not need to read from their booklets. Give time at the end of each presentation for students to ask the presenters questions about their country. When all pairs have presented their booklet, hand the booklets round the class and give students time to look at each one. The class can then vote on the most interesting booklet.

Workbook key

1 Super brains

1 a 2 has 3 means 4 has been drawing
5 has taken 6 sell 7 include
8 has also published 9 wants

b 2 is studying 3 has met 4 has appeared
5 has been exhibiting 6 is working

c Students' own answers

2 a 2 were living 3 diagnosed 4 has developed
5 began 6 had created 7 was working
8 started 9 gave 10 had called

b 2 sat 3 had tested 4 was playing 5 decided
6 had ever taught

3 a /θ/: bath, month, theatre, thin, Thursday, thirsty
/ð/: other, brother, clothes, weather

TAPESCRIPT
other bath month brother theatre clothes
thin weather Thursday thirsty

b TAPESCRIPT
1 I think their brother is thin.
2 There are three rooms with a bath.
3 I thought I saw them at the theatre last month.
4 My mother bought new clothes on Thursday.

4 a 2 Ralph was out of his mind when he resigned from that job.
3 I'm sorry, it must have slipped my mind.
4 You read my mind! Let's go for lunch now.
5 Have you changed your mind already?
6 Kay looks tired; she's got something on her mind.
7 Don't worry. Andy will speak his mind.
8 OK! I've made up my mind where I'm going on my holidays.

b 1 a 2 b 3 b 4 b

c 2 brain 3 mind 4 brains 5 brain 6 mind

5 b 1 B 2 A 3 A 4 B 5 B 6 A 7 B

c 2 h 3 a 4 i 5 j 6 b 7 d 8 f
9 g 10 e

d 1 line 6 2 line 8 3 lines 13 and 14

6 a Thanks / Don't worry / Let me know /
She keeps raving about it / Love

b Students' own answers

Unit check

1 2 playing 3 had 4 did 5 went 6 stood
7 standing 8 asked 9 told 10 forgotten

2 2 c 3 a 4 b 5 c 6 b 7 a 8 a 9 c

3 2 By the time he was 12, he ~~broke~~ had broken his leg five times.
3 Enrico's busy. ~~He studies~~ He's studying for his Maths test on Monday.
4 ~~Are you doing~~ Have you done / been doing anything good recently?
5 ~~Are they liking~~ Do they like their new school?
6 When I got home I ~~was hearing~~ heard your message on the answering machine.
7 When I arrived at the office he ~~waited~~ was waiting for me.
8 I hope ~~he's knowing~~ he knows what he's doing.
9 When the film started I realised I ~~saw~~ had seen it before.

2 Mind over matter

1 a 2 are being made 3 were guided
4 had been avoided 5 will be checked

b 2 Tree kangaroos have also been seen in the area.
3 In the past, tree kangaroos had nearly all been hunted and killed by local tribes.
4 The expedition was organised by Conservation International.
5 New types of plants will be discovered (by scientists).
6 All of their discoveries will be sent to other scientists.

c 2 b 3 c 4 b 5 d

2 a 1 operating theatre 2 local anaesthetic
3 surgeon 4 diagnosis

b 2 check up 3 symptoms 4 suffer 5 recovering
6 diagnosed 7 diet 8 get better

3 a 1 d 2 e 3 a 4 c 5 b

TAPESCRIPT
1 A placebo is a substance with no active ingredients that is given to a patient.
2 A scientist is someone who does research, usually in a laboratory.
3 A diagnosis is a doctor's opinion about a patient's illness.
4 A symptom is a sign of illness in the body.
5 A general anaesthetic is a drug that makes you sleep during an operation so you do not feel anything.

4 2 Cacao is produced in Ghana.
3 One in six people in Britain is affected by stress.
4 A British schoolgirl was chosen to star in the last Harry Potter film.
5 Old cans are recycled to make fridges.
6 11% of Americans weren't given healthcare last year.

5 a 2 The land is being bought from the Indians (by the companies) at low prices.
3 A deal is now being reached by some Indian tribes and medical companies.

4 137 plant and animal species are being destroyed by man every day.
5 Rainforest plants are being used by many medical companies in their products.
6 Less than 1% of the plants in the rainforest are being studied (by researchers).

b 2 are being considered 3 are being found
4 is called 5 were previously used 6 will be saved

6 a 2 panic 3 homesickness 4 confidence
5 exhaustion 6 envy; jealousy 7 nostalgia

b 1 e 2 a 3 d 4 c 5 f 6 b

TAPESCRIPT
Speaker 1 Tell me, how is everyone?
Speaker 2 Well Katy's in London and she's feeling very sorry for herself.
Speaker 1 That's because she's feeling homesick, I suppose.
Speaker 2 Yes. And poor Dilshan's exhausted.
Speaker 1 Why's that?
Speaker 2 He's working on a big project at university and he's over-anxious.
Speaker 1 What about Nick?
Speaker 2 His usual guilty self.
Speaker 1 Why does he always feel so guilty?
Speaker 2 He gets very jealous over Julia and then he feels guilty.
Speaker 1 What about Julia?
Speaker 2 She's depressed.
Speaker 1 Because of Nick?
Speaker 2 No. She's got no confidence in herself and then that gets her down. She cries a lot, and she isn't sleeping very well.
Speaker 1 The poor thing. And how's your grandma?
Speaker 2 Poor Grandma's really inattentive. You never get the impression that she's really with you, it's like she's in another world.
Speaker 1 Is there something on her mind?
Speaker 2 I don't think so. I just think she lives in the past. She's so nostalgic about the past, especially the 1940s when she was a teenager. She thinks life was so much better then.
Speaker 1 And that leaves Abby …
Speaker 2 Oh, Abby's always in a panic.
Speaker 1 What makes her panic?
Speaker 2 Everything! She's so absent-minded, she forgets everything and then panics. What a bunch, eh?

c 3 can 4 on 5 that 6 very 7 that 8 ✓
9 to 10 ✓ 11 to 12 at 13 ✓

7 2 c 3 a 4 b 5 d 6 b 7 c

Unit check

1 2 was prescribed 3 condition 4 were affected
5 was increased 6 were … interrupted
7 was hypnotised 8 felt 9 specialised 10 symptoms

2 2 a 3 a 4 a 5 a 6 b 7 a 8 c 9 b

3 2 Ireland was been changed *has been changed* from a farming society to an important economy.
3 1.5 billion cans have been recycled *are recycled* in Britain every year.
4 This made *is made* for us by a factory in Berlin.
5 Thousands of people have given *are given* the wrong medicine every week.
6 The TV has been repaired *was repaired* last week by a technician.
7 When we walked into the vet's surgery a dog is being examined *was being examined*.
8 Everyone are being informed *is being informed* about the risks.
9 The thief will be send *will be sent* to prison when he's caught.

3 Brainwaves

1 a 2 where 3 whose 4 which 5 that/which
6 that/which 7 whose 8 where 9 that/which

b 2 Those students who have passed their exams don't need to come to the revision course.
3 The man who Tony was speaking to is my sister's boyfriend.
4 Saturday, which is my day off, is the closing date for the competition.
5 The pasta that I had for lunch was delicious.
6 The sauce that came with the pasta was amazing.
7 I got an email from the lady who I contacted about the youth hostel.
8 I have to take a flight that stops in Birmingham.
9 The restaurant where we ate was very expensive.
10 The book that I'm reading is about the human mind.

c 2 whose 3 where 4 who 5 that 6 which
7 whose 8 what

d 2 Kate won the tennis match, which she played against Akeela.
3 I spoke to the man who works at the information desk.
4 Yesterday I met Jenny, whose sister was in my class in college.
5 They've started training for the match that/which will decide the championship.
6 Suren, who has lived next door for three years, has moved to London.
7 I asked him to post the letter, that/which I had written to my cousin.
8 My brother booked a holiday to New York, where he lived for six months.

e 1 a 2 a 3 a 4 b

f 2 his 3 that 4 what 5 ✓ 6 it 7 ✓ 8 it

2 1 d 2 b 3 c 4 a

3

a *Across*
3 goggles   5 rink   8 racket   9 league
Down
1 surfing   2 gloves   3 go-karting   4 pitch
6 puck   7 helmet

b 2 beat   3 scored   4 scored   5 draw   6 fouled
7 sent off   8 lost

4

a 1 ↓   2 ↑   3 ↑   4 ↓   5 ↑   6 ↑

5

a Statement 3

b 1 b   2 c   3 a   4 b

c 1 F   2 T   3 T   4 F   5 F   6 T

6

a Students' own answers.

b D 1   C 2   E 3   F 4   A 5
B is the extra picture.

c A   ramp / board / tricks / jump breathtakingly high / flies back down and up / protective gear / helmet / fall
C   serve / on the line / net / lob / hit / racket / smashes / backhand / volley / line / love-fifteen
D   ball / tackled / dribbles / passes / heads / pitch / goal / foul / ref / whistle / sent off
E   they're off / in side lane / gaining speed / going faster / catching up / overtake on the bend / corner / drivers / accelerating / skidding / car / race
F   beam / vault / board / jumps higher / height / balance / landing

TAPESCRIPT

1   Now Martin has the ball. He's tackled by Jones, but no, Martin dribbles past him, gets the ball past him. Martin still has the ball, and he passes to Fairhouse who heads it forward to MacColl. It's MacColl against Murphy now. They're the fastest men on the pitch. Is it going to be a goal? And ... oh no, what a foul! The ref's blown his whistle and it looks as if Murphy's going to be sent off.

2   And it's Williams to serve. Yes, it's just on the line but Smith gets to it and forces Williams to run to the net. Is she going to get it? What a lob! What a hit! But Smith manages to get her racket up and smashes the ball back across the net. But it's not powerful enough and Williams gets her backhand volley in but just outside the line. Love-fifteen.

3   And the flag is down and they're off. Collin is off to a good start in the inside lane. But Fletcher is gaining speed, he's going faster, he's catching up. It looks like he's going to try to overtake on the bend. That's the hardest corner in the race! So many drivers have fallen out of the race here ... But Collins is accelerating, he's getting faster, and oh no, he's skidding all over the place. Collin's car is on fire, and he's out of the race.

4   And now it's Summers. She takes a deep breath as she focuses her mind. After her disaster in the last part of the competition, on the beam, she'll want to do well on the vault. She's got a good speed up as she hits the board. She jumps higher than anyone else. Yes. What great height, although her balance could be better. But what a perfect landing.

5   Next one up is Jenson, the current champion. He makes his way to the top of the ramp. And he's off. He's looking cool and confident on the board today. Let's see what tricks he has planned for us today. What a jump! And now he's flying through the air. His favourite jump! It's breathtakingly high – and then he flies back down and up to the other side of the ramp ... No protective gear, no helmet, nothing, for Jensen. Is he brave or is he just crazy? Let's hope he doesn't fall.

c Students' own answers.

Unit check

1   2 whose   3 when   4 where   5 which   6 who   7 that
8 what   9 it   10 why

2   2 a   3 c   4 a   5 c   6 b   7 c   8 b   9 a

3   2 The bus ~~it~~ *that* goes to Oxford leaves in half an hour.
3 Everyone ~~what~~ *that* I asked said I should do the exam again.
4 Have you seen the camera ~~who~~ *that/which* I left there?
5 I asked her ~~which~~ *what* she was thinking.
6 There are lots of people ~~which~~ *whose* lives will be improved by the new drug.
7 Can you remember ~~whose~~ *who* introduced us?
8 The News is the TV programme ~~what~~ *that/which* I prefer.
9 She's the girl ~~who~~ *whose* bike was stolen.

4 Time travellers

1

a 2 c   3 a   4 e   5 f   6 d   7 h   8 i   9 g

b 2 Call   3 Did you take   4 I'll call   5 I saw
6 I'm going out

c 2 No, I haven't, but I'm reading the book.
3 Will you lend me the book when you've finished with it?
4 What do you know about the author?
5 The author, J. K. Rowling, has always wanted to write books.

2

a 3

b 1 took   2 's always giving   3 spends   4 've wasted

c 1 off   2 in   3 on   4 out

d 2 time off   3 take your time   4 ran out of time
5 just in time

3

a
2 He wastes <u>a</u> lot <u>of</u> time on the Int<u>er</u>net.
3 <u>Michael</u> arrived just in time <u>to</u> have din<u>ner</u> with <u>us</u>.
4 You <u>can</u> take <u>some</u> time off next week when we're not so busy.
5 <u>Have</u> you got time <u>for</u> <u>a</u> cup <u>of</u> tea?

4

a
2 a 3 b 4 h 5 d 6 c 7 f 8 e

b
2 got 3 didn't read it properly 4 take time off
5 refuses 6 read the letter

c
2 Laura recommended that I buy the latest Coldplay album.
3 Their mum warned them never to do that again.
4 She suggested going / that they go to the cinema at the weekend.
5 Jane advised me not to buy that mobile phone.
6 The instructor claimed that if we joined their gym, we'd be super fit in just a month.
7 She denied breaking / that she had broken the vase.
8 The teacher emphasised that he/she wouldn't accept homework that wasn't done on time.

5

a
3 the 4 on 5 ✓ 6 have 7 in 8 the
9 ✓ 10 ✓ 11 most 12 to 13 that 14 ✓
15 to 16 on

b
2 'I don't need a man.'
3 'I don't worry about what the world thinks of me.'
4 'There are lots of things I would like to be.'
5 'I think people should live the life they want to. It's the most important thing that they can do.'
6 You shouldn't listen to advice, as most advice is useless.

TAPESCRIPT

Dad Hello, Pete Richmond speaking.
Cathy Hello, Dad. It's me, Cathy. I was just ringing to see if you got my letter.
Dad Hi, Cathy. Yes, I got it last week. Thanks for writing.
Cathy And …?
Dad And what?
Cathy And what do you think? Did you find it interesting?
Dad Well, to be honest with you, I just skimmed through it. I didn't have enough time to sit and read it properly.
Cathy Oh, Dad! That's exactly why I wrote to you. You need to start making time for yourself. You work too hard. You need to take some time off.
Dad Now, don't tell me what to do, young lady. I'm not going to listen to an eighteen-year-old who wanted to leave school only three years ago.
Cathy That's right, Dad. But you told me to think carefully and you also told me it was your duty to tell me what you thought. Now I'm doing the same thing for you. I love you. I can't stop you working and I don't want to. But I do want you to start making some time for yourself.
Dad OK, OK. I get the message. As soon as I hang up I'll sit down and read your letter properly. Now what was the party like?

6

a It's about the future.

b 1 titbits 2 conversely 3 elegant 4 sophisticated
5 subtle 6 misinterpreted

c 1 c 2 d 3 a 4 b

Unit check

1
2 on 3 asked 4 that 5 offering 6 warned
7 spent 8 time 9 denied 10 has promised

2
2 a 3 b 4 b 5 c 6 b 7 c 8 b 9 c

3
2 Karlien promised ~~that~~ to arrive on time.
3 The teacher encouraged ~~she~~ her to go in for the competition.
4 He refused ~~to paying~~ to pay for his ticket.
5 I ~~explained Terence~~ explained to Terence how to get to the party.
6 The doctor recommended ~~for~~ that I take some rest.
7 She's taken some time ~~on~~ off to look after her mum.
8 We might catch the train if it doesn't leave ~~at~~ on time.
9 Remind me ~~that~~ to call her before we leave.

5 Personalities

1

a 1 B 2 D 3 C 4 A

TAPESCRIPT

A It was my cousin's birthday and my mum suggested that I call him to wish him a happy birthday. I rang the number and as soon as he picked up I started singing 'Happy birthday to you' really loudly. Once I'd finished I shouted: 'and have a really great day'. Imagine my horror when I heard someone saying: 'I think you have the wrong number.'

B We were playing cricket at school and I'm not really the sporty type so, when it was my turn to bat, I just swung and hoped for the best. As usual I missed the ball but I managed to let go of the bat. It went flying through the air and guess what, it hit my teacher right on the head!

C My dad's a teacher at my school. One day at assembly he was using his laptop and a projector to show everyone pictures he had taken at a school event. When he had finished he closed the program and to my horror the background was a picture of me lying on the sofa in my pyjamas. Everyone burst out laughing, even Dad. I could have killed him.

D The night before sports day I decided to put on some fake tan cream so I wouldn't look so white. The packet said the cream would make my skin go a lovely golden brown colour. It took a really long time to put the cream on, and I thought I was very careful not to put too much on my arms and legs. But the next morning my skin was bright orange. I had to wear shorts and a T-shirt all day. It was so embarrassing. The worst thing was that no one said anything to me, they just giggled and looked away.

Workbook key 117

b 2 is 3 ✓ 4 that 5 thing 6 ✓

c 2 What's very frustrating about John is that he always changes his mind.
3 What makes life difficult for her parents is that she argues a lot with her sister.
4 It's essential to do the things that the teachers ask you to do.
5 What makes that restaurant special is that it has a good atmosphere.
6 It's good to know what you should do when people are hurt.

2 a 1 What I <u>really</u> want to do is have a rest.
2 I <u>never</u> listen to what he says.
3 What really <u>impressed</u> me was her <u>presentation</u>.
4 I never know what to <u>say</u> in these situations.
5 What I would like to know is where are we all going to <u>stay</u>?
6 This isn't what you were saying last <u>week</u>.

3 a 2 c 3 f 4 e 5 b 6 a
b 1 d 2 a 3 b 4 c
c 2 a 3 b 4 c 5 c 6 a

4 a
Pisces: to repeat   Virgo: feeling
Aries: following   Libra: thinking
Taurus: to pay   Scorpio: being
Gemini: believing   Sagittarius: to think
Cancer: to meet   Capricorn: to lose
Leo: to talk

b 2 to get 3 being 4 going out 5 going 6 meeting 7 hanging around 8 to call

5 a clever, happy, loving, indulgent, excellent
b 2 a 3 b 4 b 5 a 6 a 7 b 8 b
c 1 Because her mother had died and her older sister was married.
2 They were like good friends.
3 No – 'And now that the shadow of authority had long gone away…'
4 No.
5 No – she listened to it and respected it, but did mainly what she wanted to do.
6 She did what she wanted too much and was also a little bit smug.

6 a Yes.
b 1 Text 2 is more detailed.
2 (possible answers)
He is returning to the room after not seeing it for a long time, and he is shocked at how the room has changed. He is also afraid that he won't be able to find his mother's diary.
3 It is dark and in a state of confusion. It hasn't been used for years.

4 Yes, but not for a long time.
5 He wants to find out the truth about what happened one night in the past.

Unit check

1 2 spotlight 3 excitement 4 loved 5 embarrassed 6 tried to 7 witty 8 shallowness 9 charming 10 ending

2 2 c 3 b 4 c 5 a 6 c 7 a 8 b 9 b

3 2 She always forgets what ~~she~~ needs doing.
3 ~~Which~~ What I'm trying to say is we need more money for the project.
4 ~~Shyness~~ Shy people often find it hard to speak in public.
5 ~~To make~~ Making a good first impression is what Laura does best.
6 I wish Tom looked a bit ~~scruffier~~ neater. He's always so untidy and careless.
7 He came across as ~~to be~~ quite pretentious.
8 I can't stop ~~to smoke~~ smoking, I've tried everything, but it's useless!
9 My kids are really ~~bubbling~~ bubbly in the morning.

6 In and out of fashion

1 a 2 ✓ 3 ✓ 4 ✓
b (possible answers)
2 use electricity
3 buy toys from shops
4 travel in cars and planes
5 write emails / use the phone
6 wear jeans, T-shirts, short skirts, shorts
7 listen to CDs
8 have one or two children

c (possible answers)
2 In the past, people used to use candles, but now they use electricity.
3 In the past, children used to make their own toys, but now they buy toys from shops.
4 In the past, people used to travel in carriages, but now they travel in cars and planes.
5 In the past, people used to write letters, but now they write emails / use the phone.
6 In the past, women used to wear long skirts and dresses, but now they wear jeans, T-shirts, short skirts and shorts.
7 In the past, people used to listen to records, but now they listen to CDs.
8 In the past, people used to have lots of children, but now they have one or two children.

d 2 would spend 3 used to find 4 used to be 5 wouldn't go 6 used to drive

2 a 2 craze 3 catch on 4 spread 5 overwhelming 6 hooked

b 1 c: hook – You use a hook to hang something from, or to catch fish. The other two are nouns that describe a new fashion.
2 b: overwhelming – This word describes something very great or very large. The other two describe something that you cannot stop doing.
3 a: addictive – The other two are about things that happen very quickly.
4 b: were hooked on – This describes a person who is addicted to something and is a passive verb. The other two describe trends and are active verbs.

3 a 2 The dog barked at us in a horrible way.
3 He teaches English in a fun way.
4 They listened to her with enthusiasm.
5 We found the house with difficulty.
6 He said hello to me in a friendly way.
7 We need to do this again in a different way.
8 The children waited with excitement for the clown to arrive.

b 1 in a rude way 2 with enthusiasm 3 in public
4 in a different way 5 in a fun way

4 a 2 He reads as slowly as he talks.
3 Frank doesn't work as hard as he plays.
4 She plays the guitar as nicely as she sings.
5 We arrived as soon as we could.
6 I don't speak French as well as I speak Spanish.

5 a 2 in private 3 in a hurry 4 in secret 5 in a panic
6 in public 7 on purpose 8 by accident

b 1 public 2 hurry 3 private 4 panic 5 row
6 secret 7 accident 8 purpose

6 a 2 pen 3 Dad 4 bend 5 sat 6 man

7 1 real 2 out of order 3 Besides 4 For a start

8 2 b 3 a 4 c

9 a She works as a forecaster for the Next Big Thing, a company which predicts what the next trends for young people will be.

TAPESCRIPT

Presenter Welcome to *The People Show*. This week we'll be talking to Philippa Chandler. Philippa works as a forecaster for Next Big Thing, a company which predicts what the next big youth trends will be. Philippa acts as eyes and ears for some of the world's top companies. She lets them know what their clients like and dislike and what they listen to. Her job is to keep her clients up-to-date, so she regularly interviews people on the street, goes clubbing and surfs the net. The information she gives could help her clients create the next big thing. How did she find a job like that? Well, Philippa read an article on William Higham, the founder of Next Big Thing, Britain's first trend forecasting agency. She sent Higham an email saying she was perfect for the job as a trend spotter because she was very sociable and she had answered questions such as 'Why we buy things' as part of her Cultural Studies degree. He immediately offered her a part-time job as a trainee and six months later she was part of the staff. So, Philippa tell us about your job ...

Philippa I love my job. It satisfies my curiosity but it also makes me even more curious.

Presenter How do you start your research?

Philippa I often start by surfing the net for new trends and fashions. I can spend an hour looking at a new website. It's work, but it's not really productive or useful if I spend too long on one thing.

Presenter What's your advice to young people looking for a job?

Philippa First of all they should choose a course they are going to enjoy as well as something they think will be useful for work. Then they should try to get as much work experience as they can. The more experience you have, the easier it is for you to realise what you are good at and what you really like doing. If you haven't tried something, you'll never know.

b 1 F 2 D 3 T

c 1 a 2 c 3 a 4 c

d (possible answers)
1 Something new and exciting that a lot of people will want.
2 It tells them what young people are interested in, and what the latest fashions are.
3 When she spends too long looking at one website.
4 Study something you enjoy, and get as much work experience as you can.

Unit check

1 2 popular 3 sharing 4 demand 5 group
6 are concerned 7 For a start 8 potentially
9 fashion 10 warnings

2 2 a 3 c 4 c 5 b 6 a 7 c 8 c 9 a

3 2 That was no accident, she did it ~~in~~ *on* purpose.
3 The class reacted with ~~exciting~~ *excitement* when the teacher told them about the class trip.
4 He ~~would~~ *used to* be the sales manager before he changed jobs.
5 She's won the gold medal for three years in ~~rows~~ *a row*.
6 I'm sorry, I knocked over the vase by ~~accidentally~~ *accident*.
7 He looked at me with ~~surprising~~ *surprise* when I asked him about Marco.
8 She didn't react as ~~bad~~ *badly* as we had expected when we told her the news.
9 They must have organised it ~~as~~ *in* secret because everyone was shocked.

7 Kindness matters

1 a 2 It's wonderful to be kind.
3 It feels good to see people smile.
4 It's important to say you're sorry.

5 It isn't difficult to be nice to other people.
6 It doesn't cost anything to help people.
7 It's not unusual to see people who are stressed.
8 It's difficult to understand why people don't talk to each other.

b 1 d   2 a   3 f   4 c   5 e   6 b

2 **a** 1 trial   2 properly   3 wrong   4 struggled
5 out   6 heartedly   7 easy   8 lengths

b 2 go to great lengths   3 struggled
4 trial and error   5 done something wrong
6 half-heartedly   7 did the job properly

3 **a** 2 y   3 w   4 w   5 y   6 y

4 **a** 2 a   3 f   4 h   5 b   6 g   7 c   8 e

b 2 'll   3 'll   4 shouldn't   5 can't   6 'll   7 can   8 shouldn't

c 2 can't   3 must   4 can   5 mustn't   6 wouldn't

d 1 must   2 can/may   3 can't   4 might/could/may
5 wouldn't   6 must

5 **a** A 3   B 2   C 6   D 1

b 1 b   2 c   3 b   4 c

6 **a** The correct order is: picture A, B, F, D, E, C.
Pictures G and H are not used.

TAPESCRIPT

Speaker 1 A strange thing happened to me the other day …
Speaker 2 Yeah? What was that?
Speaker 1 Well, I was just walking down the road from my place, down towards the town centre, I just needed, erm, I was going to, to the bank and I needed to get a bit of money and buy a couple of things, and I was listening to some music on the MP3 player and sort of singing along a bit. And there was this song called *Good People*, it's by Jack Johnson.
Speaker 2 Oh yeah, I know that one. It's good, eh?
Speaker 1 Yeah it's, I mean, I really like it. Anyway, I look over to the other side of the road and there's a man trying to push his car over to the side of the road, he's broken down, you know, and he's trying to get his car out of the traffic, and he's doing it on his own …
Speaker 2 Wow, that's tough …
Speaker 1 Yeah, steering and pushing at the same time, it's not easy. And anyway, I thought that, I thought, you know, about the song I was listening to, you know, *Good People* and he sings 'Where did all the good people go?' and I thought 'Good question!'
Speaker 2 Right!
Speaker 1 Yeah, and I kind of thought, 'Come on, why not? If that was me, I'd love someone to come and help me push the car' so I crossed over and went up to him and said 'Can I give you a hand?' and he said

'Yeah, thanks mate, if you give the car a push maybe it'll start' so I said 'OK'. Then the guy looked inside the car and said 'Go and help him to push', and I didn't know who he was talking to at first but then this small boy got out of the car and came to the back beside me. He was only about ten I think, a little kid, you know, so I said 'Come on, let's get your dad's car going – let's push!' and we started pushing and the car kind of started to move a bit …
Speaker 2 Where was the man?
Speaker 1 Oh he was back inside the car behind the wheel, of course. Anyway, after about 50 metres pushing, I don't know, maybe 50 or 60 metres, the car started! Great! So I stood up and then the man leaned out of the window and shouted 'You! Get back in the car!' and the little boy ran and jumped in. And I started to walk up to the driver's window to say something – and the guy just drove away! I was so surprised! No wave, no thank you, no nothing!
Speaker 2 You're kidding!
Speaker 1 No, honestly – there I am, standing in the middle of the road, all hot and sweaty, I've helped him get his car started, and he just drives away!! I mean, can you believe it!
Speaker 2 So you'll never push a car again then?
Speaker 1 Oh, no, I'd do it again. I mean, not everyone's like that, are they? You can't stop trying to help just because some people are horrible!
Speaker 2 I suppose not, but even so, it's kind of …

b 1 He was going to the bank to get some money.
2 *Good People*.
3 The car had broken down.
4 He was about ten.
5 50 or 50 metres.
6 The man didn't say thank you.

Unit check

1 2 find   3 arguments   4 lengths   5 couldn't   6 wrong
7 properly   8 must   9 struggled   10 half-heartedly

2 2 a   3 c   4 c   5 a   6 a   7 c   8 a   9 b

3 2 ~~Is~~ It's not easy to travel if you don't speak English.
3 ~~It~~ It's important to be nice to other people.
4 It ~~isn't~~ doesn't cost anything to smile.
5 It's his birthday, so we should ~~to~~ buy him something.
6 Waiter, this bill is for £10. It ~~mustn't~~ can't be right – we only had two lemonades!
7 When I was younger, I ~~can~~ could walk on my hands.
8 I don't know exactly when, but he ~~will~~ should arrive sometime in the morning.
9 She worked really hard today. She ~~can~~ must be exhausted.

8 Peacemakers

1 **a** 2 was   3 were   4 had been   5 had been   6 was
7 had been   8 were

b 2 The dog hadn't been taken for a walk.
3 The front window had been left open.
4 The sofa had been torn.
5 The washing up hadn't been done.
6 The TV had been left on.
7 The books and CDs hadn't been tidied away.
8 The letters hadn't been collected.

c 2 I opened my bag and saw that my wallet had been stolen.
3 I woke up and saw that I had been bitten (all over my body) by mosquitoes.
4 The street was very different – the trees had all been cut down.
5 We arrived too late – the tickets for the concert had all been sold.
6 When I got home, the TV had been fixed.
7 I didn't go to the party because I hadn't been invited.
8 We didn't watch the programme because we hadn't been told about it.

2

a 2 been fighting 3 been causing 4 been developing
5 played 6 become known 7 not studied 8 spent

b 2 a had/'d read b had/'d been reading
3 a had/'d saved b had/'d been saving
4 a had/'d been eating b had/'d eaten
5 a had/'d been watching b had/'d watched
6 a had/'d talked b had/'d been talking
7 a had/'d been cooking b had/'d cooked
8 a had/'d been writing b had/'d written

3

a 2 a 3 b 4 d 5 a 6 c 7 b 8 a

b 2 sort 3 stuck 4 make 5 stay 6 take
7 reach 8 resolve

4

a 1 b 2 b 3 a 4 a

5

a 2 originated/started 3 down 4 more 5 across
6 most 7 which/that 8 have 9 same 10 sing

b 4 Song name: *99 Red Balloons*
3 Song name: *War*
2 Song name: *Sunday Bloody Sunday*; Artist: U2
1 Song name: *Happy Xmas (War Is Over)*; Artist: John Lennon

TAPESCRIPT

DJ Okay, so it's time for another of my top four songs of all time list, chosen, as always, by me – so if you don't like or agree with it, well – bad luck, I guess. Today I've gone for the top four protest songs of all time. Now, of course, there were literally millions of songs to choose from and it was difficult to pick just four but, after hours and hours of listening to loads of great songs, I have come up with the top four. So get ready, here we are, it's time for today's top four.

Recorded voice Number four.

DJ And at number four is Nina with *99 Luftballoons*. Nina was from Germany and we didn't understand the title 'Luftballoon' in England, so she kindly renamed it *99 Red Balloons* for her British audience. This song sounds really sweet and like it's written for little girls, but it's actually got a really serious anti nuclear weapon message, and a warning that the world will just be 'dust' if we ever have a nuclear war. Wow, I bet she was fun at a party.

Recorded voice Number three.

DJ And at number three it's Edwin Starr and *War*. Now I like this because it's direct and to the point and it's great to shout along to. I mean there's no messing about with the message here, is there? Edwin says war is good for absolutely nothing. You know exactly what the message is with a song like this.

Recorded voice Number two.

DJ It's U2 with *Sunday Bloody Sunday*. This is a great song – you can hear the powerful feelings of protest against war and all the horror it causes ordinary people in the music, the words and in the way the band sing. Their hearts are in the music. It's also the song that made U2 into the huge international act they are today. So it's that moment of truth again. What's this week's number one?

Recorded voice Number one.

DJ And so my number one protest song is … *Happy Xmas (War Is Over)* by John Lennon, because he didn't just write a great protest song but he also wrote a great Christmas song at the same time. And it's made all the more beautiful with its universal theme of peace and love and understanding.

6

a 2

b who the person is / why they deserve the title / what charity your Samaritan supports / why your Samaritan has chosen this charity

c 1 An English teacher who teaches immigrants to the UK.
2 Because he really cares about his students and spends a lot of extra time helping them.
3 New Home – because this charity helps immigrants to adapt to their new life.

Unit check

1 2 from 3 travelling 4 arrived 5 been 6 had
7 what 8 with 9 about 10 for

2 2 b 3 c 4 c 5 a 6 a 7 b 8 a 9 c

3 2 I had been ~~waited~~ *waiting* for an hour before the doctor arrived.
3 Her eyes were red because she had ~~cried~~ *been crying*.
4 When I tried to open the door with my key, I found the lock ~~had changed~~ *had been changed*.
5 He was angry because his car had ~~being~~ *been* hit.
6 By the end of the tour, the band had ~~been playing~~ *played* in 20 different countries.
7 This ring ~~had been~~ *was given* to me by my grandmother.
8 She had ~~spoken~~ *been speaking* all day and had lost her voice.
9 When I last looked in the fridge, the cake ~~hasn't~~ *hadn't* been eaten.

9 Get involved

1 a) 2 f 3 a 4 g 5 b 6 h 7 e 8 c

b) 1 a 2 d 3 e 4 f 5 b 6 c

c) 2 had 3 goes 4 'd visit 5 didn't have
6 don't go 7 'll throw 8 had made

2 a) Across
1 involved 5 sponsored 6 sign 7 hand
8 petition 9 raise 10 leaflet
Down
2 volunteer 3 donation 4 demonstrate 6 support

b) 2 sponsored 3 volunteers 4 leaflets 5 donations
6 demonstrated 7 petition 8 involved

4 a) 2 PO 3 PP 4 PO 5 PP 6 PP

b) 1 c 4 a 6 b

c) 2 e 3 d 4 h 5 a 6 f 7 b 8 g

d) 2 If I swam well, I would have won the race.
3 If she hadn't worked extremely hard, she wouldn't be successful.
4 If my brother didn't love U2, he wouldn't have spent $200 on a ticket for their concert.
5 If I didn't hate action films, I would have gone to see *Star Wars Episode III*.
6 If my grandfather wasn't a multi-millionaire, he would have needed to work.

5 a) 1 a 2 b 3 b 4 a 5 c 6 a

b) (possible answers)
1 Because he was expecting danger.
2 Do you speak English?
3 He thinks they are playing.
4 Yes. He whistles softly (in surprise).
5 Before things started to go wrong.

6 a) 1 will make all the difference
2 speak with one voice
3 saved ancient forests from logging
4 who want to get involved
5 informs or inspires you
6 Let your imagination run wild

b) 2 F 3 T 4 F 5 T 6 F

Unit check

1 2 raise 3 donation 4 volunteers 5 I'd be 6 sponsored
7 I finished 8 support 9 handed 10 I'd finished

2 2 b 3 a 4 c 5 a 6 a 7 c 8 c 9 b

3 2 If I run too fast, I usually ~~got~~ *get* bad pains in my stomach.
3 It'd be better if we ~~would rest~~ *rested* for a little while.
4 If I were you, ~~I went~~ *I'd go* to the doctor immediately.
5 If more people had made donations, they'd ~~bought~~ *have bought* the new heart machine.
6 If more people ~~would sign~~ *had signed* the petition, the government would have changed the law.
7 If I ~~would have listened~~ *had listened* to you, I wouldn't have all this trouble now.
8 If I wasn't so lazy, ~~I'd gone~~ *I'd have gone* on the sponsored walk yesterday.
9 If John Lennon ~~didn't die~~ *hadn't died* in 1980, he'd still be writing great songs.

10 SOS Earth

1 a) 2 she'll be discussing the new Paris shop with George.
3 she'll be having lunch with Alain Dupont.
4 she'll be interviewing people for the shop manager's job.
5 she'll be visiting the Le Clerc factory.
6 she'll be looking at the new designs.
7 she'll be flying back to Manchester.
8 she'll be watching the film on TV.

b) 2 We won't be eating any natural food.
3 Children will be studying at home on computers.
4 We will be driving electric cars.
5 We won't be using telephones.
6 People won't be working more than 25 hours a week.

2 a) 2 will have found
3 will have increased
4 won't have left
5 will have been
6 will our lives have changed
7 will have sold

b) 2 The school will have disappeared.
3 The river will have dried up.
4 The shops will have become a supermarket.
5 They will have closed down the factory.
6 They will have put the car park underground.
7 People will have put solar panels on the roofs of their houses.

c) 2 have lived 3 will be doing 4 will have played
5 will be watching 6 will be sitting

3 a) In sentences 1, 3, 5, *will* is weak.

b) *will* is weak because it is not the most important word in the sentences and it can be contracted. It cannot be contracted to *'ll* if the word before it ends with an *l* sound.

4 a) 1 resources 2 temperature 3 atmosphere
4 waste 5 species 6 starvation

b) 2 dying out 3 go up 4 fouling up 5 get rid of
6 used up

5 a) swap, switch, cut, unplug, recycle, take, use, wash

b) 2 Use 3 Unplug 4 Wash 5 Recycle 6 Swap
7 switch 8 take

6 a) 2 until 3 from now 4 for 5 time 6 by

b 2 time 3 from now 4 for 5 until 6 during

7 a 1 so what 2 stuff like that 3 come off it
4 since when 5 Point taken

b 2 It's really funny, this soap opera.
3 It's a really serious problem, pollution.
4 She teaches us really well, Mrs Drake.
5 They get on well together, Mike and Sally.
6 It went on too long, that film.

9 a 1 A plan to build a new supermarket.
2 He hopes there will be a full discussion of the advantages and disadvantages.

b 1 F He can see some advantages in the proposal.
2 T
3 F He believes that the supermarket will bring jobs for young people.
4 T
5 F Lorries will be there if they build a supermarket.
6 T

Unit check

1 2 species 3 dying 4 is going 5 will have 6 time
7 until 8 will be 9 bring about 10 starvation

2 2 a 3 a 4 c 5 a 6 a 7 c 8 a 9 a

3 2 By next year, they ~~have built~~ *will have built* a new library in town.
3 Call me at four. I ~~will arrive~~ *will have arrived* home by then.
4 I can't talk now – I have to finish this work ~~until~~ *by* tomorrow.
5 She talked to me ~~during~~ *for* an hour, non-stop!
6 Fifty years ~~now~~ *from now*, we'll all be living on another planet.
7 The exam starts at nine tomorrow, so at ten ~~I write~~ *I'll be writing* as fast as I can!
8 ~~I'll leave~~ *I'll have left* school by the next time I see you.
9 I'll call you back ~~on~~ *in* 15 minutes' time.

11 Stars step in

1 a 2 ✓ 3 ✓ 4 ✓ 5 ✗ 6 ✗ 7 ✓

b 2 Here is an extract ↑ taken from the first chapter of the book. which was
3 The Great Sphinx is a famous statue of a man / lion ↑ built by the Egyptians. which was
4 Harry Potter is a fictional character ↑ created by J. K. Rowling. who was
5 The A380 plane, ↑ built by Airbus Industries, can seat over 550 passengers. which was
6 The Live 8 concert ↑ attended by 15,000 people was a success. which was

2 a 2 c 3 a 4 c 5 b 6 a

b 2 sensation 3 household 4 made 5 made
6 enjoyed

3 a 2 thought 3 way 4 concerned 5 mind 6 ask

b and **c**
2 I couldn't care less. Ø
3 It doesn't really matter. Ø
4 It's not a good idea. ✗
5 I'm completely against it. ✗
6 It can't be a bad thing. ✓

d 2 'm completely against it 5 's not a good idea
3 can't be a bad thing 6 'm all for it
4 couldn't care less

4 a 3 ✗ are you? 4 ✗ doesn't she? 5 ✗ didn't he?
6 ✓ 7 ✗ did it? 8 ✗ didn't they? 9 ✓ 10 ✓

b 2 isn't it 3 have they 4 does she 5 won't she
6 didn't they 7 shouldn't we 8 could they

c 2 did it 3 don't we 4 do they 5 will they
6 do you

TAPESCRIPT
Harry Did you see the programme about celebrity charity work last night?
Carol Yes, it was interesting, wasn't it?
Harry Not really. It didn't tell you much you didn't already know, did it?
Carol What do you mean?
Harry I mean, we know everything there is to know about Brad Pitt, don't we? People don't want to see his face on TV again, do they?
Carol Oh Harry – you can be really boring sometimes.
Harry Sorry, but you asked me what I thought.
Carol Well, yes – but if you always talk like that, people won't ask you for your opinion very often, will they?
Harry OK, I'm sorry. Let's talk about something else. I mean, we shouldn't fall out over something as silly as this.
Carol But Harry, you don't think charity work's silly, do you?

5 a 6

b 3 B 4 A 5 B 6 A 7 B 8 B

6 a 2 successful 3 cruelty 4 products 5 preference
6 activist 7 death 8 treatment 9 collection
10 belief 11 difficulties

b 1 T 2 T 3 F She thinks fur is beautiful. 4 T
5 F Madonna used to wear fur. 6 T 7 T
8 F Gucci owns 50% of her fashion label.

7 a 1 F 2 F 3 F 4 T 5 F 6 T 7 T 8 T

TAPESCRIPT
Interviewer First of all, can you tell me, erm … what is it that qualifies someone to represent UNICEF?
Expert Well, UNICEF's celebrities have a wide range of talents and achievements, you know – there are singers, writers, actors, musicians, erm, footballers of course, erm, photographers – all kinds of people. But

they all share a commitment, erm, a commitment to improving the lives of children all over the world.

Interviewer I see. And how does UNICEF pick the people to be ambassadors?

Expert Well, in each case a celebrity working with UNICEF happens because he or she has already ... erm ... shown some commitment. For example, Youssou N'Dour, the singer from Senegal, erm, he became a Goodwill Ambassador in 1991 but before that, in 1987 I think, he had already worked on a programme in his own country to immunise children, you know, protect them from diseases. And he had also, if I'm not wrong, he also took part in concerts to raise money for kids in Africa.

Interviewer Uh huh.

Expert And Shakira, the Colombian singer, had also done a lot of work and shown a lot of interest in children, especially education for children, before she became an ambassador in, erm, in 2003.

Interviewer Right. And, it's always important that they're famous, isn't it? I mean, you always ask famous people to become ambassadors.

Expert That's right. But they don't need to be famous worldwide. I mean, there are many ambassadors who are best known in the parts of the world where they are going to work, and that's extremely useful. Erm, but the important thing, you see, the really important thing is that celebrities do two things. They attract attention, when they travel and visit places, there are cameras behind them and in front of them because they're so well-known. And so the needs of children and the work of UNICEF get publicity, people know about it, this is very important ...

Interviewer And the second thing?

Expert The second thing is access – I mean, very often the fact that these people are famous means that they get access to presidents and prime ministers. These are the kinds of people who make the big decisions, who make changes. And the ambassadors can talk to them, and, you know, maybe the ambassadors can have some influence. They can argue for children, they can argue for children's rights.

Interviewer Uh huh.

Expert And that's important, I mean, don't forget that children can't vote, they don't get to choose the leaders of the country. So it can be easy sometimes for leaders, erm, politicians to, erm, not to pay much attention to children.

Interviewer Yes, indeed. And what is it that UNICEF wants children to have?

Expert Four things, basically – health, education, equality, protection. UNICEF believes that all children all over the world have the right to these four things, but in so many places they don't get it. UNICEF wants to improve that situation and the ambassadors work to achieve that.

Interviewer Is this a new idea, this idea of Goodwill Ambassadors?

Expert Not really – erm, the first person to do it was Danny Kaye ...

Interviewer The film star in the 1950s?

Expert Yes, he became 'Ambassador at Large' in 1954, so he started everything. And then later the great Audrey Hepburn, the film actress, she took the role on, and she was incredible, she worked so hard, all the years up to when she died in 1993.

Interviewer And there have been many other famous people too, haven't there?

Expert Oh, yes, the list is a very long one ...

b (possible answers)
1 They all share a commitment to improving the lives of children.
2 He took part in concerts to raise money for African children.
3 They can have some influence and argue for children's rights.
4 Because children don't have votes.

Unit check

1 2 borrowed 3 won't 4 make 5 see 6 household
7 bad 8 enjoying 9 will 10 concerned

2 2 c 3 c 4 c 5 a 6 a 7 b 8 c 9 a

3 2 They did a concert ~~attending~~ *attended* by 15,000 people.
3 You've been to Australia, ~~aren't~~ *haven't* you?
4 The cinema or the theatre? It ~~isn't~~ *doesn't* really matter to me.
5 We shouldn't listen to them, ~~don't~~ *should* we?
6 She doesn't really like me, ~~likes~~ *does* she?
7 As ~~long~~ *far* as I'm concerned, it's a wonderful place.
8 They must have been really angry, ~~haven't~~ *mustn't* they?
9 It's a competition ~~holds~~ *held* once every four years.

12 The global village

1 a 1 c 2 f 3 a 4 d 5 b 6 e

b 2 got by 3 brought ... round 4 give ... back
5 looking into 6 make up for 7 gets away with
8 put up with

c 2 I'm trying to find out.
3 They got away with being rude.
4 My parents are looking into buying a new car.
5 Sales of fair trade goods have taken off recently.
6 What can I do to make up for it?
7 Have you got enough money to get by?
8 How does your mother put up with you?

d 2 He never gave it back.
3 It's hard to put up with them.
4 I got away with it.
5 I looked it up in my dictionary.
6 The referee sent them off.
7 I didn't make it up.
8 Some songs take them back to the 1980s.

2 **a** 2 went up 3 takes ... back 4 take ... back
5 make up 6 are going up 7 came across
8 come across 9 bring ... round 10 sent off
11 send off 12 brought ... round

b 2 sent ... off 3 bring ... round 4 makes up
5 takes ... back 6 went up 7 bring ... round
8 took off

3 **a** 1 not 10% 2 not children 3 not all countries
4 not older people 5 not 25% 6 not a bad idea
7 not £25 8 not a week 9 not exactly £15

4 2 turn up 3 sit back 4 turn into 5 turn down
6 take on 7 stand up for 8 look into

5 **a** 3 ✓ 4 on 5 the 6 was 7 ✓ 8 The 9 did
10 but 11 ✓ 12 than 13 ✓

b 1 T 2 T 3 T 4 F 5 T

c 1 In 1989. 2 The rainforests and the tribes that live there. 3 19 million US dollars. 4 18.

TAPESCRIPT

Interviewee ... and of course, Sting is not only a musician, he's an actor too, he's acted in several films and he's done a Broadway play, too.

Presenter And of course he's known for charity work, isn't he?

Interviewee That's right. Erm, he's done lots of work with Amnesty International, he supports them a lot. But of course he's best known for the Rainforest Foundation which he started in 1989.

Presenter That long ago?

Interviewee Yes, I know, it is a long time ago now. Sting has always been ahead of the times. He started the Rainforest Foundation with his wife, Trudie Styler. The organisation has two objectives really, obviously the first is to protect the rainforests themselves, especially the Brazilian rainforests in the Amazon ...

Presenter Mmm.

Interviewee ... and the other one is to protect the people who live in the rainforests, the tribes, the indigenous people who live there.

Presenter Right.

Interviewee They raise money in lots of different ways, one of them is concerts, benefit concerts, that's an important way of raising money for the Rainforest Foundation, and so far, I believe they've raised something like nineteen million US dollars, something around that figure.

Presenter That's a lot.

Interviewee Yes, indeed. And the organisation has expanded a lot since it started. It started really only in the countries of the Amazon but now it's all over the place, wherever there's rainforest really, eighteen countries or so. Erm, well, the Rainforest Foundation now, it's part of an inter-connected group of organisations, you know ...

6 **a** 1 Larry Mullen.
2 Three.
3 Wearing goggle-like sunglasses and not being afraid of arguments.
4 He travels to political events because he is a social activist.
5 A screenplay.

b 1 D 2 B 3 A 4 B or E

Unit check

1 2 countries 3 trade 4 farmers 5 get by 6 make up
7 less 8 put up 9 started 10 brought round

2 2 c 3 c 4 a 5 c 6 c 7 a 8 b 9 a

3 2 You've had my books for a week – please give ~~back them~~ them back.
3 It's so noisy in here – I can't put ~~it up with~~ up with it any more.
4 He ~~came~~ came across some old letters ~~across~~ in a drawer.
5 The referee sent three players ~~out~~ off.
6 The police are looking ~~up~~ into last night's bank robbery.
7 I don't believe you – you're making ~~up that~~ that up!
8 It's not possible to get ~~through~~ by on £25 a week.
9 He's never even tried to make up ~~it for~~ for it.

13 Language

1 **a** 1 are known to be
2 is believed to be used
3 are also thought to have
4 is believed to have
5 is known to be
6 are known to be able

b 1 DT 2 PT 3 PT 4 NT 5 NT 6 DT

c 2 are believed to be spoken 3 is said to be
4 is thought to be 5 are known to have
6 is said to be

d 2 past 3 past 4 past 5 present 6 past
7 present 8 present

e 2 ✓ 3 are 4 ✓ 5 ✓ 6 but 7 being
8 had 9 who [first occurrence] 10 ✓
11 to [second occurrence]

2 **a** enough, tough, rough = stuff
through = blue
cough = off
though = know

3 **a** 2 gist 3 lost 4 totally 5 out 6 get

b 2 I'm managing to understand most of it.
3 I can just about catch the gist.
4 I understand a lot of what he's saying.
5 I can't make out very much.
6 The talks he gives are totally incomprehensible.

c) 1 4   2 3 and 5   3 1 and 6

4
a) No, he didn't.

b) 1 c   2 c   3 c

c) 1 line 1   2 line 3   3 lines 12 to 14   4 line 21
5 line 24

d) classrooms and lessons

e) 1 is small and slimy
2 are made out of glass
3 makes the tea

5
a) Paragraph order: 5, 2, 4, 1, 3

b) 1 T   2 T   3 F   4 T   5 T   6 F

Unit check

1 2 speaks   3 to speaking   4 would   5 trying   6 paid
7 to speak   8 make   9 catch   10 which

2 2 b   3 b   4 a   5 a   6 c   7 c   8 a   9 b

3
2 This painting is thought to ~~have be~~ *be* very valuable.
3 I didn't ~~got~~ *get* very much of what he was saying.
4 The whole lecture was ~~very~~ *totally* incomprehensible.
5 The thieves are believed to ~~leave~~ *have left* the country yesterday.
6 The Rolling Stones are said ~~being~~ *to be* the greatest band in the world.
7 I caught the ~~understanding~~ *gist* of what she said but not the exact details.
8 He had a strange accent. I couldn't make ~~off~~ *out* what he was saying.
9 William Shakespeare ~~said~~ *is said* to have spent a night in this bed.

14 The wonders of the world

1
a) 4, 5 and 7 are correct.

b) 2 Hugging the hillsides behind me, the city of Rio de Janeiro is one of the most beautiful places I've ever seen.
3 Having booked into a cheap hotel in the Gloria district, we made our way immediately to the beach.
4 Having spent all day in the sun, Dave spent all night complaining about sunburn.
5 Having hired a deck-chair and an umbrella on the beach, I spent most of the time reading my Rio de Janeiro guide.

2
a) 2 Lake   3 Canyon   4 mountain range   5 cliffs
6 Desert

b) 2 Bolivia and Peru   3 the USA   4 South America
5 England   6 China

3
a) 1 a   2 a   3 b   4 a   5 a   6 b

b) 2 g   3 a   4 d   5 c   6 b   7 h   8 f

c) Students' own answers

4
a) 2 away   3 on   4 on   5 to   6 off   7 for
8 into   9 off   10 out   11 for   12 on   13 off

b) 2 taxi   3 this afternoon   4 horse   5 the airport
6 bus

5
a) TAPESCRIPT/ANSWERS
1 She <u>bit</u> her sandwich.
2 I'll <u>heat</u> the chicken.
3 Can you <u>feel</u> it?
4 The <u>ship</u> is leaving in the morning.
5 The <u>pitch</u> was in bad condition.
6 Where did you put the <u>beans</u>?
7 Did he <u>leave</u> in the car?
8 Don't <u>slip</u>!

6
a) 1 Take it easy.
2 How does that grab you?
3 a bit of a nightmare
4 Get out of here.

b) 1 a bit of a nightmare
2 Take it easy
3 Get out of here
4 How does that grab you

8 1 1,000   2 75   3 43   4 toes   5 sandcastle   6 friends
7 17   8 47   9 Good weather   10 Hawaii

TAPESCRIPT
It's official – the beach is America's favourite place for a quick getaway. In an online survey of 1,023 people, three quarters of those who completed the questionnaire said that they would definitely or very likely visit a beach in the coming year. That's 75% – about 700 people – that's a lot of people! What's really interesting is that 43% chose the beach as their ideal destination for a perfect holiday, just higher than the number of people who chose the mountains. Holidays shopping in the city don't seem to interest people so much according to this questionnaire! Big cities had a much lower score. And we have even more holiday information from the survey. When asked if they would be going into the sea for a swim, 68% of the questionnaire respondents said they definitely would, while 27% said they would at least put their toes into the water. This means that 5% of everyone who replied have no intention at all of getting anywhere near the water! But when you look at the results for favourite activities, you realise there is more to do at the beach than just swim in the sea. The most popular beach activity is to have a beach party or a barbeque, with 44% choosing this. This was followed by building a sandcastle – 39% of all the people who replied said they would definitely make one of these. For themselves or for their children, we'd like to know! Relaxing was quite high on the list too. 32% said they would just like to lie on the beach with a good book. 21% of all the people who replied said they would like to be with their friends – aaaah! And flying a kite was a choice for 17%. They'll have to find somewhere windy! Maybe another reason why those 5% don't fancy getting into the sea at all is because 39% of Americans are afraid of jellyfish when they go

swimming. This was the top answer in the 'beach fears' category. Amazingly, people are more afraid of jellyfish than they are of sharks. Only 37% said they wouldn't swim because of the risk of becoming shark food! The sting, it seems, is mightier than the bite. Finally, internet users were asked what they look for in a beach. Here they were allowed to choose more than one category. A clean beach was the top answer. This was chosen by just under half of all the people who replied. Just one percent below, with 46%, was having a good view. Good weather was thought to be very important by 34% and warm water by 23%. We imagine this was not that 5% who refuse to get into the sea at all! Oh, and before I forget, the nation's favourite beach is Waikiki in Hawaii – now there's a surprise! OK, I'm packing my barbecue and beach hat – hope to see you there!

Unit check

1 2 islands 3 ever 4 beaches 5 reefs 6 on 7 for 8 thunder 9 off 10 in

2 2 b 3 b 4 b 5 b 6 a 7 c 8 b 9 c

3
2 I was going to phone her but I ~~needn't have~~ *didn't need to* because she called me.
3 We're going ~~for~~ *on* holiday tomorrow. I can't wait.
4 Having ~~eating~~ *eaten* dinner, we turned on the TV.
5 We got in the car and drove ~~for~~ home.
6 ~~Whistle~~ *Whistling* a happy tune, he walked out of the house.
7 I wasn't hungry so I ~~needn't have eaten~~ *didn't need to eat* until dinner.
8 ~~Have~~ *Having* got into the car, we drove off.
9 I'm just going out ~~on~~ *for* a quick walk.

15 Movie magic

1
a 2 e 3 a 4 c 5 f 6 d

b 2 so as to 3 in order not to 4 in order to 5 to 6 so as not to 7 in order not to 8 to

c
2 We got to the stadium early in order not to miss the start of the game.
3 I phoned Michelle so as to invite her to my party.
4 I didn't tell Ahmed about the accident so as not to worry him.
5 I took the train in order not to get caught in a traffic jam.
6 I'd like to speak to her so as to apologise.
7 He's saving all his money to buy a new computer.
8 Can you speak quietly so as not to disturb other people?

2
a 2 such 3 so 4 so 5 so 6 such

b 2 so 3 so 4 such 5 such 6 so 7 so 8 so

c
2 Nigel's so careless that he breaks something every time he comes to my house.
3 We set out so late that we didn't arrive until midnight.
4 That's such a nasty cough that you should see a doctor.
5 United played so badly that they were beaten five to one.
6 Rob's such an intellectual person that it's difficult to understand everything he talks about.
7 The sponsored walk was such a great success that we're going to organise another one.
8 He snored so loudly that I couldn't get to sleep.

3
a 3 con<u>front</u> 4 confront<u>ation</u> 5 <u>problem</u> 6 problem<u>atic</u> 7 a<u>dapt</u> 8 adapt<u>ation</u> 9 recom<u>mend</u> 10 recommen<u>dation</u>

4
a 1 f 2 c 3 h 4 d 5 a 6 g 7 e 8 b

b Students' own answers

c 2 laughing 3 screaming 4 sitting 5 chuckling 6 biting 7 crying 8 jumping

5
a They give information about the festivals' places and dates, their prizes, their history and some other interesting facts.

b 1 Venice 2 Cannes 3 London 4 Cannes

6
a *The Purple Rose of Cairo*: director – Woody Allen; leading actors – Mia Farrow, Jeff Baxter
The Truman Show: director – Peter Weir; leading actors – Jim Carrey, Laura Linney, Ed Harris
EDtv: director – Ron Howards; leading actors – Ellen DeGeneres, Matthew McConaughey

b a 5 b 4 c 6 d 2 e 3 f 1

Unit check

1 2 order 3 so 4 a 5 about 6 such 7 not 8 which 9 chuckled 10 should

2 2 c 3 b 4 c 5 a 6 a 7 b 8 b 9 c

3
2 I wrote him a quick email in order ~~tell~~ *to tell* him when I'll arrive.
3 We left early so ~~not as~~ *as not to* be late.
4 It was ~~so~~ *such* a boring lecture that I left half-way through.
5 I didn't eat all the fish to ~~leaving~~ *leave* room for dessert.
6 That's ~~such~~ *such a* good film that I've got to buy the DVD when it comes out.
7 I studied for three weeks ~~on~~ *in* order to get a good grade in the exam.
8 He speaks ~~such~~ *so* fast that I don't understand a word of what he says.
9 I didn't say anything ~~for~~ *so* as not to upset him.

16 Music in the air

1
a
2 Do you know how much this costs?
3 Can you tell us what time the film starts?
4 Can you ask him what grade he got in the test?
5 Do you know when they arrived? / Do they know when you arrived?
6 Do you know who I can speak to?

7 Can you tell them who the teacher will be?
8 Do you know what his name is?

b) 2 How much does this cost?
3 When does the film start?
4 What grade did he get in the test?
5 When did they/you arrive?
6 Who can I speak to?
7 Who will the teacher be?
8 What's his name?

c) 2 b 3 c 4 g 5 d 6 h 7 e 8 a

d) 2 what type of music is popular in the early mornings?
3 what you played this morning when you opened the gym?
4 what people like to listen to while they exercise in the afternoons?
5 what time it starts getting busy again?
6 what kind of music we can hear then?
7 how many clients the gym has got at the moment?
8 how many complaints you have had about the music you play?

2 a) 2 Elvis Costello
3 Keane
4 Coldplay
5 Echo and the Bunnymen
6 New Order
7 The White Stripes
8 Fat Boy Slim

b) 2 nearly 3 lot 4 just 5 far 6 a 7 nothing
8 better

3 a) 2 export 3 increase 4 increases 5 in<u>s</u>ult
6 <u>in</u>sult 7 <u>pre</u>sent 8 pre<u>sent</u>

4 2 lyrics 3 live 4 tune 5 hum 6 muzak
7 recorded 8 Instrumental

5 a) 2 when 3 how 4 where 5 why 6 what

b) 1 g ... happy. 2 c ... that? 3 h ... live?
4 f ... year. 5 d ... party? 6 b ... went.
7 a ... works. 8 e ... went?

c) 1 where I put my pen.
2 why it doesn't work.
3 who sent me this card.
4 why she did that.

6 a) 2

b) b spontaneous c sampled d re-released
e vocal improvisation f hits g remixed tracks
h extended

c) 2 T 3 F 4 T 5 F 6 F 7 T

TAPESCRIPT
Sister Sledge are, as their name suggests, all sisters. Imagine having all that talent under one roof! They were born and raised in Philadelphia in the USA and started singing at an early age. They were taught by their grandmother, Viola Williams, who was herself an ex-opera singer. As well as singing at their local church, Viola got the sisters to perform at charities and civic and political gatherings. Their grandmother must have been proud of them as the name she gave the group at this time was 'Mrs. William's Grandchildren'. As the girls got older they probably realised that this name wouldn't make them famous in show business. So they came up with the name Sisters Sledge. One night, they were announced on stage as Sister Sledge and the name stuck from then on. With the new name came success. Their breakthrough album *We are Family*, which was released in 1979, was a huge hit and featured a number of hit singles. The album was number one in both the pop and R&B charts. During the 1980's, the group continued to enjoy success with hits like *Love Somebody Today*, *Reach Your Peak* and *Frankie*. They became one of the world's most successful female groups. They toured the world extensively, visiting Asia, Africa, Europe, the Middle East, South America, Australia and the United States, playing to full audiences wherever they went. Although some of the original members have since left, the group still continue to tour and make music together.

7 a) 1 The Rolling Stones, The Black Eyed Peas
2 Keith Richards, Mick Jagger
3 *Start Me Up, Rough Justice, Miss You, Satisfaction, Jumping Jack Flash, You Can't Always Get What You Want, It's Only Rock 'n' Roll*

b) A 5 B 6 C 1 D 2 E 3

Unit check

1 2 sensation 3 charts 4 best 5 far 6 household
7 name 8 live 9 which 10 success

2 2 c 3 a 4 a 5 b 6 b 7 b 8 c 9 a

3 2 Can you tell me who ~~is she~~ she is?
3 It's ~~far difficult~~ far more difficult than I thought.
4 I can't remember where ~~did I meet~~ I met him.
5 Do you know where ~~have they~~ they have gone?
6 I'm thinking about how ~~should we~~ we should tell her.
7 It's easy to see why ~~are they~~ they are so rich.
8 Can you remember when ~~do we meet~~ we met?
9 She's ~~very~~ far/much happier today than she was yesterday.

Acknowledgements

The publishers are grateful to Pentacor**big** for: text design and layouts

Meredith Levy: editorial work

Annie Cornford: Workbook key